T0283292

A former primary school teacher, S[...] about her ancestors took her all the way to a PhD in Aboriginal history.

———————

'Compelling and courageous truth-telling, so necessary in Australian history.'

Dr Jackie Huggins AM,
historian and author

'Children stolen, homes resumed, authorities spying, ASIO snooping. Bostock's family has it all—yet she can still see the funny side. This is why we need family histories. This is why we need truth-telling.'

Professor Peter Read AM,
Australian National University

'Bostock sees such truth-telling as a great unshackling. This brilliantly researched, difficult-to-put-down history demonstrates how five generations of a multi-talented Aboriginal family made their worlds anew. Although pummelled by colonialism, across the generations, courageous individuals emerged to reshape the nation's cultural and political future. Through her engaging narrative, Bostock continues their illuminating legacy.

Readers will hear a very different story of who made the Australia of today. Visual and visceral, this book will rumble the ground of what constitutes family history, if not what connects us, the Australian people as a whole.'

Professor Ann McGrath AM,
Australian National University

REACHING THROUGH TIME

FINDING MY FAMILY'S STORIES

Shauna Bostock

ALLEN&UNWIN

SYDNEY·MELBOURNE·AUCKLAND·LONDON

First published in 2023

Allen & Unwin
Cammeraygal Country
83 Alexander Street
Crows Nest NSW 2065
Australia
Phone: (61 2) 8425 0100
Email: info@allenandunwin.com
Web: www.allenandunwin.com

*Allen & Unwin acknowledges the Traditional Owners of the Country on which we
live and work. We pay our respects to all Aboriginal and Torres Strait Islander
Elders, past and present.*

 A catalogue record for this
book is available from the
National Library of Australia

ISBN 978 1 76106 798 3

Set in 13/17 pt Granjon LT Std by Midland Typesetters, Australia
Printed and bound in Australia by the Opus Group

10 9 8 7 6 5 4 3 2 1

 The paper in this book is FSC® certified.
FSC® promotes environmentally responsible,
socially beneficial and economically viable
management of the world's forests.

Contents

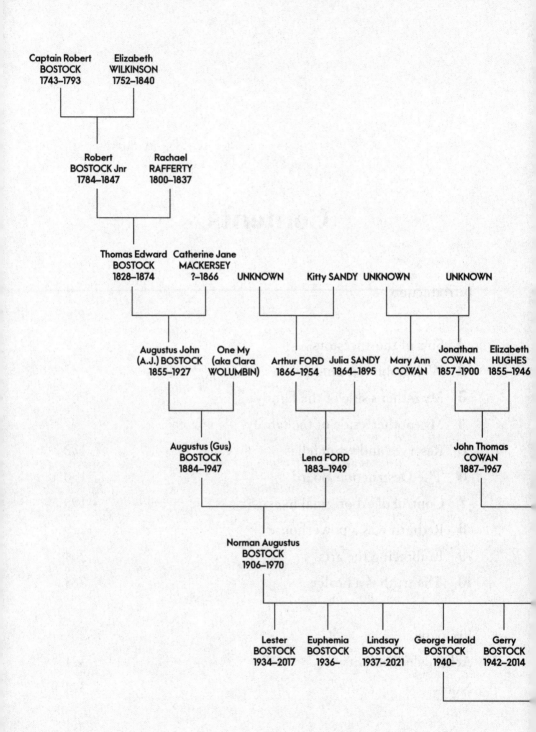

Family Tree

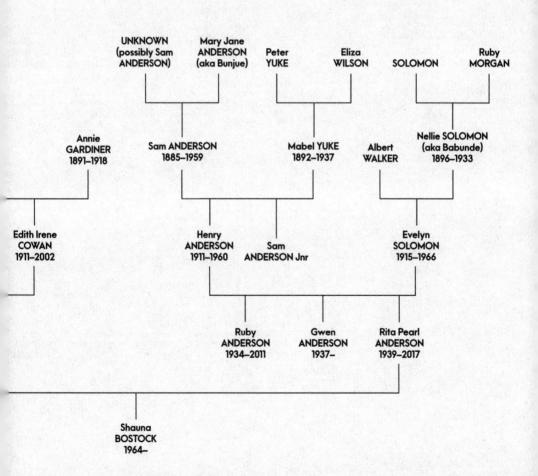

UNKNOWN (possibly Sam ANDERSON)

Mary Jane ANDERSON (aka Bunjue)

Peter YUKE

Eliza WILSON

SOLOMON

Ruby MORGAN

Annie GARDINER 1891–1918

Sam ANDERSON 1885–1959

Mabel YUKE 1892–1937

Albert WALKER

Nellie SOLOMON (aka Babunde) 1896–1933

Edith Irene COWAN 1911–2002

Henry ANDERSON 1911–1960

Sam ANDERSON Jnr

Evelyn SOLOMON 1915–1966

Ruby ANDERSON 1934–2011

Gwen ANDERSON 1937–

Rita Pearl ANDERSON 1939–2017

Shauna BOSTOCK 1964–

To my daughter,
Brenna Janna Bostock Smith
(I love you way more than a hundred and fifty-two!)

Introduction

I am Bundjalung. I am an Aboriginal Australian and I come from Bundjalung Country on the southern border region of Queensland and in the Northern Rivers region of New South Wales, on Australia's east coast. In the Tweed River valley, a sacred mountain called Wollumbin stands majestically as the first place on mainland Australia to receive the sun's rays each day. It is my family's ancestral home. My ancestors woke up in that sunshine, drank from crystal-clear streams, hunted game, were guardians of the forests and the mountains, and maintained and preserved sacred sites of Earth magic. As an urban Aboriginal woman who lives in the present, I yearned to connect with my ancestors from the past, learn their history and tell their stories. I have travelled on a long and exhausting journey, for over a decade, to find a way to bridge these worlds.

Why don't you know?

I vividly remember how shocked my fellow student Lynda looked, how the mortification in her voice made her sudden question sound more like an interrogation rather than the urgent, truth-seeking inquiry that she intended. She whacked

1

me on my shoulder and gasped, 'Did you *know* this!' I responded sadly, 'Yes . . . Why don't *you* know?'

I have never forgotten this small exchange, which took place in 2003, directly after one of the lectures on our Indigenous History course for my Bachelor of Education degree. We had just sat through a tough lecture about Aboriginal segregation on Aborigines reserves and missions, and the indenture of young Aboriginal teens into so-called 'apprenticeships' as domestic servants and labourers. Lynda and I were part of a small subgroup of mature-aged students who had just begun four years of study to qualify as primary schoolteachers. I was about to turn forty, and my new university friends were in their mid-to-late thirties when they, for the first time in their lives, were learning about Aboriginal history.

The instant Lynda asked me that question, I was struck by the realisation that at that time there were still generations of white Australians who did not know the history of Aboriginal people in this country. I am 58 years old now, and countless times in my lifetime I have witnessed non-Indigenous people's shock at revelations about Aboriginal history. When that happens, they almost always say exactly the same thing, 'We were never taught about that when I was at school.' Whenever I hear those familiar words, I sigh. It comes from a deeply personal, ancestral place in my heart. It's like a twinge of pain from an old injury. It is a recurring reminder that, even after all this time, there still lingers something that needs to be properly healed.

I'm not the first person to write about this widespread lack of knowledge about Aboriginal history. Historian Henry Reynolds wrote about it two decades ago in his 1999 book called *Why Weren't We Told? A personal search for the truth about our history*. 'Why weren't we told?' was a question that people from all over the country frequently asked him after his history lectures. Reynolds confessed that he was 'ignorant of protective and repressive legislation and the ideology and practice of white racism beyond a highly generalised view that *we* had treated *them* rather badly in the past'. His acclaimed book was written from the perspective of a non-Indigenous historian who went on a personal journey towards realising that he, like generations of Australians, grew up with a distorted and idealised version of history, and he urged Australians to continue to search for the truth about our past.[1]

Similarly, this book is an account of a personal journey to search for the truth about our past, and I too have written with the goal of counteracting the widespread lack of knowledge about Aboriginal history. But this book differs in that it is written from the perspective of an Aboriginal historian who has researched her ancestors. I began my research journey with the goal of tracing my four Aboriginal grandparents' family lines as far back as I could in Australia's written historical record, which was just after white settlers arrived in northern New South Wales.

My research covers five generations of my family history and examines my ancestors' experience of the continuing encroachment of white settlement through to the present day.

This research journey culminated with receiving my doctorate from the Australian National University, but the greatest, most heart-warming reward has been the discovery of an unbroken connection to my pre-colonisation ancestors—and time immemorial. I discovered that family history research was a way to bridge these worlds. This book is the story of my personal research journey.

History of Aboriginal history

The reason generations of Australians never learned about Aboriginal history was that it only started to be given attention as recently as 1981—too late for anyone, like me, who was completing their schooling at that time. In his 1968 Boyer Lectures for the Australian Broadcasting Commission (ABC), well-known anthropologist W.E.H. Stanner first used the term 'The Great Australian Silence' to highlight how the Aboriginal experience of colonisation and white settlement had been left out of the national narrative. He said that Aboriginal people had been reduced to little more than a 'melancholy footnote' in Australia's history and he concluded that inattention on such a massive scale could not simply be explained as absentmindedness. Stanner believed that it was a structural matter:

> A view from a window which has been carefully placed to exclude a whole quadrant of the landscape. What may well have begun as a simple forgetting of other possible views turned under habit and over time into something like a cult of forgetfulness practised on a national scale.[2]

In this famous quote, Stanner held up a mirror to Australian historians, so that they could see their own culpability in the erasure of Aboriginal people from the written historical record. His criticism inspired young non-Indigenous historians like Henry Reynolds. Nearly twenty years before he wrote his book *Why Weren't We Told?*, Henry Reynolds' first ground-breaking book, *The Other Side of the Frontier: Aboriginal resistance to the European invasion of Australia*, paved the way for the burgeoning field of study now known as Aboriginal history.[3] His work profoundly changed the way in which Australians understood

4

relations between Aboriginal people and European settlers. Another distinguished historian who also came to prominence in 1981 was Peter Read. His research revealed the Australian Government's policy of the removal of Aboriginal children from their families, and he coined the phrase 'The Stolen Generations'. Peter Read was one of my PhD supervisors.

As historians systematically uncovered shocking truths about the nation's past, some conservatives in Australia became infuriated. In 1993, conservative historian Geoffrey Blainey created the term 'black armband' to describe what he and others called an exaggerated, negative view of Australia's history. This term was adopted by the mainstream media and prominent conservatives, including Prime Minister John Howard. What followed was a series of public arguments between academics and the media that later became known as the 'history wars'.

In 2002, historian Keith Windschuttle published a book called *The Fabrication of Aboriginal History, Volume One: Van Diemen's Land, 1803–1847* and in 2009 he followed it up with another book on this topic, *The Fabrication of Aboriginal History, Volume Three: The Stolen Generations 1881–2008*. Windschuttle accused historians, including Henry Reynolds and Lyndall Ryan, of 'misrepresentation, deceit and outright fabrication' of frontier violence and race relations in North Queensland and Tasmania.[4] He also questioned the work of Peter Read and the accepted account that Aboriginal children were removed from their families in large numbers as a result of fundamentally racist government policies.

Archives can be wielded in powerful ways, and I was surprised to learn from historian Victoria Haskins that Keith Windschuttle had only accessed limited historical records.[5] I remember seeing him on television interviews emphatically declaring, 'I've seen the archives!', and no one ever questioned which archives he was referring to. Years after this, Haskins noted, 'Keith Windschuttle's very flawed work on the Stolen Generations was based on his limited access to the Board's Ward Registers (which were once open to all and have since come under restrictions)'.[6] I remember the disdain that was directed at academics and the false perception that experiences of the Stolen Generations were exaggerated. Although Windschuttle's books produced a range of responses, from condemnation to support for his work, one of the negative outcomes that I remember was that the naysayers of Aboriginal history used his 'flawed work' to justify their refusal to accept the deep racism in Australian society and decades of mistreatment of Aboriginal people.

During the 'history wars', writers of Aboriginal history were struck by waves of rebuttal, and although the force of the waves diminished over time, there seems to be an ever-present potential for them to rise again. During the time I have been writing this book, I have noticed some mainstream media again denying the importance of Aboriginal history. There appears to be a national exasperation that the subject has surfaced yet again, and I think that comes from a misconception that history is an unchanging, static body of knowledge.

But history is always changing. Narratives of the same historical event can be remarkably different depending on the perspective of the historian, or the people they are writing about. The discovery of 'new' archival material can also dramatically change our understanding of the past. This book contains an enormous amount of information sourced from such rare archival discoveries.

A balanced view

I have always joked that my family members are the 'Forrest Gumps' of blackfellas. In every era, there was usually someone immersed in, or witness to, most of the milestones of Aboriginal history since European invasion. This book is written for people who want to know our history from an Aboriginal perspective. I place this multi-generational story of my family history in the context of Australian history. Of course, in my family's history there is a plethora of stories about racism, oppression, hardship and outrageous injustice, but this book is not only about the negative circumstances and events in Aboriginal history. There are also beautiful, heart-warming examples of non-Indigenous kindness and humanity.

My goal has been to provide a truthful, balanced view.

Henry Reynolds said, 'Truth-telling is the ultimate gesture of respect. It indicates a willingness to listen, to learn and to concede that the stories should be heard of those who have been victims of great wrongs.'[7] I would like to acknowledge and express my deep gratitude to you, the readers of this book. Our stories need to be heard, and I am thankful for your willingness to listen and learn about the historical experiences of my ancestors and other Aboriginal people in Australia's history.

1

Sins of the ancestors

'Those white ancestors of ours must be rolling in their graves knowing we turned out to be a mob of blackfellas!'

UNCLE GERRY BOSTOCK

We're a superstitious mob, but I don't think it's an exclusively Aboriginal reaction to instantly think *Who's died?* when the phone unexpectedly rings late at night. That night in 2008, my trepidation rose quickly when I heard that it was my Uncle Gerry, from Sydney, who was on the line. But instead of sounding mournful, he sounded strangely . . . incredulous. 'I've just been on the phone with a Bostock woman, a "white" Bostock woman from A.J.'s side of the family. You won't believe what she told me about the white side of the family!'

Immediately I knew he was referring to Augustus John Bostock, my non-Indigenous great-great-grandfather, whom Uncle Gerry had long ago nicknamed 'A.J.' Uncle Gerry explained that the elderly caller's name was Thelma Birrell, but her family name, like ours, was Bostock. He told me that Thelma was an avid genealogist who had been researching the Bostock family tree for over 30 years. She told him that she knew of her family's rumour that her great-grandfather's cousin, Augustus John Bostock, had *taken up with* an Aboriginal woman in the 1800s, but she didn't know if there were any descendants from that union. Incredibly, after seeing Uncle Gerry's photograph online, an obviously Aboriginal man with the Bostock family name, she somehow tracked him down. In their long conversation, Thelma told him that she had traced the Bostock family line back to the 1600s in England.

'Guess who our white ancestors were?' Chuckling to himself, Uncle deliberately paused for dramatic effect before he blurted out: 'They were slave traders! A couple of generations of slave traders! Can you believe it? Imagine that!' A deep, loud belly laugh erupted down the line, and he snorted as he added, 'Those white ancestors of ours must be rolling in their graves knowing we turned out to be a mob of blackfellas!'

Up until that time, Augustus John Bostock was known to us only as 'the whitefella who gave us our family name', but on hearing this new information about *his* family history, a burning desire to find out more was suddenly ignited in me. Thelma had given Uncle Gerry her phone number, and I was surprised to find that she lived only a little over an hour's drive away from me on the Sunshine Coast. When I rang Thelma we chatted easily on the phone, and by the end of the call, she kindly invited me to come and visit her next time I was up that way.

Thelma was a lovely, elderly lady who, years earlier, with her husband, Matthew, had travelled to England and to Australia's southern states many times to collect her treasure trove of historical, archival and church records. We spoke on the phone many times, and I enjoyed my face-to-face meetings with her over several cups of tea and delicious sweet treats. She was thrilled that I was interested in her work, and so proud to gift me a copy of her self-published book *Merchants, Mariners . . . then Pioneers*.[1] Thelma thoroughly enjoyed telling me all about the history of the non-Indigenous Bostock family prior to Augustus John's birth. She had been able to trace the Bostocks back to an ironmonger called Jonathan Bostock, who lived in Chester in late seventeenth-century England. Jonathan Bostock was the father of Peter, Peter was the father of Robert, and Robert Snr was the father of Robert Jnr. The two 'Roberts' were the slave traders.

Thelma explained that after slave trading was abolished, the British Government arrested Robert Bostock Jnr and his business partner, John McQueen, and sentenced them to 'transportation' to the colony for fourteen years. She was quick to tell me that not long after they arrived here, 'Governor Lachlan Macquarie pardoned them'. I had never heard of 'pardons from the Governor' in Australian history, until Thelma showed me her transcription of the colonial secretary's documents, in which the last sentence of the pardon declared:

> By virtue of the power and authority Given and Granted unto me the Governor in Chief of the said Territory of New South Wales under such Warrant and conformally to the tenor thereof I do hereby order and direct that Robert Bostock therein named be forthwith discharged out of custody accordingly and he is hereby . . . restored to all rights and privileges of a free subject. Signed, L. Macquarie, 1st January 1816.[2]

In later research, I found that in the *Historical Records of Australia* there are other records about this correspondence, stating that the pardon was 'By Command of the Prince Regent' (later George IV) and was forwarded by Earl Bathurst to

Governor Macquarie, with 'Despatch No. 44, per ship *Fanny*: acknowledged by Governor Macquarie, 18th March 1816'.[3]

Confused by the pardon, I remember asking Thelma for confirmation. 'But Robert Bostock really was a slave trader, right?' She patted my hand and answered in a hushed voice, 'Ooh yes, he was a very naughty boy.' Silently, Thelma handed me the pretty floral matching teacup and saucer and busied herself pouring us more tea, then once seated she enthusiastically told me tales of Robert Bostock's exploits after he arrived in Australia—about how he became an excellent merchant in Sydney, and married a beautiful maiden, and then moved to Van Diemen's Land, and expanded his business interests in Hobart, and became a very wealthy landowner, and lived in a grand mansion.

Most precious to Thelma were the stories about his children, who left Van Diemen's Land and settled in southern Victoria. She was so proud of the white Bostock's narrative of dashing pioneers and nation-building settlers—but I wanted to pause the story and go back to understand more about the two 'Roberts' who were slave traders. I had so many questions, but her reluctance to discuss them was palpable. In her book, she explained that even though Robert Snr had a number of ships and was successful to some degree, he was regarded as a small operator. Thelma wrote that 'he exhorted his captains to treat the slaves well at all times' and she pointed out that 'Robert [Snr] died 20 years before slave trading was actually abolished', and that 'trading in slaves continued up to the 1860s in different parts of the world'.

Thelma's writing moved on to present her outstanding genealogical research, and her proud narrative of the pioneering lives of the non-Indigenous Bostocks. After the initial excitement of finding Uncle Gerry and connecting with me over cups of tea, Thelma and I continued to chat on the phone every now and then, but unfortunately a year or so later, contact between us gradually faded away. But before we lost touch, she introduced me to the slave-trade historian Emma Christopher.

Emma's field of expertise is the transatlantic slave trade, Pacific Islander labour, West African and historical slavery, and modern slavery. When a fellow historian told her that a mansion built by a convict transported for slave trading still existed in Tasmania, Emma was astonished, because after years of extensive research, she had never heard of any slave traders in Australia. Her response was like mine: she was gripped by the need to know more about the two Roberts. As the Australian expert on Bostock genealogies, Thelma was a major contributor to a website for Bostock descendants all over the world, and that is how Emma found her.

Being a spiritual person, I paid close attention to the intriguing way that we all connected with each other. Seemingly out of the blue, Thelma found Uncle Gerry on the internet, then Uncle Gerry contacted me, and this led to my contact with Thelma; Emma was told about Robert Bostock, then found Thelma on the internet, and this led to her contact with me. My intuition was telling me that this synchronicity was somehow orchestrated, that it was all part of God's plan that I met Thelma and Emma.

Back then, I was focused on filling in the gaps in my family tree chart and finding out how Robert was related to my great-great-grandfather, Augustus John Bostock, whereas Emma, an established PhD historian and a published author, wanted to know all about the global legacy of the transatlantic slave trade. I now smile at the trivial nature of my little project in comparison to Emma's extraordinary and globally important work. Yet despite our contrasting levels of academic knowledge at that time, our common interest in the history of the Bostocks quickly led to us becoming good friends. She helped me to see how interesting history can be when you push through the surface level and delve more deeply.

When Emma and I met, she was compiling research for a book about Robert Bostock Jnr and his business partner, John McQueen, who were the only two convicted slave traders to have ever been transported to Australia. Emma was surprised when Thelma told her about the Aboriginal branches of the Bostock family. I say the plural 'branches' because George Bostock, the cousin of my great-great-grandfather Augustus John Bostock, lived in the Northern Territory of Australia and had children with a Jingili woman, who, in the historical record, was only recorded as 'unknown F/B' ('F/B' meaning 'full-blood'; the use of this term will be discussed later). So, it turned out that my family are not the only Indigenous descendants of Robert Bostock.

In 2018, Emma's book *Freedom in Black and White: A lost story of the illegal slave trade and its global legacy* was published, and it is a meticulous examination of the lives of the two Roberts, their tragic human merchandise and their captive African workers.[4] As with Thelma's book, I devoured every word. The fates of the African captives who worked for Robert Bostock Jnr, and his Aboriginal descendants, are essential to Emma's final discussion on the global legacy of the transatlantic slave trade.

Out of the blue, Emma said, 'It must be a shock to be an Aboriginal Australian, a woman of colour, and find out that your ancestors were slave traders.' After what seemed like an excruciatingly long time, I realised that I simply did not have the words to describe how I felt. Frowning, I lamely said, 'I don't know what to say . . . I feel numb about it—I just wish I had better words to say.'

That was over twelve years ago; after advancing my education, and undertaking intense study and archival research, it is only now that I am in the position to be able to present my research and provide answers to complex questions such as the one Emma posed. The book you are now reading is evidence that my wish for 'better words' was granted. At the beginning of my research journey, I imagined that my future book would be exclusively limited to my Aboriginal family history and would not include any of the non-Indigenous side of the family. It was only when I was completing my PhD, and had read Emma's extraordinary book, that I realised how integral my slave-trading ancestors are to the conclusion of this history of my multi-generational Aboriginal family.

Captain Bostock

The two sections on Robert Snr and Robert Jnr are sourced entirely from Emma Christopher's book—and for the following section, called 'The pardon', I bounced back and forth between Emma's book and Thelma's book to weave a comprehensive narrative of Robert Bostock's post-transportation life. Taking large chunks of another historian's work and paraphrasing it is something that is frowned upon in academic scholarship, but the circumstances here are an exception. How many family history researchers have a distantly related genealogist extraordinaire and a world-renowned transatlantic slave-trade historian who just happened to have done extensive research on the individual lives of their ancestors?

Emma travelled all over the world to research Captain Robert Bostock and Robert Bostock Jnr's history as traders in the transatlantic slave trade and I have to thank her and Thelma for allowing me to draw on this information. Emma searched through archives in the United Kingdom, Sierra Leone, Cuba and Australia to find information on the global legacy of the two Roberts. I learned that there was so much that I didn't know about the transatlantic slave trade. Throughout her book, Emma frequently used the term 'the middle passage' and straight up I have to admit that I had no idea what that was. It proved to be slave trade terminology for the middle sector of the standard slave traders' three-leg voyage. During the years of the transatlantic slave trade, a common route taken by slave traders was to circumnavigate the North Atlantic Ocean. After leaving England or Europe, they headed south down Africa's west coast, sailed west across to the Caribbean Islands and North America's east coast, and then completed the circuit when they arrived back in England or Europe.

On the first leg, cargo ships were loaded with manufactured goods such as iron, cloth, brandy, firearms and gunpowder, and sailed to Africa. It was the second leg of the slave traders' triangular voyage that was known as the infamous 'middle passage', with the terrified captives packed into ships to be transported from Africa to the Caribbean Islands and America. Those who survived the middle passage were sold to wealthy plantation owners as slaves. For the third leg of the voyage, the slave traders' ships were loaded with raw materials such as sugar, rice, tobacco, coffee and cotton, to be sold in England and Europe.

When Captain Bostock was a boy he joined the Royal Navy, and later, as a young man, he was drawn to Liverpool and the slave trade. The first slave ship that Captain Bostock commanded was the tiny sloop *Little Ben*, which set sail in 1769 for Cape Mount, a county in what is now known as Liberia.

He then transported 79 captives across the seas to Dominica, an island in the Lesser Antilles on the eastern side of the Caribbean Sea. There was a second voyage in *Little Ben*, and then another in a larger ship called *Townside*, accompanied by *Little Ben*. By 1773, Captain Bostock was the master of a much larger vessel called the *Burrowes*. In 1784, the year Robert Bostock Jnr was born, his father took 239 captive Africans across the Atlantic in the *Bloom* and sold them in Antigua, another island in the Lesser Antilles.[5]

Thelma's book mentioned a specific trip that highlights the amount of money to be made from the trade. In 1783, Bostock sailed from Africa to America and back to Liverpool as the master of the *Bloom*, having been employed by Foxcroft & Co. to pick up and deliver slaves for the owners. The voyage lasted about one year and netted Foxcroft & Co. £9600, with the captain's commission being £360 pounds. The slaves would bring £35 to £45 each, depending on their condition.[6]

I was curious about what these figures would look like in today's money, so I keyed them into the UK National Archive's online (historical) currency converter. Based on 2017 currency rates, that one voyage by Foxcroft & Co. was worth approximately £827,000. Captain Bostock's commission was worth approximately £31,000 and the slaves were priced at between £3000 and £3800 each. When you add to that the knowledge that Captain Bostock went on to own a number of vessels, this currency conversion makes perfectly clear how lucrative the slave trade was.

The wealth of the slave traders depended on the 'cargo' surviving the middle passage, and that was not always a fait accompli, given that slaving vessels were breeding grounds for diseases that originated in Europe, Africa and America. The slaves were laid flat close beside each other, with no sanitation, and exposed to alarming diseases to which they had no resistance. Slaving vessels were hothouses of hookworm, tapeworm, ophthalmia, diarrhoea, dysentery, malaria, measles, yellow fever, smallpox, scurvy, elephantiasis, trypanosomiasis, yaws, syphilis and leprosy. Slaves also suffered from friction sores, ulcers, and injuries, and wounds resulting from accidents, fights and whippings.[7]

As free Africans, these people were used to eating an abundance of palm oil and pepper, with meat and fish, roasted plantains, ears of corn, and dates. They drank either water or palm wine. Onboard the slave ships, palm oil and pepper were limited rations, and often too much salt was added to coarse European provisions. Some refused to eat, resulting in harsh punishment or death. Slaves who tried to starve themselves to death might have had a *speculum oris* jammed into their mouths. This metal device wrenched open their jaws and forced the captive Africans to eat. The slave traders were fierce in ensuring that their valuable commodities survived the middle passage and did not escape their intended fate.[8]

Captain Bostock and other slave traders used the manufactured goods from England or Europe to buy enslaved African people from local traders. Some successful slave traders had large compounds, within which they erected barracoons—covered holding yards or pens made for the temporary confinement of slaves, with the sides open to the scorching sun and torrential rain. These vast bamboo cages were too flimsy to imprison people, so captives were tethered individually to stakes, one foot in stocks, which were basically logs with a hole in the centre for the foot, a peg driven in sideways to confine it. As an extra deterrent to escape, high mud walls were erected all around the compounds.

The slaves were forced on a long journey from their homelands to the coast. Often the oldest women the merchants bought were still in their twenties; the majority were younger. It is upsetting to imagine the indignities these young women may have suffered, and heartbreaking to know that three-fifths of the captives were children just eight, nine or ten years old. They suffered from loneliness, hunger and exhaustion and must have been terribly distressed wondering about their parents and siblings. Emma wrote about one woman whose daughter was born on the long walk to the ocean.[9]

Captain Bostock was a mariner, and did not own a barracoon, instead relying on African dealers to supply him with captives. He and his crew anchored at the Banana Islands off the coast of Sierra Leone and would meet the local African chief—the son of a slave trader and a local woman—James Cleveland. He promised Captain Bostock good deals and they had exclusive business dealings for over sixteen years, but Cleveland was a ruthless man. The chiefs were like terrorists and warlords in their own dominions. Chief Cleveland expanded his territory by marrying a sister of a neighbouring rival (another warlord), Chief Charles Caulker, and then beheading him.

After slaving on the *Jemmy* in 1787, Captain Bostock decided to retire from the sea and leave younger men to the dangerous and dirty side of slave trading. He became a merchant in Liverpool, which was a natural progression for slave traders, but he made an unusual decision which he lived to regret for the rest of his life. He traded solely with his old friend James Cleveland, and after years of working well together, Cleveland suddenly decided to withhold money. In May 1790, 'Captain Bostock wrote to Cleveland complaining that he was so "much distressed for money at present" that he could "scarce keep my credit up". I have "so much property in your hands," he wrote, "I hope you will take it into consideration and release me from these difficulties as soon as possible."[10]

It all went horribly wrong, and by December 1790, his bank account at Heywood's Bank in Liverpool was overdrawn by nearly £1400 and his business was failing, but he still hoped it could be saved if Cleveland would repay him. In 1791, when Robert Jnr was just seven years old, one of Captain Bostock's ships brought the dreadful news that Chief James Cleveland had passed away. It signalled a terrible reversal of fortune for the Bostock family and Captain Bostock was close to ruin. In 1792, Captain Bostock became ill, and while many in Liverpool held firm in their support of the slave trade, in the rest of the country abolitionism was becoming a very popular cause, with an unprecedented one in six citizens signing a petition against the slave trade between 1787 and 1792. The abolitionists celebrated their first parliamentary victory in 1792 with a bill ensuring a gradual abolition of the slave trade, which was passed in the House of Commons. Unfortunately, it failed to become law because it was blocked by the House of Lords.

By January 1793, Britain declared war on republican France. The abolitionist movement was temporarily silenced, and all maritime commerce was halted by the war. Crisis gripped the country and Heywood's Bank was forced to borrow money from the Bank of England. Captain Bostock was sick and desperately anxious, and the financial burden took its toll on his health. In September 1793, he died at the age of 50.

It was a terrible financial blow for his family, and his wife, Elizabeth, was forced to work when their oldest son, John, was lost at sea in a shipwreck. The nine years between Captain Bostock's death and his son Robert's coming of age were a tumultuous time in Britain's history, and a time of hardship for the family.[11]

Robert Bostock Jnr

Seafaring and slave trading had always been in his family, and when Robert Bostock turned eighteen, he followed in his father's and older brother's footsteps. In 1802 he decided to set sail for the Banana Islands. His father's money was still there, but in Liverpool Captain Bostock's will remained unresolved. Robert hoped to vindicate his family's claim, and his timing was perfect, because Britain and France had just signed the Treaty of Amiens, a temporary truce that brought an upsurge in maritime trade. The French revolutionary government had abolished the slave trade, but Napoleon Bonaparte re-introduced it. A year later, in America, South Carolina would open its ports to slave ships.

Robert arrived at the Banana Islands, and found himself in the middle of a war between two African mafia-style criminal families: the Clevelands and their arch enemies, the Caulkers. Alone in Africa, with the chance of recovering his father's money disappearing, the possibility of slave trading was open to Robert. In true Godfather style, Chief Stephen Caulker made him 'an offer he couldn't refuse'. He would be his patron on the condition that Robert marry his daughter to secure his loyalty. It would cause great offence if Robert refused, so he married the daughter of the powerful Caulker family. For the next few months, the Caulkers were his in-laws, his patrons and his financiers, and the Banana Islands was his home.

While working for the Caulkers, a new opportunity opened up for Robert. Lancelot Bellerby, a slave trader who owned a 'slave factory', or multiple compounds, in the Gallinas region (on the Kerefe River), offered Robert a job as his second-in-command. Robert accepted Bellerby's offer and took his new young African wife on the short voyage to Gallinas. Bellerby's business was booming. Robert based himself there and did big business with the big names in slave trading at the time: ships belonging to one of North America's most avid slave traders, the De Wolfs of Rhode Island, patronised the factory.

Bellerby and Bostock had received information in 1804 that the Society for Effecting the Abolition of the Slave Trade had again been meeting in Great Britain. Other slave ships brought news that bills to prohibit slave trading were once again being introduced to parliament. Bellerby decided to leave Africa to link up directly with the De Wolf family. This left Robert Bostock, at 21 years of age, in charge, a ruler of his own slave-trading business. While other slave traders gave up and sailed home, Bostock continued in the trade. Hungry slave markets in Cuba and Brazil demanded to be fed, and increased risks meant higher profits. This market attracted new men, like American slave trader Charles Mason. Gallinas was once again an attractive destination for slave ship captains, but they were precariously close to the enemy, the abolitionist governor of the British colony of Sierra Leone, Mr E.H. Columbine.

Such was the impact of the slave trade that, at Gallinas and further south, even the landscape began to change. Imperceptibly at first, the previously cultivated land began to return to a dense forest of timber trees covered with vines and brushwood. It was said that thousands of miles were without inhabitants because so many had run in terror. Stories of those taken had spread like wildfire, with people lamenting those they had lost. It wasn't just the landscape that changed; the cultural structure of the people's everyday lives changed too. So many lost their kin that cultural clan identifications dissolved as groups moved from smaller hamlets into bigger settlements for their own protection. They made pacts to be brothers against the enemy and defend each other. While others came from places nearer to the coast, the birthplaces of some of those sold at Gallinas was around 450 kilometres from the coast. The cultural impact was a human disaster.

By the end of 1810, a new barracoon was raised on the shore at Gallinas, but Bostock and Mason were greedy and envisioned even greater profit, so they planned expansion. Both men agreed to establish a factory at St Paul River, a little further south. Bostock would stay at the factory, and 'sell, barter, ship, and dispose of the property as he may think most advantageous to the risk and benefit of both parties'. Charles Mason decided not to stay at their Gallinas business. His part of the agreement stated that Mason would 'go off with such property as may appear to be shipped on the account of the said parties and he shall make use of the property that may appear to rise from the same to the best of his judgement'. Both Bostock and Mason laid down a £1000 surety, and with Mason gone, Bostock needed someone to help him, so he hired John McQueen, who had been apprenticed to a slave trader from the age of ten or eleven.[12]

In March 1813, one of the Royal Navy's anti-slavery patrol ships, HMS *Thais*, captured the De Wolf vessel *Rambler* at Cape Mesurado as it cruised offshore from Bostock and Mason's St Paul factory. Substantial prize money had been paid to the crew of the *Thais* and they were jubilant. At the helm was Captain Edward Scobell, and he knew that extensive slave trading was being carried out nearby, by one or two Englishmen.

Scobell decided to go and investigate, and arrest the two men if he found anything suspicious. The Caulker family, Bostock's allies, heard of the plan and quickly sent men in canoes to charge ahead and warn him.

Frantic, Bostock ordered the factory slaves to unshackle the rest of his captives and take them to nearby warlord Chief Bagna's compound. In one last desperate move, the barracoon was put alight. Though they always denied it, and the marines admitted they did not know what happened, several others there that day said Bostock and McQueen ordered it. With the barracoon in flames, they ran away in the billowing smoke. Explosions boomed as the fire hit their vast store of rum, and barrels of gunpowder also exploded, creating fireworks visible for miles around.

Bostock and McQueen knew the game was up. Chief Bagna handed them over, claiming that they had been 'taken in the woods by the natives' rather than admit he had been hiding them. Both were handcuffed and rowed out to the *Thais*. Bostock and McQueen left behind the ruins of the slave factory they had constructed only eighteen months before.[13]

On 11 July 1813, apparently convinced that if they admitted their crime and begged for forgiveness they would walk free, Bostock and McQueen decided to plead guilty. They made a point of mentioning how long they had been involved in the slave trade, hoping that since they joined the trade before it was abolished, they would be able to alleviate their guilt. They were tried under the *Slave Trade Felony Act 1811*. Judge Robert Purdie, after hearing the testimonies of the crew of the *Thais*, proclaimed the two men guilty and quickly passed sentence. They were to be transported to Australia, Britain's prison colony, founded in 1788, for a term of fourteen years.[14]

Bostock and McQueen were told that they were being sent to England to have their sentences actuated and were ordered to re-board the *Thais*, which set sail on 4 August 1813. Neither Bostock nor McQueen would ever set foot in Sierra Leone again. As the weeks became months, they began to learn that the world they left a decade ago had changed. Abolitionism was such a force that it was changing the social landscape of Britain. Slave trading was not just illegal; it also had come to be recognised as immoral—and the view that it was so *un-British* it was on the verge of being traitorous had taken a firm hold. Opposition to the transatlantic slave trade had become a mark of self-acclaim, similar to today's 'virtue-signalling'. Abolitionism was a way in which the British, in their own self-regarding rhetoric at least, could 'save' the world's second-largest continent. As well as having the laws and statutes to contend with, Bostock and McQueen were also pitted against this phenomenon.

In August 1814, Bostock and McQueen were still languishing in Portsmouth gaol. They decided to go right to the top and wrote to the Prince Regent, who had taken over from his increasingly mad father, King George III, under the Regency Act of 1811. They wrote that they were 'sinking under the heavy sentence which has been passed upon them', lamenting their 'broken constitutions' after years in Africa, and that they had been 'dragged from Africa as felons'. Then they flattered that the example set them by Britain, 'this most humane, great, and united Kingdom', had already been 'most beneficial'. Finally, with a sense of full entitlement to forgiveness, they wrote that the way they had been shipped to Britain on the *Thais* had been 'disgraceful', since they been made to wear 'heavy irons' and, without irony, they exclaimed that it was 'insulting to the munificence of Britain', a country whose 'philanthropy and protection

so powerfully comforts the humble African'. 'Confined with
the dregs of society with felons of the worst description' in
Portsmouth jail, they dramatically signed off 'death will be a
welcome visitor'.[15]

When four convict transports set sail for Australia and
they were not ordered aboard, they were hopeful of a pardon,
but luck ran out when they were sent to the *Retribution* hulk,
and, in October 1814, loaded on to the convict transport
Indefatigable.

The pardon

In what can only be seen as a travesty of justice, after they arrived
in Sydney Cove in late April 1815, Bostock and McQueen
landed on their feet and deftly began new lives free from
hardship. Unlike other convicts who were allotted as private
servants for white settlers in outlying areas (such as Liverpool,
Parramatta or Windsor), or as labour for the colony's works,
Bostock and McQueen remained in Sydney, New South Wales.
Governor Lachlan Macquarie, whose vision was to establish
Sydney on seaborne trade, utilised the expertise that Bostock
and McQueen offered. Emma revealed that 'The opportunities Macquarie offered to convicts were so controversial that
in 1819 Britain sent out Commissioner John Brigge to investigate what on Earth was going on . . . Brigge was horrified by
what he found: lax rule and little intense agriculture'. Prior
to Brigge's arrival, New South Wales was the ideal environment for convicted men to start over again, so Bostock and
McQueen had plenty of time to set themselves up comfortably
before Brigge came.[16] There was huge demand for imported
goods and luxury items, and Bostock and McQueen became
busy, wealthy merchants. In January 1816, a convict ship called

Fanny delivered a cargo of 171 male prisoners, the news that Napoleon Bonaparte had been defeated at Waterloo, and pardons for Bostock and McQueen.[17]

Five days after the *Fanny*'s arrival, 31-year-old Robert married fifteen-year-old Rachael Rafferty at St Phillip's Church. She was the daughter of an Irish convict woman called Elizabeth Rafferty and a ship's captain, Robert Rhodes, who sailed away before Rachael was 'born free' in New South Wales. Rachael was a renowned beauty and it is likely that Robert Bostock was awaiting his freedom before marrying her so as not to harm her status as a freeborn woman through marriage to a convict. There were three men for every woman in the colony, so it was no small matter to attract a woman, and rarer still to win the hand of a freewoman. Bostock's African wife was forgotten.[18]

Records do not reveal how Bostock became so successful immediately upon his arrival in Sydney in April 1815, but by the time he married Rachael in January 1816, he was already a respectable colonial merchant and had set up a profitable shop. Bostock's business soon became a well-known emporium at 14 Hunter Street, where Sydney's first church had once stood. John McQueen worked as his assistant and they sold everything from furniture to food stuffs; beer, wine and liquor; apparel of all kinds, including hats, umbrellas and parasols; all manner of ironmongery; a vast assortment of cloth; tobacco and snuff; stationery and trunks; and even grand pianos and bird cages. Soon Bostock owned homes on Hunter and Bligh streets. By the end of 1816, Governor Lachlan Macquarie had given him his first land grant. Certainly, he would have received letters and news from England via the ships that pulled into the harbour. Perhaps it was his family in Liverpool who informed him that he and McQueen were mentioned in a controversial new book by Robert Thorpe. It was Thorpe's belief that Bostock and McQueen's arrest was illegal.[19]

Judge Robert Thorpe was Judge Robert Purdie's predecessor, and while sitting on the bench at Freetown in Sierra Leone, he had always stood firm against the slave traders—but after he published a book in the form of an open letter to William Wilberforce, he was removed from his post in absentia and never allowed to return to the colony. Furious, Thorpe had become an avid advocate for the slave traders. He quoted the Slave Trade Felony Act to argue that Bostock and McQueen (or Bostwick & M'Quin, as he called them) had a claim for wrongful arrest purely on the grounds that Cape Mesurado was not British territory. None of this raised any doubt that Bostock and McQueen had been illegally slave trading. In fact, Bostock himself never denied it. The British Government, however, did know that they had been wrongly convicted, because it was an oversight on their part that actually led to the conviction being overturned.

Before Bostock and McQueen's arrest in 1813, the British Government failed to send out a new commission to Sierra Leone to allow them to try those captured for slave trading if they were beyond British boundaries and on land rather than on seas. Without such a commission, Bostock and McQueen should have been sent back to England for trial. It wasn't so much about being convicted in error, as it was about being tried in the wrong location. The British Government had little choice but to overturn the conviction. Much more than the free pardon that arrived in New South Wales, this made Bostock a free man with no past convictions on his record. His slave-trading past was officially erased.

By late 1817, having been married to Rachael for nearly two years, Robert heard about three slave dealers arrested in 1814 who had won their cases to have their convictions overturned. One of them had been awarded £20,000 compensation from Governor Maxwell for his losses, and another was claiming £50,000. Robert decided that he would make his own case to hopefully get his record expunged and gain a vast sum of money in compensation for the losses he suffered while a convict. Passage back to Britain was expensive and it is surprising that Robert had already earned enough money to take his wife and baby daughter. Few convicts were ever able to return. Robert and his young family set sail on the *Harriet* a few days before Christmas in 1817, but some convicts had stowed away on board, so they had to make an unscheduled stop, sailing into the harbour at Hobart, Van Diemen's Land, to offload them. The stopover was only for a few hours, but it was long enough for Robert to see a bit of the town, and it took his fancy.

Robert Bostock claimed £50,000 damages, the same sum that slave trader James Dunbar had successfully claimed. Governor Maxwell was now 'financially embarrassed', so Bostock and Thorpe decided to launch a suit against Edward Scobell, the captain of HMS *Thais*. However, Scobell had retired. The British Government, smarting from having to pay countless claims of wronged slave ship captains, including having to bail out Maxwell, therefore agreed to an 'out of court settlement'. Since it was a behind-closed-doors agreement, there is no record of what Bostock received. He then applied to the secretary of state for a free settler certificate for Van Diemen's Land. The British Government must have been pleased that what he wanted the most was a free settler certificate and, as a result, perhaps he received a smaller amount in cash.[20]

The more I learned about colonial times and the social stigma associated with being a convict, the more I could see that what Bostock had done was a very wise move.

Van Diemen's Land

At the end of February 1821, Robert, Rachael and their three children arrived in Hobart, Van Diemen's Land. It was three years and two months since he had left Sydney as an emancipated convict. Now carrying a certificate from the English secretary of state for the colonies that declared he was a 'free settler', Robert could persuade people that he had never been a convict at all. Returning to Sydney, though, was not an option. There were too many people there who knew he had been a convict, and he was keen to go somewhere where he could make a new start.

Ever the money-making entrepreneur, Bostock carried with him an assortment of merchandise from England. He placed an advertisement in the *Hobart Town Gazette* for the sale of brandy, gin, cloth and clothes of various kinds. He then set off for Sydney to settle his affairs with McQueen, who had faithfully been running their joint business. McQueen was doing very well; he was married with two children, had applied for an auctioneer's licence and had the means to buy out Bostock's share of the business. McQueen was an agent for businessmen who lived out of town, and one of his clients left him an incredible bequest of a schooner called *Endeavour*, which he had refitted and, through his old friend, he began trading with Van Diemen's Land.

When Robert returned to Hobart, he applied for a land grant. The amount of land given was dependent on the amount of money a settler had, and these figures were usually exaggerated. So, when Robert listed his assets, he professed to have £1800 of merchandise and cash on hand, the houses in Hunter Street and Bligh Street in Sydney, worth £1200 and £300 respectively, and another £1800 from the proceeds of the business with John McQueen. In Van Diemen's Land, Lieutenant Governor Sorrell handed out land grants on a scale never before witnessed, and in just the single year of 1821, he allocated a massive 47,180 acres (19,100 hectares) to white settlers. The land that Sorrell granted to Robert Bostock is still a prize plot of land—Hobart's twelve-storey Grand Chancellor Hotel (formerly the Sheraton Hotel) stands there today.[21]

Robert Bostock's second business venture, in the heart of town, thrived by importing all manner of goods for the young colony's social elite, who were trying to recreate British-style culture in the colony. Robert and Rachael were at the forefront of dignified colonial society, with Robert remaining utterly silent about his past. Rachael, who travelled with him to England, must surely have been aware of his conviction, but his children were never told of their father's earlier career. Robert wasn't just hiding his slave-trading past; he was extremely anxious about hiding from 'the convict stain'. Free white settlers were almost religious in their claims of moral superiority over convicts and emancipists. He needed to distance himself from the convict and ex-convict world as much as possible. This wasn't just about his and Rachael's hopes of entertaining 'the better sort' as dinner guests. This was critical to their children's chances in life. There were stories of children being thrown out of school when it was discovered their long-dead mother was a convict. Robert wanted nothing of the kind for his growing family.

By 1826, when Robert was given another generous land grant north of Hobart on the South Esk River, he and his wife Rachael had six children. There he built his mansion called Vaucluse, named after a 125-acre (50-hectare) property on a Sydney headland that Rachael's mother, Elizabeth Rafferty, once owned. Within a few years of settling in, he had eleven children, and another adjoining 1800 acres (730 hectares) had been granted to him. He built a home as well as a barn, granary yards and stables, and soon owned 63 cattle, 2500 sheep and eight horses. Robert was allotted an assortment of convict servants, mostly petty thieves, to work for him in the fields and in the house. Once merino sheep were found to flourish in Australia, the colonists had a product that was in huge demand globally, could be transported long distances cheaply, and proved astonishingly profitable.

The Black Line

Robert Bostock lived a relatively quiet life, concentrating on his farming and providing for his family; however, he was involved in a certain affair that it is important to relate. In the late 1820s and into the 1830s, his home on the South Esk River was on the frontier of the Black War between white settlers and Indigenous inhabitants of the region. The traditional inhabitants of the land were fighting for their survival as their access to food evaporated, but the settlers were intent on proclaiming the land theirs, and deaths of both settlers and Aboriginal people resulted from the violent encounters that occurred. In 1826, the *Hobart Town Gazette* reported Aboriginal people as the lowest form of humanity and lamented that 'we might entertain some distant hopes of civilising them, had they any affinity to the African negro—who is both docile and intelligent'. This article openly stated that if Aboriginal people were 'collected and removed to some island in the Straits where they could have an equal chance, as here, of animal support, without the molestation of white men, we think the happiest results would ensue'.[22]

So, Robert Bostock, in his late thirties, was required to stand on what became known as 'the Black Line'. It was a truly immense and desperate operation that would require a mass mobilisation of able-bodied men to defend the colony. They would stand together to form a huge chain across the island and walk in a pincer movement towards the sea to capture all the native people who were still living. The 'chain of posts' that showed the lines to be marched passed straight through Robert Bostock's land. Emma Christopher writes,

> The plan was an utter failure, but nevertheless, here at the end of the world we find a baffling but related image, a final glimpse of the man who once had been a fair-haired boy hearing his father's stories of slave trading in Africa. Now the former slave trader and his sons stood with rifles in an attempt to rid his new land of dark-skinned people.[23]

Antipodean roots

Once settled into post-convict life as a free settler, Robert Bostock was able to establish the roots of a new Antipodean family tree, with branches that spread all over Australia. The abolition of the transatlantic slave trade, and Robert's eventual arrest for illegally trading slaves, had in effect uprooted him from his English family and their slave-trading legacy.

Rachael Bostock gave birth to eleven children in her lifetime, the births occurring when she was 16, 18, 20, 22, 24, 26, 28, 30, 33, 34 and 37. Sadly, she died young, just after she had given birth to her eleventh child, James, in 1837. There were ten surviving children when Rachael died, and Robert had enough wealth and servants to provide each of them with an affluent, privileged life.

As his children grew into adulthood, Van Diemen's Land became fully grazed and Robert encouraged his son George to follow the tracks of his neighbour John Batman and other pioneers who had gone to Victoria to seek 'greener pastures'. Later, he encouraged his other sons, Thomas, Ernest, Augustus and James, to do the same. Robert frequently visited them, and they returned home often enough to maintain relationships with young ladies whom they had grown up with, and would later marry. Robert Bostock's health declined only a short while before he died at Vaucluse on 10 June 1847 at the age of 63. By that time, almost all of his children's families had moved to the Western District or Port Phillip in Victoria.

Robert Bostock's last will and testament was very different from the usual ones of the period, where the eldest son, and his son, and so on down the generations, were the beneficiaries of all real estate. Instead, Robert bequeathed an equal distribution of his wealth to each of his children following the sale of Vaucluse.

Emma Christopher wrote that 'Robert Bostock's life was an exemplar of what middle-class men with entrepreneurial talents and vast amounts of luck could achieve. But if viewed from a perspective that stretches far beyond Australia's shore, it is also clear that he was the recipient of heady doses of white privilege, one of the legacies his former trade bestowed upon the world.'[24] His obituary lauded him as a pioneer settler and gentleman whose 'kindness of heart' had won him many friends. Perhaps his descendants and others would argue that the transformation from being a slave trader to becoming a model citizen was enough to redeem him. Does living a good life atone for long-forgotten crimes of the past? Although one might accept that 'the sins of the father' should not be 'visited upon the child', the refusal to acknowledge those sins, and/or erasure of those sins, surely serves as an incredible injustice to the humanity of the people against whom those sins were committed.

Augustus John and One My

Thomas Edward Bostock was the first of Robert and Rachael's children to be born at Vaucluse, in 1828. He married Catherine Jane Mackersey, and the third of their eight children was my great-great-grandfather, Augustus John Bostock. Thelma told me that when Augustus John's mother died he was eleven years old, so the family sent him to England to be educated at a wealthy private boarding school and later, at the age of eighteen, he returned to Australia.

It is not known when Augustus John Bostock travelled north to Bundjalung Country, but at around 27 years of age he married my great-great-grandmother, an Aboriginal woman called One My. I know this because on his death certificate, in the section marked 'Marriages: Where, at what age and to whom deceased was married', the corresponding details recorded were 'Tweed River ... about 27, One My otherwise Clara Wolumbin'. Her name, this record and other archival documents (which name her), as well as confirmation from Bundjalung Elders, indicate that she was a traditional Aboriginal woman from the Wollumbin/Mount Warning people. Finding One My was incredibly exciting for me, because I actually had the name of one of the traditional Aboriginal ancestors from whom our 'mob of blackfellas' is descended.

We always knew we were Bundjalung, and my father had frequently told us, 'Our mob are from the Tweed', but he didn't know much else. Now I had a starting point for my research journey. Uncle Gerry's late night phone call, then meeting

Thelma and Emma, and finding out about the slave traders in the family, felt like I had turned the ignition key on a vehicle to take me on this journey. My burning curiosity was the fuel that propelled me forward on my quest to find everything I could get my hands on about the experience of my ancestors, from colonisation to my generation.

2

Wollumbin onslaught

'Begone, begone . . . you have the river and the open country and ought to be content, and leave the mountains to the black people. Go back—keep the plains, and leave us the hills. Go, go, begone!'

TOOLBILLIBAM, AS RECOUNTED BY EDWARD OGILVIE, 1842

When my father said to me, 'Our mob are from the Tweed', he meant the Tweed River, which is very close to the border between New South Wales and Queensland. At that time, I didn't know where to begin researching my family history, so around 2009, I took myself to the Tweed Heads Historical Society. Their premises is a charming little historical cottage, right on the banks of the stunningly beautiful river. Behind the counter was an elderly lady, and I told her that I was researching my family history and looking for any records with the Bostock name. I explained to her that my great-great-grandfather was a white man who married an Aboriginal woman, and that I am a descendant of the local Bundjalung people. She became really animated and said, 'Oh, what a shame you just missed Bill.' Unsuccessfully trying to access the computer, she gave up and began searching through the filing cabinet, all the while chatting about how Bill had meticulously organised their records—he had whole sections on 'the pioneers' and 'the Aborigines'. It was obvious that she wanted to help me, but didn't know where to look, or what to do. Excruciatingly long minutes passed until I suggested that perhaps she could give me Bill's phone number so that I could give him a call. She immediately stopped rummaging through the files, looked directly at me and said, 'Oh no, Darl. Bill died two weeks ago.'

Bill Bainbridge was formerly a senior bureaucrat in the Victorian Education Department. Upon retirement he moved up to the Tweed River region to enjoy the warmer climate in his advancing years. He was very interested in local history, especially Aboriginal history. Bill helped out at the historical society, and privately accumulated a huge collection of archives and information. The lady at the historical society gave me the name and phone number of Bill's friend, Ian Fox, saying that he and Bill did a lot of 'that history stuff' together.

When I rang him, I found out that Ian was actually a professional heritage consultant who, not surprisingly, was completely engrossed in local history. He told me that he knew my uncles, Lester and Gerry Bostock, and was delighted to help me find out more about my family history. Before he died, Bill had instructed his daughter to make sure that Ian got copies of whatever he wanted from his vast collection. Ian had added Bill's paperwork to his own private collection of historical information, which he called his 'library'.

Ian Fox sounded as interested in my family history as I was. I told him that our family has always known that we were descended from a non-Indigenous man called Augustus John Bostock, who married an Aboriginal woman, and that our family was from the Tweed. I also told him that Augustus John's death certificate states in the 'marriages' section that my great-great-grandmother's name was recorded as 'One My otherwise Clara Wolumbin'. There was a long, silent pause before he quietly asked me to repeat what I had just said. I obliged, and then he said, 'Well—that is certainly a significant piece of information. There are plenty of traditional Aboriginal people recorded in the historical record, but only a handful have the Wollumbin name, and there are plenty of people who will be very interested to hear this news. Sounds to me like she was one of the traditional Wollumbin/Mount Warning people.'

Mount Warning is the name that maritime explorer Captain Cook gave the strikingly majestic mountain that towers over the region. It is nestled in a caldera, the remains of the huge sides of the volcano that it once was. Captain Cook gave it the name 'Mount Warning' to warn mariners of shallow water where the caldera extends into the ocean—but the traditional Bundjalung name for Mount Warning is (and always will be) Wollumbin.

Next, I asked Ian if he had any information about Augustus John Bostock. I could hear the faint sound of keyboard keys clickety clacking and could tell he was searching for something. I waited patiently until he said, 'Okay—interesting. Bill put together a list called "Tweed Valley Land Records 1868 to 1918", and on the top of the list is Augustus John Bostock. It says his land was in the Parish of Burrell, and the year recorded is 1882. Going back that far, it would have to have been a CP.'

Not knowing what a 'CP' was, I asked Ian to explain. He answered, 'Have you ever heard of a pioneer's selection, and the way the government distributed land in the 1800s?' I had seen a (1995) movie starring Leo McKern and Geoffrey Rush called *Dad and Dave: On our selection*, so I had a vague idea that a 'selection' had something to do with land. Ian explained, 'Well, it's officially called a conditional purchase, hence me calling it a "CP". A settler could purchase a piece of Crown land for a reasonably cheap price, but the government placed conditions on it, like putting up a fence and making improvements. If you can get hold of a copy of Augustus John's CP, then we can look up where his land was. I have a great collection of maps in my library, including all the county and parish maps. You'll have to come down to Burringbar for a visit.'

Nineteen counties

To understand how land was distributed in the 1800s, I first had to learn about new concepts (for me) such as conditional purchases, Crown lands, 'limits of location', government land Acts, pastoralism and free selection—so it was important to go back half a century to fully comprehend what led to Augustus John Bostock's conditional purchase of land, and how the encroachment of white settlers actually happened.

In New South Wales, the 'limits of location' were defined by Governor Darling in 1826 in accordance with a government order from Lord Bathurst, the British secretary of state for the colonies from 1812 to 1827. By 1829, the boundaries were extended to 'the nineteen counties' around Sydney. This meant that land grants would only be issued within this boundary, and all land outside these boundaries was considered to be Crown land.[1] Searching the internet, there are plenty of maps of 'the nineteen counties', but they might best be described as follows: the boundary of the nineteen counties looks like something really big had opened its mouth over Sydney, and taken a bite out of the side of New South Wales. From Sydney, the perimeter of the semi-circular *bite* goes up the coast as far north as

Taree, then curves out to the west and south, skirting the town of Orange, before circling further south and east, and into the coast at Bateman's Bay. People who chose to settle on unoccupied land outside the jurisdiction of the nineteen counties were classed as 'squatters'.

The term 'squatter' first appeared in 1828 and, other than being the first European person to settle on the land, the squatters had no legal title to it. Squatters were usually wealthy people of high social prestige who could afford to spend large sums of money on expeditions to stake out claims, and later drove large numbers of livestock to graze on pastoral land. Successful squatters were among the wealthiest people in the colony, and they came to be described as the squattocracy. They were the new rural aristocracy of the colony.

In the 1830s, a rapidly expanding colonial capitalist economy meant that the nineteen counties' boundaries became redundant. With wool becoming the colonies' staple export, it offered emancipated convicts and free settlers employment in the pastoral industry, and the demand for labour soon outweighed supply. The government attempted to reduce the monopolies on the land held by squatters, but they were up against the mutual interests of the squatters and the merchants. Nonetheless, the government's implementation of land Acts can now be seen as a long-sighted attempt to create fairer acquisition of land and to increase the number of players in the pastoral industry. Governor Bourke's *Crown Lands Unauthorised Occupation Act 1836* was the first Land Act to control the squatting trend, by issuing licences costing £10 to pastoralists, which allowed them to use Crown land beyond the nineteen counties for grazing.[2]

To clarify, 'squatters' (or squatting) refers to the illegal way they took up the land, and 'pastoralists' (or pastoralism) refers to the way they used the land as graziers. But not all the Europeans who penetrated Bundjalung Country were interested in pastoralism or farming.

Cedar getters

Most of the Tweed River and Richmond River regions were covered with rainforest that became known as 'The Big Scrub'. The rainforest was nearly impossible to walk through except for occasional grassy areas where the tree canopy opened up to the sunlight. The forests that had stood undisturbed for centuries were soon under threat because the timber they contained, especially the red cedar, was as valuable as gold to merchants in Sydney. The men who came to Bundjalung Country and cut down the giant cedar trees were called 'cedar getters'.

Once it had begun, the invasion of the cedar getters into the Tweed Valley went ahead very rapidly. The forest echoed with the sounds of shouting men, 'the ring of axes, the rasp of a cross-cut saw, and the thunderous crash of forest giants'.[3] When the first cedar getters arrived on the Tweed River, they had whale boats. The long boats were an essential mode of transport up the river because, at that early stage, the cedar getters had no knowledge of the Aboriginal tracks. The harvesting of cedar began in 1844 and the abundance of cedar was such that they didn't have to penetrate upriver until years later. The density of the forests made it impossible to utilise bullock teams, but the plentiful supply could be accessed by rivers and waterways. Huge quantities of red cedar were shipped from the Tweed Valley between 1845 and 1870, and it wasn't until after 1870 that the lack of cedar trees forced the trade to end.

In 1857, Captain W.A.B. Greaves, Grafton-based district surveyor and Crown lands commissioner, described the Tweed as being virtually grassless and wrote: 'For grazing purposes it was worthless being covered with an impenetrable scrub.'[4] The Big Scrub was a vast, untamed, unmapped territory and the cedar getters were described as being 'by and large, a reckless, rum drinking lot'. Just like the landscape, cedar getters were recorded as being wild and uncivilised.

There were some respectable cedar getters, but they were usually those who preferred the anonymity of the forest. Only a few of the men took their women and children with them. The density of the cedar forests was so incredibly thick that the overhead canopy allowed only minimum sunlight to get through. Reverend Cole Childs, the Grafton vicar, wrote that he came upon a creek and 'where the sawyers are, were seven huts, men, women and children all in the brush under immense trees, the women and children are quite pale with a yellow tint'. Frontier violence between Aboriginal people and cedar getters was not uncommon, with revenge attacks and punitive reprisals following murders of both cedar getters and Aboriginal people. Until the 1860s, the denseness of the rainforest made overland travel difficult for white settlers and discouraged permanent settlement.[5]

But it wasn't just The Big Scrub that was in the way of white settler dreams of future prosperity on Bundjalung Country. Large numbers of squatters had claimed land in the New England Ranges area, but baulked at traversing the treacherous eastern escarpment of the Great Dividing Range to reach the abundant river valleys below.

Ogilvie and Toolbillibam

Two decades before permanent settlers arrived in the Tweed River Valley, talk of a 'Big River' reached the elite gentlemen's group known as the Australian Club. Consisting of exclusives and emancipists, Whigs and Tories, who were 'prepared to make common cause', it was formed to promote 'the social and literary interests of individuals resident in the colony, and for country gentlemen'. The list of 64 foundation members included some prestigious names, such as Hannibal Macarthur, Richard Jones, Alexander Macleay, and the three Blaxlands. Other members included Dr John Dobie, James and John Mylne, J.H. Grose and (Frenchman) Francis Girard. Once a radical crusader, the gruff William Charles Wentworth (of Vaucluse) was an interesting omission, having previously called the exclusives 'the yellow snakes of the Colony'; but, as the largest landowner of them all, he was later admitted.

Although Governor George Gipps was named the Australian Club's patron, the members saw him as a threat to their landowning ambitions. Retired naval captain William Ogilvie, his oldest son Will (William Jnr) and his second son Edward, Hunter Valley pioneers and pastoralists, were invited to join the Australian Club. The Ogilvies felt they had finally arrived. The Australian Club was a handy place to pick up information, and word had got to its members that there was a region 'protected from the outer world by steep rugged mountains, possessed of fertile grazing lands without a hoof on them, a warm climate, unlimited water, and untouched forests'. It was 'beautiful beyond description'. With all that high praise, it was surprising that the Big River had remained virtually unknown.[6]

The colonisation of the region happened fairly late in the settlement of Australia. In 1839, Governor George Gipps changed the name of the 'Big River' to the Clarence River in honour of the previous king, William IV, Duke of Clarence. A year later, at 26 years of age, Edward Ogilvie and his younger brother Frederick set out to take up a pastoral run on the

Clarence. They came down from the New England region and, in their haste to beat other squatters, they suffered a harrowing experience and near starvation, before pushing on to the Clarence to take up the Yulgilbar Run.[7]

Edward's father had taught him an interest in Aboriginal languages and he learned one of the Bundjalung languages from a boy called Pundoon, whom he found after 'one of the encounters' (a terrible massacre) with local Aboriginal people. Ogilvie discovered Pundoon hiding in a hollow log. The lad's mother presumably died in the shooting. He put him on his saddle and rode home. He took him back to the two bark huts that he and Fred had built for themselves, treated him with kindness, and took him everywhere he went, even on the long-distance journey to Merton, his father's run in the Hunter Valley, to buy sheep and drove them back to Yulgilbar. A visitor to Merton, pastoralist Charles Tindal, wrote a letter home to his family, stating, 'there is a wild black down from the Clarence River. He was taken prisoner by the Ogilvies some time back. He cannot yet speak a word of English; but is fond of Edward, who speaks their language well.'[8]

Edward Ogilvie wrote a remarkable letter to *The Sydney Morning Herald* on 8 July 1842 that offers incredible insight into how Aboriginal people felt about the settlers' encroachment on to their land. I have not done the research to find out if the following account is the first time that a traditional Aboriginal person's conversation with a colonial settler in an Aboriginal language was translated and transcribed for non-Indigenous Australians to read, but I find this letter a truly fascinating read.

By learning to speak the dialect of Toolbillibam's traditional language group—then translating his encounter and recording it in writing—Ogilvie has captured a moment in history that has been liberated from language barriers. We cannot know for sure whether this exchange is exactly as it happened, but Ogilvie's motivation and his determination to learn the language are supported by others. George Farwell, author of 22 books, and biographer of Edward Ogilvie, wrote that 'On Edward's own admission, this was the chief reason for adopting the boy. He recognised that the key to mastering these wild tribes was to learn their language. Ogilvie's sister Ellen said he spoke the language fluently in a remarkably short time, and even produced a grammar. No trace of this has since been found. Edward was a very determined man'.[9]

Although this letter, written for Sydney newspaper readers, is quite a long one, its content warrants reproducing it in its entirety. A transcription of the original correspondence was given to me by a retired academic and former senior lecturer at the Southern Cross University, Mr Maurice Ryan. It was typed on an old-fashioned manual typewriter, and the paper is so old it is starting to crumble and fall apart. In his book, George Farwell has edited out small parts of the original letter, and I believe this copy is the full, unedited transcription of the original letter that Edward Ogilvie sent to *The Sydney Morning Herald*.

To the Editors of the Sydney Herald.

Gentlemen: I am induced to send you an account of a rather interesting interview which I had some days ago with a party of aborigines on the upper part of this river, being of the opinion that insertion of the particulars in the columns of your widely circulated paper may be productive of some good results, as far as may tend to remove the belief that these people are an utterly irreclaimable and ferocious set of beings, and throw light upon their real character and disposition—a subject very little known or understood.

Since the hostile encounters with the blacks, which took place upon this river about a year ago, in consequence of the murders committed by them, they have rarely shown themselves, but have kept among the mountains, and avoided all intercourse, always making off as fast as possible if accidently seen, they have occasionally crept unobserved upon the huts, and carried off the shepherds blankets and axes. I had previously several times tried to find them and bring them to a parley, to endeavour to establish a better understanding between them and ourselves, but always without success, until upon the occasion abovementioned, when, having seen a smoke arising amongst the hills some miles distant, my brother and myself mounted our horses, and set out to make another attempt. After clambering about the hills for some time, we entered a narrow valley, which we had not explored far, when we suddenly came in sight of a camp situated upon a small flat, surrounded on three sides by a creek, and backed by a mountain. Instantly setting spurs to our horses, we galloped across the creek into the camp; we found it untenanted, however, except for a woman with an infant at the breast, and a child apparently about four or five years old. On our approach they fled up the mountain, the woman carrying her child astride upon her neck. As we neared them they cried out in great fear, and upon our coming close the woman took the infant from her shoulders, and clasping it to her bosom, threw herself upon her knees and bowed her face to the ground thus concealing and protecting her little one with her body: the other child crouched at her side and hid its face in the grass.

They uttered no sound, but their long drawn respiration showed that they were in great terror. I dismounted, and taking the child by the shoulders, raised her face from the ground, but she set up such a terrible squalling, that I let it go again, when she dropped quite stiff and stark into her former position, and was again silent. I sat down near them, and having some knowledge of their language, which I had gained from a young boy called Pundoon, who was taken in one of the aforementioned encounters, and who has since remained with me, I addressed the woman, telling her not to fear, as we had no hostile intentions, and would not harm her etc. etc. After a time she raised her head and looking steadfastly at me for a little while, resumed her former position, but she seemed to have been reassured by the scrutiny, for she presently raised her head and began to speak. She first asked if we were hostile or angry, and being again assured that we were not, she said that she was afraid of the horses, and asked if they would not bite her. We told her that they were harmless, and lived upon the grass; upon which she seemed to lose all fear, and became quite chatty, answering all our questions, and saying a great deal more that we could not understand. We learned from her that the men were hunting upon the surrounding mountains, and after a great deal of shouting and calling, in which the lady joined (though not until she made me repeat several times that I was not an enemy), we heard an answering shout from a hilltop; all was then silent again for some time, and, as we felt assured that the blacks were reconnoitering, we concealed our only gun in the grass, and assuming as unwarlike an appearance as possible, we sat down upon the grass beside our horses.

48

We had long remained thus, when we were roused by a sudden shout upon the mountainside, and as we got upon our feet, two men, armed, but perfectly naked, came in view over the shoulder of the hill, about one hundred and fifty yards above us. One of them, a large, finely proportioned man, immediately stood forward, and waving one arm in the direction of the river, in a most undaunted and uncompromising manner, told us begone. I called out to him that our intentions were friendly, that we were unarmed, and that I wanted to speak with him, but he talked so loudly himself, that he could not hear me. He also spoke so rapidly that I could but partially understand what he said, which was, however, something to this effect: 'Begone, begone, and take away your horses;—why do you come hither among the mountains to disturb us? Return to your houses in the valley;—you have the river and the open country, and you ought to be content, and leave the mountains to the black people. Go back,—keep the plains, and leave us the hills. Go, go, begone'—with a great deal more in the same strain.

Having at length induced him to attend, I advanced some distance towards him, and after again assuring him that my intentions were not hostile, and calling upon him to observe that I was not armed, I said, 'Lay down your weapons and approach me.' He regarded me for a moment, and then, with great deliberation, threw from him his spears and his boomerang, and came forward a few paces, retaining his parrial (or wallaby stick), in his hand. I told him to put that down also—he did so with some reluctance, but would not consent to come any lower down the hill. I therefore slowly ascended towards him, keeping a steady watch upon his movements.

As I approached, he seemed uneasy and went behind a tree, but, as if ashamed of this, he soon stood out again. By this time I was near enough to distinguish his features, and feeling satisfied from his bold and open expression that he might be trusted, I walked straight up to him and took him by the hand. He asked 'Are we friends?' and I again assured him that we had none but friendly intentions towards him. He appeared to be much delighted at finding me speaking his own language, and soon became quite at ease. His companion, who had till this time remained some distance in the rear, now threw down his weapons and joined us. They, however, still showed a great fear of the horses, and would, on no account, consent to their being brought near; my brother, therefore, fastened them to a tree, and came up the hill, carrying in his hand a tomahawk that we brought with us, and which he presented to our tall friend, whose name we found to be Toolbillibam: he was overjoyed at the gift, and leapt and shouted with delight. We were now upon the best terms possible, and Toolbillibam began to shout loudly for the rest of his tribe, who, he saw, were upon the surrounding mountains, to come in and see us. I now asked him if he knew anything of Pundoon; at hearing the name, his countenance brightened, and with great earnestness of manner, he told me he was the boy's second father, or uncle, and that the father was at hand among his companions, to bring whom to me, he now redoubled his shouting. In a short time five of them made their appearance, running along the mountainside towards us. Toolbillibam called out to them, telling them how matters stood, and they instantly threw their weapons out of their hands.

He pointed out one of them as Pundoon's father, calling him by his name of Pundoonban. The old fellow, upon Toolbillibam calling out to him that he had news of his son, came running down, with outstretched arms, and coming first up to my brother, gave him the full benefit of a most literally sweet embrace, as the old gentleman had evidently dined upon honey, and for want of a spoon, had used his fingers, besides having smeared his face a good deal more than was pleasant. He asked me many questions about his son, much more quickly than they could be answered, and upon learning that he lived in a house and ate bread, and wore clothes like ourselves, and that we would soon bring him back to the river, and that he should see him, the old fellow's joy was unbounded. Having, by this time, eight or nine of the blacks about us, we told them to sit down in a row, and made them a regular harangue.

We said, that we made war upon them, because they had killed white people, but that now our anger was gone, and that we wished to live in peace with them; that we wanted nothing in their country but the grass, and would leave them their kangaroo, their opossums and their fish. Toolbillibam here interposed, to know if we would not leave them the honey also. We assured him that it was quite at their service, and that he might make himself perfectly easy about rats, bandicoots, grubs and all other small game.

All this appeared to be extremely satisfactory to our audience. We told them that if they would not rob or injure our people, nor kill our sheep, that no person would harm them; but on the contrary, would give them bread when they came to the stations; and we promised that if they conducted themselves peaceably for a time, that we would give each of them a tomahawk. We pointed out to them the direction of all our stations, and told them that when they visited them, not to sneak from tree to tree, but to walk up openly and call out to give notice of their approach, and put their weapons out of their hands—all this they promised to attend to. The sun was sinking, therefore, after distributing amongst them, our pocket knives, our handkerchiefs, and such articles of our dress as we could spare, we told them that we must go.

They all rose and accompanied us to the camp, which lay in our route, Toolbillibam walked before, and with much care parted the long grass with his hands, and cleared away all obstacles from our path.

Before parting with our wild looking friends, we remained a few moments to examine their household goods and utensils which were in the camp. Hanging near each fire was a large bag, about the size of a two bushel sack, very ingeniously fabricated of grasses and rushes woven together, which appeared to contain all their property. Some spears were piled against the trees, and clubs, boomerangs and shields were scattered about.

Of opossum cloaks they appear to have a very scanty supply, as I saw none but the very old well-worn ones, but as a kind of substitute they had large bunches of the skins of flying squirrels tails tied together, which they used as a covering at night. The blacks appeared uneasy at our taking so much notice of their valuables, we therefore, having attempted in vain to have some of them accompany us home, took our leave.

Toolbillibam, who was evidently the head of his tribe, again preceded us, clearing our path as before, until he had conducted us as far from his camp as was consistent with his notions of politeness. None of these people could speak or understand a single word of English, and some had possibly never seen a white man before. I have not since seen them, but they have visited some of the outstations, always approaching as they were desired, calling out to give notice of their approach, and laying down their weapons. I shall not fail to follow up this first step by all means in my power, and hope it may improve the commencement with a friendly intercourse with the natives of the River.

The only apology I can offer for occupying so large a portion of your valuable space, is, that without entering into the details I could not have attained the object I had in my view, namely, to show the very placable disposition and unrevengeful spirit of these people, and to convince those who are in the habit of looking upon them as little better than wild beasts, that they are mistaken.

With an appeal, therefore, to the patience of your readers, I beg to subscribe myself, Gentlemen,

Your obedient servant, E.O.

Clarence River, June 4 – 1842.[10]

Land Acts

Whether knowingly or unknowingly, Edward Ogilvie's letter to *The Sydney Morning Herald*—and his translation, which included Toolbillibam's demand that they 'leave the mountains to the black people'—not only presented the wider Australian public with a vivid story of first contact between a white man and a 'full-blood', traditional Aboriginal person, it also presented Toolbillibam's expectation that land should be left for him and his people to occupy.

With the ending of slavery in the British colonies in 1833, the Anti-Slavery Society and other humanitarian reformers turned their attention to the plight of Indigenous peoples in the British colonies. They began to investigate and advocate for the Maoris in New Zealand, the Indians (as First Nations people were then referred to) in Canada and Aboriginal people in Australia. In Australia, the Land Act of 1842 began to regularise the sale of land in the colony, but at the same time it reflected rising British concerns about Aboriginal people and their access and rights to land. For the first time, the Act allowed for Crown land to be reserved for the use of Aboriginal people.[11]

Because squatters increasingly began to regard these contested areas as property that belonged to them—when in fact they were only the licensed occupiers of Crown land—Governor Gipps attempted to devise a way for the government to control and profit from pastoralism without impeding its growth or giving the squatters permanency of tenure. Gipps believed that the colony was gripped by 'land-mania'. The *Imperial Waste Lands Occupation Act 1846*, brought into operation by an Order-in-Council, replaced earlier restrictions and gave the squatters far more security than Gipps wanted. Yet the Act did reiterate the 1842 power to create reserves for the benefit of Aborigines.[12]

This system remained in place until the *Crown Lands Alienation Act 1861*, and the *Crown Lands Occupation Act 1861*, both known as the Robertson Land Acts after John Robertson, the premier of New South Wales. The Robertson Land Acts were a new system of land occupation where all Crown land, including that held on pastoral leases, was open to free selection. This Act forced the squatters to have to buy the freehold land that they had previously held by lease. Some squatters with vast amounts of land had to go deeply into debt to protect themselves from the 'selectors'. The Robertson Land Acts released land from pastoralism, and opened up Crown land for the selectors, the regular, everyday people, rather than just the wealthy squattocracy who made their fortunes 'on the sheep's back'. Selectors could choose any block of land, which they would be entitled to own freehold if they were able to meet low repayments and residence qualifications.[13] That is how the land ownership agreement between the government and the selector came to be called a 'conditional purchase'.

A.J.'s land

Ian Fox and I spoke on the phone a few more times, but months passed before I could meet him in person. I live in Brisbane, Queensland, and his home was in Burringbar, northern New South Wales, nearly two hours' drive away, so there was no point in visiting until I had a copy of Augustus John's conditional purchase document. That took quite a bit of time to organise long-distance, as the archives were in Sydney. Once I had received the parcel of photocopies from the New South Wales archive, I was finally able to head down to Burringbar, on Bundjalung Country. Interestingly, the archives parcel contained two conditional purchases. Augustus John Bostock applied for one in 1882, and another in 1888. Given that in our phone calls, Ian had revealed himself to be so knowledgeable of history, especially local history, I was looking forward to the visit to find out more.

Ian and his wife, Teena, lived on rural acreage a short drive from the tiny one-street town of Burringbar and I was a welcome guest. Their house had a steep, high-pitched roof, and the loft area was where Ian housed his library. It was impressive. Apart from shelves and shelves of books, there were also shelves packed tight with black-spined, numerically ordered lever-arch folders filled with papers and archives. In addition to a large worktable, a computer and printer, and a huge map cabinet that had a large number of wide, shallow drawers, he had on display his amazing rock collection from his days as a geologist.

Augustus John Bostock's conditional purchase (CP) files were jam-packed with historical information. The first CP, dated 1882, was 18 pages in total and the second CP, dated 1886, was 34 pages. Each file contained pages of Department of Lands correspondence and filled-out forms, as well as hand-drawn illustrations by surveyors. A number of the forms were filled in with some of the most beautiful old ink-quill calligraphy that I had ever seen. Other pages were covered in government department date stamps, signatures, and vertically and diagonally scribbled notes, with even this scribble calligraphically beautiful. (Oh, to be able to write like that!) I was pleased when Ian said, 'Let's look at the details of these later, after we find out where his selections were.' I too was curious about the location of A.J.'s land.

Ian's map cabinet included colonial maps, terrain maps with contour lines, Aboriginal language group and dialect maps, and much more, all focused on Bundjalung Country. Searching through his map-cabinet drawers, he found what he was looking for. 'Ah, here it is. This one's got all the parishes and counties.' I had placed the pages of each of Augustus John's CPs back-to-back into a display book, so, rather than have pages scattered everywhere, I could flip the plastic sleeve pages with ease. Ian laid out his large map on the table and then opened the CP display book, skipping through the written pages to find the surveyors' drawings.

Augustus John's first attempted purchase of land was a CP of 40 acres (16 hectares), recorded as 'Portion 3, Parish of Burrell,

County of Rous'. It was selected, applied for with a deposit of £10, paid for on 16 November 1882 and officially received by the agent for the sale of Crown lands, Mr Joshua Bray. This CP was forfeited on 18 November 1886 'on account of non-fulfilment of condition of residence'. Then, on 22 November 1888, A.J. applied for another CP of 80 acres (32 hectares), which was the previous 40 acres of 'Portion 3' and the adjacent 40 acres of 'Portion 9, Parish of Burrell, County of Rous'.[14] The second CP was forfeited on 5 August 1890 because 'the prescribed conditions of residence and fencing have not been fulfilled'.

Seeing the surveyors' drawings, and knowing the parish and the county, Ian set aside the CPs and slowly slid his finger over the map until it stopped on the location of Augustus John Bostock's land. It was situated near Wollumbin Creek on the road to Tyalgum. The road to Tyalgum runs straight past the base of Wollumbin/Mount Warning. Thinking aloud, Ian said, 'Interesting,' and then he tapped the map with certainty. 'See here', his finger traced a line, 'that's the road to Tyalgum, and see here', he pointed to a squiggly blue line, 'that's Wollumbin Creek. I remember something significant about that place.' He went to one of his black folders and flicked through the pages, then said, 'Yes, here it is. There was an early settler who lived to be between 90 and 100 years old, and in a letter he identified that location as one of the original camps of the traditional Wollumbin/Tweed Aborigines. So, by "traditional", I mean it was a place where they had a pre-colonisation camp that the [Aboriginal] people chose, and not a post-colonisation camp that whitefellas pushed them out to.'[15]

On its own, the fact that Augustus John Bostock married One My at a time when such interracial marriage was a rare occurrence is very interesting. However, the additional information that on two separate occasions he tried to secure land located at the traditional camp of his wife's people—and the fact that no further record can be found of an attempt to secure land elsewhere after the forfeiture—led me to wonder if he was sympathetic or close to his wife's people, the Wollumbin group. If that was the case, then this would be in stark contrast to his family's slave-trading heritage.

Joshua Bray

Joshua Bray was the agent for the sale of Crown lands who signed Augustus John Bostock's CP paperwork, but—well before the many roles in the Murwillumbah community he undertook later in his life—as a young man he was one of the first white people to settle on the north arm of the Tweed River, known as the Rous River. In 1863, he accepted an offer from his sister Mary's husband, Samuel Gray. The offer was a partnership in a run of 16,000 acres (6500 hectares) called Upper Wolumban, a lease that was purchased by Gray at the auction rooms of the government auctioneers Dean & Co. in 1862.[16] The land was cleared by Joshua with the help of the local Aboriginal people—my ancestors, the Wollumbin people—and he built a homestead, which he named Kynnumboon.

When he went to work on his Upper Wolumban run, Joshua Bray wrote detailed diaries as well as letters to his fiancée Gertrude in Sydney. In a letter to Gertrude dated 26 June 1863, Joshua relates the story of his journey to Kynnumboon. He wrote:

> Mr Fawcett the Police Magistrate was very kind. He sent me
> to see if any of the Tweed blacks are anywhere about, to get
> one to show me the short way over the Tweed—the short

way is a road Mr Gray cut through the scrub from the Upper Tweed to come here. I would have to go thirty miles before I came to that, and if I did not find the exact spot, I would not be able to get that way, for it is utterly impossible for a footman to go through the jungle—it is a mass of vines like ropes all through the larger trees. Mr Fawcett strongly advises me not to go that way. There are two men here, Mr Boyd and his brother—they are what is called Merchant Sawyers. They employ men to cut cedar and send it to Sydney . . .[17]

Joshua Bray was enlisted by local man Wollumbin Johnny at the cedar getters camp at Terranora, to guide him for the final leg of his journey. They travelled along the ridge line above Bilambal to Dungay, and then down to the plain where Samuel Gray had sited a house on the north arm of the river. On the way Joshua had shot a wonga pigeon through the head with his Colt revolver—a deed that he reported impressed the local Aboriginal people. In July 1863, Joshua wrote that although he had white employees living and working on the property:

I get all my work done by the blacks—I have sixteen or seventeen at work every day, they can split timber mortice posts, pull the boat, trench the ground, and anything I put them at—they dug a drain a mile long, eight feet wide and three feet deep—in fact, they do nearly all my work but I have a good deal of trouble looking after them . . . their camp is 100 yards from the house, there are about 80 or 90 at this camp—old men, women and children. This would put you much in mind of a slave establishment, but I always have to carry my loaded revolver with me.[18]

In a later letter to Gertrude, Joshua Bray described the scene of a war party preparing for battle. The following account is a vivid description of Aboriginal warfare and mourning at this time, but this letter may also be one of the first records of Aboriginal exclusion and restriction from their own land on Bundjalung Country.

> My blacks never go away without asking my permission. I often give three or four of them a day to hunt—I let some go one day and some another. A brother of one of them was killed by another tribe about 20 miles from here. The news came yesterday. I have given them all permission to go and give the other tribe battle. About 30 soldiers will start in the morning. If they come to an engagement I will give an a/c of it in my next. They are roaring out murder and crying— they could be heard a mile away—that is how they mourn their dead. You can imagine about 100 savages within about 70 or 80 yards from the house making a most unearthly yell all night—but they will stop it before morning. I never let any but the workmen come near the house. I intend to put a paling fence around the house before my sister comes and never allow them inside of it.[19]

The words that Bray uses to stamp his perceived 'ownership' and 'authority' stand out pointedly, with his description of 'My blacks' and his declaration that they 'never go away without *my* permission'. I was astonished by Bray's next comment: 'This would put you much in mind of a slave establishment'. This is a telling indicator that Bray immediately saw the Wollumbin group as his very own workforce. Both his diaries and the language he uses give weight to this observation. It was his 'slave establishment' comment that got me thinking about Augustus John Bostock's motivation for securing his CPs at Wollumbin Creek. Was I naïve to think that Augustus John was sympathetic to his wife's people? Did he also see One My and the Wollumbin people as his potential workforce?

Joshua Bray's writing brings attention to the importance of the boundary fence in settler colonial life. Bray was determined to install a fence around the house before his sister arrived to settle on the Tweed. It was his way of controlling the chaos that settlers typically perceived in the landscape. In a sense, the fence was his way of civilising his property, the Kynnumboon homestead, and the Aboriginal people on and around 'his' land. I imagine the local Aboriginal people must have looked upon this senseless structure as a ludicrous absurdity, but, at the same time, confronting and offensive—like a racial stranger (without warning or permission) coming into your house to barricade a portion of your lounge room off for their own personal use.

Wollumbin Johnny

Ian Fox later told me that Joshua Bray's mention of the 'brother of one of them' who was killed by a neighbouring tribe refers to Wollumbin Charlie, Wollumbin Johnny's brother, who, up until then, was the leader of the Wollumbin group. With his brother's murder, Wollumbin Johnny was now the leader of the Wollumbin people. Around 2009, my Uncle Gerry told me he was certain that our family were related to Wollumbin Johnny, but other than my great-great-grandmother's name being recorded as 'One My, otherwise Clara Wolumbin', I had not found any definitive evidence that linked us to him. Wollumbin Johnny was often called 'King Wollumbin Johnny' by the early settlers and he was highly regarded. A local history enthusiast in the 1940s, J.J. Byrne, wrote an article for the *Tweed Daily* that described Wollumbin Johnny as 'the Kings of Kings' and 'the greatest of all the kings', and he differentiated Wollumbin Johnny from other Elders who were awarded their titles by the white settlers. Byrne wrote in a newspaper article that 'King Johnnie was of good appearance, being about 5ft 11 in height, of dignified mien, athletic, of a quiet temper, low voiced and kind. He was well looked up to by his people and evoked considerable respect from the whites'.[20] The first reference to Wollumbin Johnny that I could find was the one mentioned above in the letter Joshua Bray wrote to Gertrude in 1863. The latest reference I could find about Wollumbin Johnny was a newspaper article written in 1885.[21]

A scan of a photograph of Wollumbin Johnny was given to me by Joshua Bray's great-granddaughter, Mrs Beverly Fairley, once she had sought permission from the photograph's owner, her very elderly aunt, Mrs Noella Elworthy (née Bray). At the time, Mrs Elworthy was one of the two surviving grandchildren of Joshua Bray. Although I forget when the conversation took place, I do not think I will ever forget what a distant relative and friend of mine, Aboriginal anthropologist Michael Aird, said when I mentioned to him that 'we might be related to Wollumbin Johnny'. He broke into laughter and responded dryly, 'Every blackfella within a ten-kilometre radius of the mountain wants to be related to Johnny!'

Ann Curthoys and Ann McGrath, both historians, wrote that in family history research 'the possibility of finding a famous or infamous ancestor can spark great interest'. British family history researchers covet a connection to royalty; and for Americans, having a family connection with the 'founding fathers' or the Pilgrims on the *Mayflower* is highly prized. In

Australia, trends have changed drastically over the generations, from wanting the same kind of ancestors as the English, such as royal or titled gentry, to becoming obsessed with finding a convict relative.[22] I would say that the Australian Aboriginal equivalent would be finding out that one of your ancestors was a great warrior, cleverfella or kurradji, respected Elder, freedom fighter or resistance leader.[23]

Changes on Country

Augustus John Bostock's CPs were forfeited because inspectors reported that he did not reside on the land. I examined Augustus John's CPs thoroughly and found that during the years he was on his selections, from 1882 to 1890, he frequently had to change his location for employment that paid for his conditional land purchases. The Crown lands inspectors and a police constable reported in 1882 that Augustus John Bostock was 'working on the South Arm at Murray's'; in 1888, he 'had another house 6 miles away from where he lives'; in November 1888, he was 'in the employment of Mr Langley'; in 1889, he was 'living at the Tweed'; and at the end of his second CP, in 1890, he had 'left the Tweed and was at home on the Mid Arm (of the Tweed River) near Kelly's'.[24]

Settler encroachment onto Bundjalung Country occurred with incredible speed: in the nine years from 1880 to 1889, there were 683 CPs sold, and most of the accessible land to the east and north of Murwillumbah had already been taken up by settlers;[25] in the nine years from 1900 to 1909, the number of CPs had nearly doubled to 1224.[26] In 1895, Mary 'Ellen' Bundock (Edward Ogilvie's sister), who lived on Wiangarie Station to the south-west of Wollumbin/Mount Warning, commented on the detrimental effect this rapid encroachment had on young local

Aboriginal men. Her acute observations sadly emphasised the changes that settlement brought to Aboriginal culture, and she lamented, 'They do not use the spear or the boomerang as their fathers did. They work spasmodically on the stations and like riding and work amongst the cattle, but drink and gambling are their curses.' Referring to all of the Aboriginal people on Wiangarie Station with empathy and inclusion, she stated, 'our tribe is fading away, though we do all we can to save them. I fear another generation will see few or any left'.[27]

3

My father's side of the family

'There are many people who advocate intermarriage. It is sheer madness. I have heard it even from the pulpit. Show me the minister who would like his daughter to marry an aborigine, or his son a black gin. Nature seems to scream out—Don't do it!'

PASTORALIST CUNNINGHAM HENDERSON[1]

We tend to forget that for generations coloniser and colonised had sex, courted and married each other. Australian historical narratives have tended to separate Indigenous and non-Indigenous pasts, but in fact they are intimately interwoven.[2] The family names of my four grandparents were Bostock, Anderson, Cowan and Solomon, and in the process of tracing the origins of their family lines as far back as I could in the written historical record, I found some interesting stories of interracial liaisons. The Solomon family originated from a 'full-blood' Indigenous couple; the Bostock and Anderson families originated from the marriage or 'physical union' of a white Australian man and an Aboriginal woman; and the Cowan family originated from the marriage of an Aboriginal man and a white Australian woman. So, contrary to pastoralist Cunningham Henderson's ideas about nature, and social propriety . . . my ancestors certainly *did* do it!

I have already explained that the Bostock family descend from a white Australian man, Augustus John Bostock, who married a traditional Bundjalung woman from Wollumbin/ Mount Warning called One My. Early in my research journey, I saw the name 'Clara Wolumbin' used as a way of Anglicising her name to align it with the European practice of using a first name and a last name. Although grateful that at least the name 'Wolumbin' was retained, for a cynical second I at first thought that her name, like everything else for Aboriginal people, was being colonised. Looking at Augustus John Bostock's death certificate more closely, however, the family 'informant' was recorded as being his daughter-in-law Lena Bostock. If my (Aboriginal) great-grandmother Lena was responsible for ensuring that both of One My's names were recorded, perhaps she insisted because one was her Ab-*original* name, and the other identified her as a Wollumbin woman.

Queensland DEATH CERTIFICATE		REGISTRATION NUMBER 1927/ 2219
DECEASED		
Name and surname	Augustus John Bostock	
Occupation	Old Age Pensioner	
Sex and Age.. .		
Date of Death.. .	24 August 1927	
Place of Death	Brisbane Hospital	
Where born and, if not born in Australia, period of residence in Australia..	Campbell Town, Tasmania	
PARENTS		
Name and surname of father	Thomas Edward Bostock	
Occupation	Landholder	
Name and maiden surname of mother . ..	Catherine Jane Mackersey	
MARRIAGE(S)		
Where, at what age and to whom deceased was married	Tweed River, New South Wales, about 27, One My otherwise Clara Wolumbin	
CHILDREN		
Names and ages	Augustus 43 years	
	3 females deceased 1 male deceased	

To summarise the other three family lines: the Anderson family originated from the union of a white Australian man believed to be named Samuel Anderson and a 'full-blood' Wakka-Wakka woman originally from Crow's Nest, near Esk, Queensland. Her traditional name was recorded as Bunjue, but later she was known as Mary Jane. The earliest record that I could find about the Cowan family traces back to a Bundjalung man called Jonathan Cowan, who married a white Australian woman called Elizabeth Hughes in 1883. Lastly, the Solomon family can be traced back to an Aboriginal 'full-blood' couple, Ruby Morgan and Solomon, who lived at Kyogle Aborigines Reserve. In my quest to discover everything I could possibly get my hands on about the lived experience of my ancestors, I quickly realised that before I could even begin to look at their histories, I first had to construct a detailed family tree chart.

The starting point of any genealogical family history research is collecting official birth, death and marriage certificates (commonly known as BDMs) about your ancestors. BDMs provide numerous pieces of information other than just the date of the event. Apart from information about when the ancestor was born, who their parents and siblings were, who they married and when they died, extra information on BDMs includes places where people were born, churches where people were married, cemeteries where people were buried, witnesses to (and informants of) these events, and even medical causes of deaths.

The great thing about BDMs is that where you don't have information about an ancestor or their family group, other BDMs can provide vital clues. For example, if there is no birth certificate for an ancestor, then subtracting their age at marriage from the year their marriage took place provides an approximate year of birth. Additionally, if a family group's first child is born in one location and then the next three children are born at another distant location, the time of the family's move can be assumed to be somewhere between the first and second children's births.

I was able to use BDM details to construct family tree charts, and map my ancestors' movements on Country. From reading archives about them, knowing the changes to their lifestyle that came with colonisation, and knowing the historical, social and political climate of their times, I could gain a very clear picture of the lived experiences of my ancestors throughout the decades. Family history research is in fact a way to counteract my Aboriginal ancestors' erasure; it's enabled me to pull them out of the collective noun 'the Aborigines' used by white Australians and restore their individual humanity. It's a deep, heartfelt, spiritual resurrection.

The early Bostocks

The Aboriginal Bostock family had only seen my great-great-grandmother's name recorded as 'Noumie' on her son's marriage certificate. My great-grandfather Augustus Bostock Jnr married Lena Ford, and on their marriage certificate his parents were recorded as 'Augustus John Bostock and Noumie (Native)'. I vaguely remember Uncle Gerry pronouncing it as 'Now-mie' (rhyming with 'pie'). I now believe that the recording of her name as 'Noumie' was a transcription error for her true name, 'One My'.

Uncle Gerry told me that One My was just blackfella talk for 'first born'. He said English was a second language for my ancestors and they spoke in simple, broken English in those days. He added that 'Two My' meant 'second born' and so on. Uncle also said that a 'mie' in the Bundjalung language means sleeping place, dwelling, or gunya. Later, I found a 1925 newspaper article that backed up what he said. It was an interview

Conjugal status	Birthplace	Age	Father's name, mother's name and maiden surname	Father's occupation
Bachelor	Tweed River N.S.Wales	Years 31	Augustus John Bostock Naumie (Natino)	Labourer
Spinster	Southport Queensland	22	Arthur Ford Julia Bandy	Farmer

This Marriage was solemnised between us { Augustus Bostock / Lena Ford   By me, Victor Clarence Bell
Officiating Minister or Registrar.

In the presence of us { Ina Bostock / Emma Bell

Received and Registered by me, this 22nd day of November 1905.

W. Arnott ___ District Registrar.

with one of the oldest surviving pioneers of the Byron Bay district, Mr William Flick, who said that the local Aboriginal people 'would rather live in their hut or gunyah or "mie-mies" than a house'.[3]

One day, out of the blue, Ian Fox sent me an email alerting me to yet another archival record of Augustus John and One My's names. He told me that the Grafton Diocese of the Anglican Church had begun digitising their historical records, and my great-great-grandparents' names were recorded there. Ian and I became good friends through our common interest in Bundjalung history, and not only was he generous with his extraordinary knowledge, and the use of his personal library—he was, like me, always on the lookout for tantalising new pieces of information. He taught me everything I needed to know about how to become (like him) a genuine, bona fide history nerd.

After receiving my email inquiry and contact details, Charmaine, an archivist at the Anglican Church Diocese office in Grafton, phoned me. She was helping the minister to digitise all their historical records, and she rang to say that she had found the records that I was after. Charmaine loved to talk, and she went on to chat about what the registry books looked like, describing in detail the beautiful writing using ink quill pens, some pages that had ink-pot spills, blurred writing from water damage and dirt smudges that were evidence of the tough times they had endured. As if painting a picture, she spoke in awe and admiration about how, in the 1800s, the then Church of England clergy would ride on horseback over rugged bushlands and flowing creeks to get to settlements to perform church services, marriages and baptisms for the diocese. 'Can you imagine what these books have seen? I can just picture them poking out of saddle bags, and being splattered with mud.' She then suggested, 'You should come down here and see them for yourself.'

From my home in Brisbane, driving to Grafton and back is a seven-hour return trip. It's a huge commitment to drive that far just for the purpose of seeing the archives in person. I enjoy going on road trips, and will happily jump in the car and head interstate just for the heck of it, but there was another reason I felt compelled to go. The moment Charmaine suggested I visit, my scalp tingled a little, and goosebumps appeared on my lower arms. Spiritual intuition was telling me to go, but it wasn't until I returned home that I fully understood why.

Baptisms found

My parents were born in 1939 and 1940, and my experience is that records of the births of my Aboriginal ancestors beyond my parents' generation are rare, if not impossible to find—and beyond my grandparents' generation, Aboriginal births were simply not recorded. Of my four Aboriginal grandparents, born roughly between 1906 and 1916, I have managed to locate only one official birth certificate. I calculated the approximate birth years of my other three grandparents by subtracting the age they identified being at the time they were married from the year the marriage took place. Of my eight great-grandparents, there are no official birth certificates to be found, therefore I had no records of birthdates for any of them, so I was thrilled when I found a baptism register entry that recorded my great-grandfather Augustus Jnr (aka Gus) Bostock's *actual* birthdate.

When I arrived at the Anglican Church's Grafton office, Charmaine directed me to take a seat at a large table, and a little while later the dusty, smelly birth register book was put on the table before me. It was a huge bound book that was once covered in navy blue material but had since faded like old denim jeans. The cover was stiff and warped with age. Charmaine showed me the entries recording the baptism of Augustus and Meta Bostock. I didn't know that Gus had a sister, let alone that her name was Meta. Their baptisms were recorded on two consecutive pages and later Charmaine gave me large A3 photocopies of both pages in full.[4] Their parents' (my great-great-grandparents') names were recorded as 'Augustus J & Wonmie'.

When Baptised.	When Born.	Child's Christian Name.	Parents' Names.		Abode.	Quality or Profession.	By whom the Ceremony was performed.
			Christian.	Surname.			
November 1 1894		Charlie	Nannure...bulgun			Labourer	H.C. Reynolds at St Peter's ...bulgun
November 1 1894		Louie	Howie		.	Labourer	H.C. Reynolds
November 1 1894		Jennie	Fiji	.			H.C. Reynolds
November 1 1894		Maggie	Selokee				H.C. Reynolds
November 1 1894		Mary Ann	Vanbern				H.C. Reynolds
November 1 1894	May 20 1884	Augustus	Augustus J / Wonmie	Bostock	Bungalora	labourer	H.C. Reynolds

Arriving home late in the afternoon, I sat down and examined the photocopied pages more closely. Reverend Reynolds had baptised Gus and Meta Bostock on 1 November 1894, and as my eyes scanned other entries on both pages, I was struck by the large number of baptisms Reverend Reynolds had performed on that one day. Later, my father came for a visit and, as I showed him the photocopies of the baptism register pages, he told me the other children who were baptised on that day were all Aboriginal or Pacific Islander kids, because he recognised their surnames as families that he had grown up with. How interesting.

I rang Ian Fox to tell him about these findings, and Ian said that what Reverend Reynolds had done was known as a 'bulk baptism'. A bulk baptism was explained to me as a kind of public call, where Reverend Reynolds put the word out to the local Aboriginal and Islander communities to bring their children to a designated location to be baptised all at once. I immediately had an image in my mind of a Monty-Python-and-the-Holy-Grail-style (Black Plague) 'Bring out yer dead!' call. Reverend Reynolds put out a similar, but racial, call. The Reverend probably had many miles to cover in the diocese, so I am guessing that bulk baptisms were infrequent events. Meta was eleven years old and Gus was ten years old when baptised.

My great-great-grandmother's name in the baptism register was spelled W-o-n-m-i-e, and this became the fourth way her name was recorded in the historical record. Now there was Noumie, One My, Clara Wolumbin and Wonmie. Of all the children baptised that day by Reverend Reynolds, there were only a few parents' names recorded. Meta and Gus are the only children who have an actual date of birth recorded. I imagine this was because of Augustus John Bostock's education, and the likelihood is that the other parents could not read or write.

Under the 'parents' column, most of Reverend Reynolds entries record only the family names of the children. Apart from 'Augustus J & Wonmie', I noted that Tommie and Maggie Selokee were the only other parents whose first names were recorded. To my ears, 'Selokee' sounds Islander rather than Aboriginal. South Sea Islander cane cutters intermarried with Aboriginal people in northern New South Wales and many families have that connection. Reverend Reynolds seems to have spelled their surname phonetically. From memory, I recall that there are Indigenous families in northern New South Wales and further south today with the name 'Slockey'. If they do have South Sea Islander heritage, I wonder if the two-syllable 'Slock-ey' family name has been Anglicised over time from its original three-syllable 'Sel-o-kee' name? The three-syllable name 'Selokee' has a more Islander sound when spoken out loud than the name 'Slockey'. Of course, that's just me musing on the sounds of words, but what is important to note here is the power of the transcriptions of white Australians (including the clergy) in determining the retention or adaptation of Indigenous family names.

So, why the goosebumps? Why did I experience the compelling need to go and see these records with my own eyes? The answers to these questions are in the writing. Had I not gone to see the baptism records for myself, Charmaine would probably have sent me a photocopy of just the Bostock information on its own, and I would not have been able to see the other families' names. If I didn't have the full (A3) photocopies of the baptism register's pages, I would not have known about the large number of baptisms being conducted on the same day, or that it was a bulk baptism for Aboriginal and Islander people. If I had not seen the Selokee name written that way, then the Slockey family would not have come to mind. Lastly, if Tommie and Maggie are indeed their ancestors, and if there is a South Sea Islander connection, then seeing their family name spelled this way might be helpful to them if they want to research their South Sea Islander family history.

My little jaunt to Grafton taught me not to give up hope. Regardless of our ancestors' omission from historical records, if you venture into community records you may be lucky enough to stumble upon more information than you first expected to find.

Arthur and Julia

My great-grandparents on my father's side were Gus Bostock and Lena Ford; Lena was the daughter of Arthur Ford and Julia Sandy. Arthur Ford was born at Kynnumboon, the pioneer Joshua Bray's selection on the Rous River, where the majestic Wollumbin/Mount Warning towers nearby. His mother's name was Kitty Sandy, and she was the only Aboriginal great-great-great-grandparent I could find in all my research. The fact that Arthur Ford's mother and wife both had the last name 'Sandy' raised questions that I could not find answers for. All I can say, however, is that there were (and are) a large number of Aboriginal families with the last name 'Sandy'.

Remarkably, the mother of Kitty's grandchildren, Julia Sandy, gave birth to eleven children (including two sets of twins) before she died at the very young age of 32. I discovered that she was buried in the Aboriginal cemetery located near the former Deebing Creek Aborigines Reserve Station.[5] In fact, only one grave marker has survived in this location since the 1890s, and that solitary headstone was for my great-great-grandmother

Julia. A 1975 newspaper article titled 'Blacks Want "Relic" Back' describes how the local Beaudesert Aboriginal population wanted the burial ground at Deebing Creek and Julia Sandy's headstone to be classified as relics to be preserved and owned by the local Aboriginal community. The article included a transcription of the headstone's engraving: 'In loving memory of Julia. Beloved wife of Arthur Ford. Died 17th of August 1896. Aged 32 years.'[6]

When I first saw that transcription of the writing on the headstone of Julia's grave, I kept reading and re-reading it to check I had read it correctly. The date that my great-great-grandmother Julia Sandy died, and her age at death, is exactly the same date and age that *I* was when I married on the 17th of August 1996, aged 32 years—*exactly* 100 years to the day after Julia died. We're a superstitious mob, and this made my scalp tingle and my arm hair stand on end. Regardless of whether it was an incredible coincidence or a synchronous spiritual message from the universe, I decided that the best I could do was delve into whatever information was available about Julia.

Like non-Indigenous Rachael Bostock (Robert Bostock Jnr's wife in Van Diemen's Land/Tasmania), Aboriginal Julia had eleven children, but her circumstances would have been vastly different from the affluent life that Rachael lived. Of her eleven children, Julia lost three children in infancy (a three-month-old, a two-year-old and a one-year-old). My great-grandmother Lena, Julia's oldest child, was thirteen years old when her mother died. There was a younger sister, Seaver Rosilie. With two infant deaths, there was a gap between Seaver Rosilie and the littler ones. When their mother died Curtis was eight, twins Lexie and Esther were five, Jessie was four, then a third infant death, Arthur Francis was two, and lastly there was the baby, Julia.[7] I imagine that Lena would have had to look after her seven siblings while their father found work.

We don't know for sure if Julia (like Rachael) died in childbirth, but I suspect that, as her youngest child was born the same year she died, and the child's name was Julia, that may have been the case. I doubt Lena would have been completely alone and imagine that the Aunties and Beaudesert and Southport Aboriginal communities would have come in to help where possible. A year after her mother died, Lena's father, Arthur Ford, married Eva Williams. Arthur was 31 and Eva was nineteen, just five years older than his daughter. Arthur and Eva went on to have fourteen children. Astoundingly, my great-great-grandfather, Arthur Ford, fathered 25 children altogether.

A story that has often been told in our family is that on 21 November 1905, the day Gus and Lena were married in Murwillumbah, Lena was approached by a woman called Lily Williams, who was carrying a three-month-old baby in her arms. Lily told Lena that Gus was the father, and she was unable to care for the baby girl. Lena then took the baby, known as Lillian, and raised her as her own. The baby grew up alongside my grandfather, Norman, and my father and his siblings always knew her as 'Aunty Lilly'. While researching Gus and Lena's early life, I re-examined their marriage certificate and discovered that it yielded the unexpected revelation that Augustus John Bostock, like his son Gus, also had a relationship and a child with another Aboriginal woman.

A.J.'s other Aboriginal woman

It was a tiny detail on Gus and Lena's marriage certificate that led me to discover that Augustus John Bostock had not one, but two Aboriginal women in his life. I came to find out about Augustus John's second relationship by being curious about a woman called Ina Bostock, who signed her name as one of the two witnesses on Gus and Lena's marriage certificate. The baptism record revealed that Gus had a sister called Meta, but did Gus have another sister whom I knew nothing about? I had never heard that name before, so my investigation yielded the first of many family history 'surprises' that I was to experience throughout my research journey. Ina's death certificate revealed that she was indeed Augustus John Bostock's daughter, but her mother was not One My. Her mother was Jessie Unarn Walumba. Jessie was another Aboriginal woman from the Wollumbin group who, like One My, adopted the Wollumbin name. Ina was married in 1906, a year after Gus and Lena, when she was eighteen years old. This makes her year of birth 1888, so she was four years younger than my great-grandfather Gus.[8]

I immediately assumed that my great-great-grandfather was a polygamist. Although I am aware that polygamy existed in Aboriginal culture, British common law (the basis of our Australian legal system) does not recognise polygamous marriage. While monogamy was a part of white-settler culture, my great-great-grandfather Augustus John, and other white settlers, disregarded societal norms when it came to relations with Aboriginal women. I'm sure Cunningham Henderson would have been horrified by such outrageous impropriety! Perhaps Augustus John Bostock and other white settlers thought that the reach of British law did not extend as far as the frontier, or that such laws did not apply to relations with Aboriginal women.

Both Gus and Ina identified their mothers on their marriage certificates. The usual practice in recording BDM registry entries is that if one or both parents of the bride or groom were deceased, the parent's name would still be recorded with the word 'deceased' enclosed in brackets after the parent's name; for example, 'Jane Doe (deceased)'. As '(deceased)' was not written after their names, I assumed that both women were alive at their children's marriages. I cannot know whether Augustus John Bostock maintained a relationship with both women at the same time, and there is no proof to state that he did, but looking at their children's ages, I couldn't help but wonder if One My and Jessie knew each other, or if their relationships with Augustus John occurred at the same time or overlapped. Professor Ann McGrath supervised my PhD, so I was keenly interested in what she had to say about the subject of polygamy in her book *Illicit Love: Interracial sex and marriage in the United States and Australia*.

Ann noted that the possible factors that contributed to white men gaining opportunities to freely obtain a sexual partner among Indigenous women could be that there were fewer white women on frontiers, and a single white man had less compulsion to act with propriety or to be monogamous than in his previous social environment. She added, 'by having more than one Indigenous wife, or by "sharing" a wife with an Indigenous man in a polygamous marriage, many coloniser men effectively became cross-cultural practitioners of polyandry, polygyny, or both'. Two of her points that I find very interesting are that 'white Australian men were well aware of Indigenous polygamous marriage practices and contrasting attitudes toward women's sexual options', and Indigenous kin and family protocols in polygamous marriages 'potentially enabled the outsider man to enhance his strategic and economic position, and to gain expanded networks of influence'.[9]

Perhaps Augustus John Bostock had some kind of transactional arrangement with the Wollumbin people? The question then arose: 'How could Augustus John Bostock have benefitted from polygamous relationships with One My and Jessie?' Ann wrote that 'Observers tended to view the white man, as a coloniser man, to be in the superior, controlling position. He might feel the same, but this was not always so. He might be smitten. He might also be ensuring the sustenance of a large extended Aboriginal family or community.' Although I am curious about my great-great-grandfather's relationships with One My, Jessie and the Wollumbin people, and his motivation for trying to acquire land at that location, historical records are frustratingly unable to answer such precise questions.

But where archival documents and records fail, a researcher might be lucky enough to discover a photograph that sheds light on history. In my experience, it is indeed a very rare occasion to locate a photograph that validates, confirms or, at the very least, adds weight to possible scenarios that archival records and documents cannot substantiate. I was therefore struck speechless when, out of the blue, Michael Aird gave me a copy of the only photograph of Augustus John Bostock known to exist. Aunty Lilly, Gus Bostock's firstborn, showed Michael the photograph several years before she passed away. She pointed to the tall, bearded man standing by himself behind the fish crates and said, 'That's my grandfather.' Michael then verbally confirmed that Aunty Lilly was identifying Augustus John Bostock. It is disappointing that the clarity of the image is so poor, but a group of dark-skinned women and children can be seen standing nearby to the left.

Mother Lena

My great-grandmother Lena Bostock was well known for her mothering. Family oral history stories were told of how

'Granny Bostock' was like a community social worker. Apart from taking in many children who were not her own she also acted as a midwife for many Aboriginal women. The local police, unofficially, of course, donated some funds for her to help Aboriginal people who had come upon hard times or were just out of prison.

In 1910, Lena gave birth to a daughter, Meta Julia Onemy, whose death certificate records that 'Mita' died in 1911 when she was only six months old. There's no doubt that the baby's middle names are both her maternal grandmother's name (Julia) and her paternal grandmother's name (One My). Then, in 1912, Lena gave birth to another girl, named Meta Adelaide, and this baby died when she was a little over eight months old. I knew from the baptism record that Gus Bostock's sister's name was Meta, and clearly Gus's wife Lena Bostock was trying to continue the Meta/Mita name.

I found a historical record of an early Aboriginal woman from Beaudesert called 'Matilda aka "Mitta" Sandy' whom I immediately suspected was Lena's mother's mother (Julia Sandy's mother), but I cannot know for sure. The first thing you need to do if you suspect that two people have a 'mother and child' relationship is to check if the suspected child's birth year falls within the range of the suspected woman's child-bearing years. The dates of the birth and death of Mitta Sandy seem to fit with the possibility that Mitta Sandy *could* be Julia's mother. She died in 1929, aged 90, so that would make her birth year around 1839.[10] Mitta would have been 25 years old when Julia was born, so she *could* be Julia's mother, but I cannot prove that to be true.

Mitta was only three years old when Bathurst grazier William Henry Suttor obtained the depasturing licence in 1842 and named 'his property' Beau Desert. It wasn't until 1851 that W.D. White acquired the station and built a homestead on the present site of the Beaudesert township.[11] Mitta's family was on Mununjali Country and bore witness to the time that Aboriginal traditional societies and white settlers came in contact. Wouldn't she have some stories to tell! But if I were to write a list of the names of the ancestors I would most like to interview, my great-grandmother Lena Ford Bostock would be at the top of the list.

She was born in 1883 and died in 1949 at 65 years of age, during a period that saw great change in the lives of Aboriginal people in Australia. To summarise her life, Lena was the oldest child born into a very large family, and when her mother died young, she helped raise her siblings. Lena was sixteen years old at the turn of the century, and later she saw two world wars come and go. When her siblings died young, she raised their children, and her care extended to her whole Aboriginal community. My dad told me that she was 'one of those tough old Aboriginal women, you know the type, those old black women who didn't muck about'. He went on to tell me about when he and Uncle Gerry were little and couldn't swim, she just picked them up and threw them into the Tweed River. He said they came up to the top gasping and spluttering, trying to dog paddle. Dad said, 'So that's how we learned to swim, no mucking about!'

Drifting off into a daydream, I imagined her peering over my shoulder, reading the sentence *My great-grandmother Lena Bostock was well known for her mothering*, then rolling her eyes, letting out an exasperated 'hmph!' and mumbling under her breath as she walks away. If I did manage to chase after her and beg her to speak to me, I wouldn't be surprised if she shrugged her shoulders and said something like, 'Kids gotta be fed, work gotta be done.' Her life story exemplifies an Aboriginal cultural practice of child adoption. I have found numerous documents about and BDMs of Aboriginal people that contain the phrase 'was raised as', or 'known as', or 'went by the name of'. Often when a child of the extended family did not have a mother, an Aunty stepped in to honour the role, accepting a relative's child (or even a friend's child) as her own. I have seen many instances where Aboriginal people 'took in' children that were not their own—no questions asked, no seeking white Australian Government approval or legal authority, it was just done.

Aboriginal people often address older Aboriginal women as 'Aunty' regardless of whether they are a biological aunt or not. We perpetuate this terminology today as a sign of respect, but I like to think of it as an important way of remembering the important roles Aunties played in caring for children who were orphans or needed to be cared for. Lena cared for her own children, as well as some of her deceased siblings' children. Claude McDermott was the youngest of five children and was born in 1921, the same year that his mother, Jessie (Lena's sister), died. Lena's other sister, Alexandra, had a son called Edward ('Ted') Andrews, and he was raised alongside Claude, Aunty Lilly, my grandfather Norman and his siblings.

Ted Andrews used the last name of Bostock up until he enlisted in the Second Australian Imperial Force. Lena received telegrams notifying her of her adopted nephews' wellbeing during the Second World War. Uncle Ted was wounded in action and Uncle Claude was taken as a prisoner of war. It must have been such a worry for her. Not only was Uncle Claude a POW, but the experiences Australian soldiers endured as prisoners of the Japanese were so horrendous that the chances of surviving were severely reduced. In his personnel dossier from the Australian War Memorial library archive, I found a letter where he had written, 'I also was in F-Force which worked on the Burma Siam railway. We came back to Changi with less than half our force, cholera hit us pretty bad.'[12]

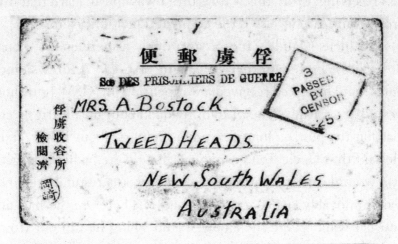

Claude McDermott's War Records reveal that, prior to enlisting, he lived with Gus and Lena and 'contributed half his earnings' to them. When he enlisted, he registered his uncle, Augustus Bostock, as being 'Wholly dependent' and organ-ised an 'allotment' for Gus, stating he was 'old and infirm and unable to work'. From 1941 to 1946 (when he was discharged), my great-grandparents received financial help from their nephew Claude. At one stage, the Australian Army inquired as to what income, if any, my great-grandparents' 'household' was receiving. From this war record, I was able to learn that my great-grandparents also received invalid pensions from 1943.[13]

In Uncle Claude's file, a document also refers to Lena Bostock as 'Foster Mother and Aunt of E. A. Andrews' and states that Uncle Ted received a war pension for 'GSW [gunshot wound] Forearm'. When I told my dad about this, it triggered (pardon the pun!) a long-forgotten memory about Uncle Ted. He said that Uncle Ted's arm and elbow were badly damaged by a wound sustained during combat and, as a result, his elbow was immovably fused at an odd angle. Therefore, he had an unusual walk where the elbow would swing in and out from his body as he walked. My father shook his head in disapproval, but smiled as he remembered, 'As kids, we used to call him Uncle Wing-ee.'

The early Cowans

In researching the Cowans (my father's mother's family), I've found remarkable photographs. Finding a photograph of an ancestor, especially one you have never seen before, and gazing into their eyes, brings extraordinary feelings, ranging from joy and delight at seeing a family member's happiness, to deep, heartfelt sadness that feels akin to witnessing their suffering. It's a bit like what happens on the television show *Who Do You Think You Are?*, where descendants—having only just seen a photograph of their ancestor for the first time—break into tears moments later on hearing sad stories about them. Old photographs seem to connect ancestors spiritually to present-day family members. It's as though a switch has been flicked on, and suddenly an emotional connection is activated.

One of many historical photographs with which I have felt such an immediate connection was a photograph called 'Mary Ann of Ulmarra', which was taken by famous photographer J.W. Lindt in the early 1870s. German-born John William Lindt was one of Australia's pre-eminent photographers and had a career spanning 60 years. His work encompassed a range of photographic genres, including portraiture, landscape, architectural and ethnographic subjects. Lindt lived in Grafton from 1863 to 1876, and it was here that he produced his first significant portfolio, titled 'Australian Aboriginals' (1873–74).

I first heard about Mary Ann's photograph in 2013 when I received an unexpected phone call from my father, insisting that I watch a documentary on the ABC because 'it's all about your research!' Intrigued, I quickly changed the channel to catch an episode of *Australian Story* called 'The Light of Day'.[14] It told the story of how, in 2004, a collection of 37 Lindt photographs, the most complete collection of this series in the world, was about to be auctioned and was likely to be bought by an overseas gallery or private collector. A *Sydney Morning Herald* newspaper article described the distress of the Gumbaynggirr Yaegl and Bundjalung Aboriginal communities, who were upset that they could not raise the money needed to buy the photographs and keep them in Australia. After reading the newspaper article, Sam and Janet Cullen decided to purchase the collection through an auction in London, and gifted them to the Grafton Regional Gallery, with the stipulation that the identity of the (nameless) Aboriginal people in the Lindt photographs be found. The Aboriginal communities of the Clarence

River Valley gratefully accepted the gift and the Lindt Research Project was formed.

The Lindt Research Project enlisted the help of a genealogist and historian, Nola Mackey, and when she compared historical photographs of Cowan family members with the 'Mary Ann of Ulmarra' photograph, she saw 'a striking family resemblance between these family members'. Ulmarra is just outside the town of Grafton on the Clarence River, and it seems that Mary Ann Cowan was the only Aboriginal 'Mary Ann' that could be found in that area at that time. As she was in her early twenties at the time Lindt took the photograph, the conclusion was that it is likely that 'Mary Ann of Ulmarra' was indeed Mary Ann Cowan.[15]

I gasped out loud when I heard this. I had been researching my family history for a few years by then, and I knew that Mary Ann Cowan was my great-great-grandfather's older sister. This exciting news had a profound effect on me. It was as though this lovely photograph had reached through time and altered my perception of her today. She has now magically transformed from an abstract entity—a name on her marriage and death certificates—into a real life, flesh and blood young Aboriginal woman.[16]

Mary Ann was no longer just a disembodied memory triggered by a two-dimensional archival record; I could now see her three-dimensional humanity. I was captivated by her face for what seemed like forever. I intuitively felt in my heart that she was Mary Ann Cowan. I had completely forgotten that Dad was still on the phone. In almost a whisper he said, 'Doesn't she look like Mum.' The more I stared at her photograph, the more information seemed to be coming through. I could see that she had scarification on her chest; this told me she was an initiated woman. 'Initiated' in this context means that Mary Ann had gone through a traditional ceremony of change, a rite of passage called the initiation process and it creates scars. In one example I have read, the girls were observed as being 'anxious to have the ceremony performed and took great pride in the scarred evidence of their womanhood'.[17] Scars can also be an expression of 'sorry business', which means mourning loved ones who have passed away. Another Lindt photograph shows two women who had the tips of their left-hand pinky fingers removed. This was also a female initiation practice. (From memory, I read somewhere that they weren't chopped off. A very strong, string-like grass was used as a ligature until they dropped off.) In the famous Lindt photograph of Mary Ann, she is wearing the vertebrae of a snake around her neck and a dingo's tail on her head.

The dingo-tail headband was traditionally worn by initiated men, but Lindt made the women wear them for his photographs. There are a number of early photographs currently held at the Richmond River Historical Society that captured traditional young men wearing this adornment.[18] Mary 'Ellen' Bundock wrote a manuscript called 'Papers of the Bundock Family, 1835–1898'. Included is a copy of Mary's handwritten memoir, which she called 'Notes on the Richmond River Blacks'. Here she wrote:

> I never saw the women wear any ornaments in those days, these being reserved for their lord and masters who, beside the shell and cane ornaments, wore necklaces of dog's teeth and coloured beans while the skin of native dogs tails fastened around the forehead was a favorite [sic] decoration amongst the younger men.[19]

Lindt utilised many props in his Grafton studio, including dead kangaroos, snakes, dirt, trees, logs, woven dilly bags, spears, boomerangs and dingo tails. He also had landscapes painted onto large sheets to be used as fake backdrops to situate his Aboriginal subjects in 'nature'. I imagine it would have been puzzling for Mary Ann and other 'subjects' to come and be adorned with culturally inappropriate props and artefacts at Lindt's strange and bizarre indoor studio.

The colonisers' moral values prohibited nudity, and white settlers' wives would often give Aboriginal women clothing to cover their bodies from the gaze of white men. White women's clothes were prized possessions, but cumbersome, and Aboriginal women often wore only the white woman's long skirt. Sometimes they were bare-breasted, but most early photographs on Bundjalung Country capture Aboriginal women wearing the skirts as a dress. They placed the waistband of the skirt under one arm, and buttoned it on the opposing shoulder, creating a one-shoulder-bare dress.

Lindt must have provided substantial incentives for the people in his photographs. These were extremely difficult years for Aboriginal people, and I imagine Lindt would have coaxed them in with food rations or some form of payment, because nearly all of the people who participated look utterly miserable, like they don't want to be there.

The emergence of affordable, palm-sized cards with photographs called *carte de visite*, or visiting cards, became an international craze. This prompted an international trade in photographs of celebrities and different 'types' of people from all over the world. Photographs of Aboriginal people ended up in scientific collections everywhere. Photographers like Lindt recognised the popularity and on-sell capabilities that *carte de visite* photographs of Aboriginal people would generate. Michael Aird, the curator of an exhibition of these photographs at the Brisbane Museum called 'Captured', explained that 'the photographers wanted the Aboriginal people to look as exotic or savage as possible to have something interesting to sell in these postcards'. Some European people and early settlers had vast collections of *carte de visite* postcards in elaborate albums to be displayed in their front parlours when guests visited.[20]

These photograph collections and photo albums provided a way for non-Indigenous people to observe Aboriginal people from a distance, in much the same way that glass separates visitors from zoo exhibits or museum dioramas. Although *carte de visite* images of Aboriginal people resided in photograph albums in the front parlours of settlers' homes, I have no doubt that few Aboriginal people, if any at all, were physically allowed past the front door in real life.

The interest in the *Australian Story* documentary and the Lindt collection of photographs was phenomenal, so the Grafton Regional Gallery hosted a special event, with a screening of the documentary, in March 2013 for the descendants to share family history information. A year or so earlier, my family history research had enabled me to find two previously unknown relatives, Aunty Pat and Aunty Esmay. They are the granddaughters of Edith Cowan Snr, whom my grandmother was named after. We became friends as well as family and shared our family history research with each other. As soon as I heard about the event, I asked my father, Aunty Pat and Aunty Esmay if they would like to join me on a road trip to Grafton, with an overnight stay, to attend the event at the gallery. They accepted without hesitation.

On the long drive to Grafton, we had wonderful conversations, and I began to realise the significance of this journey to the three Elders in my car. It wasn't just a fun, nostalgic road trip to where my father was born and where Aunty Pat and Aunty Esmay had lived in their childhood. It was so much more. These dear old souls just wanted to connect with their Country. It was extremely important to all three Elders that the Aboriginal relatives in Grafton knew that, although their lives had taken them away from there, Grafton and the Clarence River would always hold a special place in their hearts.[21]

After the screening, I had time alone to examine each of the photographs on display closely. I had already met a distant cousin, Debby Taylor, who lived locally. While I was standing there staring at the faces, she came and stood beside me. Debby said quietly, 'You know, we look at these faces and we can rattle off all the local family names.' Pointing to one of the people, she said, 'This one here, he looks like a [family name], and this woman is definitely a [family name], and that fella there, well the [family name] are his mob.' Then she sighed heavily and said, 'Look at their faces. Don't they all look just so sad!'

Elizabeth and Jonathan Cowan

My great-great-grandfather Jonathan Cowan was the younger brother of Mary Ann and, in 1883, about ten years after Lindt's photograph 'Mary Ann of Ulmarra' was taken, he married a non-Indigenous woman called Elizabeth Hughes. My great-great-grandmother Elizabeth's choice to marry Jonathan came at a cost though, and through our family's oral history, we are told that Elizabeth's family disowned her because she married a blackfella.

In the many colonial histories that I have read, and just as the excerpt of Cunningham Henderson's memoir above illustrates, there existed a racial stigma in Australian society that denounced and condemned sexual relations between Aboriginal people and white settlers—and, specifically, written histories about relationships between white women and Aboriginal men are hard to find. White women who lived with or married Aboriginal men often received pity. The desire of white society was to rescue them, and it was mingled with revulsion, abhorrence and fear.[22] The rarity of unions between Aboriginal men and white women, as opposed to those between white men and Aboriginal women, was simply about biology, because the consequences of these relationships were very different. A white woman, unlike a white man, would be literally left holding the baby.[23]

My great-great-grandmother Elizabeth wasn't just left 'holding the baby' (Roy), she was also left with five other children. In 1900, at the age of 43, my Aboriginal great-great-grandfather Jack Cowan died, leaving Elizabeth with six children under the age of fifteen. I have often wondered how Elizabeth, a white woman with six mixed-race children, survived after 1900, particularly with the government's Aborigines Protection Board gaining frightening control over the lives of Aboriginal people, and especially the lives of Aboriginal children.

Harold/Arthur

The current Elders in Grafton told me that Elizabeth and her children lived out of town, but when her son Harold Arthur was about seven years old, he broke his leg and had to be brought into Grafton for medical treatment. Around that time, Elizabeth had to escape with her other children to hide from the government's Aborigines Protection Board. Elizabeth's children were considered to be 'half-castes', meaning that they were half Aboriginal and half white, and they would have been prime targets for child removal. Poor Elizabeth was forced to leave Harold Arthur behind. He was left with his Aunt Mary Ann, who eventually adopted him.

My inquiry found that Harold Arthur was four in 1900, when his father died, so it must have been 1903 when he broke his leg. Mary Ann Williams was previously Mary Ann Cowan, the same Mary Ann whom we saw in the Lindt photographs. Harold Arthur remained in the care of his aunt and was known by the name of Arthur 'Codger' Williams'.[24] In 1917, during the First World War, Arthur joined the Australian Imperial Force, at the age of 21. His military records list 'Mrs Mary Ann Williams' as his next of kin. To enlist, Arthur Harold Williams had to change his name back to his biological name, Cowan, and although his birth name was Harold Arthur Cowan, in the army he was known as Arthur Harold Cowan.[25]

It was wonderful to find out about Arthur, but as I was continuing my family history research, I always had Arthur's mother (my great-great-grandmother), Elizabeth Cowan, on my mind. She was lost from history. No matter how much I searched, I could not find any historical records about her after her husband's death in 1900. What on earth had become of her? That poor woman, the widowed mother of children whom the government's Aborigines Protection Board called 'half-castes', children whom the Board targeted for removal. My extraordinarily active imagination conjured up all sorts of scenarios, and she was constantly in my thoughts.

Less than six months, in *my time*, had passed between me losing Elizabeth's trail in 1900 and 'finding her again' two decades later—in 1920—but in the interim I could not help but worry about her and wonder what happened to her children. I prayed that she did not suffer too greatly. She was probably a social outcast and no doubt trying to survive with five hungry 'half-caste' children to feed during drought, depression and increasing Aborigines Protection Board removals of Aboriginal children. Given her circumstances, it must have been a terrifying, uncertain time for her. My insignificant little first world problems vaporise immediately when I think of the hardship she must have endured to survive.

The Aborigines Protection Board

There were government bodies in most Australian states to administer the lives and affairs of Aboriginal people. The Aborigines Protection Board operated in New South Wales for nearly 90 years, from 1883 to 1969. Its principal legacy is one of deep bitterness among New South Wales Aboriginal people over their treatment by those who were entrusted with their welfare. The impact of the Protection Board's policies of segregation, assimilation, child removal and wage withholding would endure for decades, and the damaging results of the Australian Government's directives are still visible today. For many Aboriginal people of that time, including members of my family, the Aborigines Protection Board was not about protection at all; it was about persecution.

The depression of the 1890s and drought that later affected most of New South Wales through to the early 1900s caused high unemployment in most areas. There was no government unemployment relief, so unemployed Aboriginal people were forced to rely on the Aborigines Protection Board for basic rations, which usually consisted of a small dole of dry goods such as flour, sugar and tea. There was never meat, as Aboriginal people were expected to hunt and fish for themselves. Many previously self-sufficient Aboriginal people were forced to move to Aboriginal reserves, and the rise in the general white-settler population considerably diminished their potential for self-sufficiency.[26]

The need for Aboriginal people to come forward and collect rations also put them under the Protection Board's spotlight. The Protection Board became increasingly alarmed that people of mixed descent were not separating themselves from the Aboriginal community. In 1907, the Board wanted new legislative power to remove all authority Aboriginal parents had over their children and for this authority to be handed over to the Board *in loco parentis* (meaning 'in place of the parents').[27] As the campaign for more power *in loco parentis* became more frenzied, the Protection Board began to lease out reserve land for its own revenue, to fund future plans for training homes for Aboriginal children.[28] Robert Donaldson, a Board member since 1904 who helped draft the *Aborigines Protection Act 1909*, crafted an amendment to this Act that would see the removal of Aboriginal children from their families without the consent of the court. Although the Act was not officially amended until 1915, from 1912 the Aborigines Protection Board began removing as many children as it could.[29] The impact on Aboriginal families was devastating.

Elizabeth Cowan/Olive

Family history research can become a consuming passion and, with hindsight, I realise now that I began to care about my ancestors in ways that I hadn't previously anticipated. To say that I was holding my breath waiting on more news of Elizabeth would be a dramatic over-statement, but I was hugely relieved when more information about her life and children surfaced six months after my previous discoveries. I discovered that Elizabeth's children had survived childhood and, upon reaching adulthood, almost all of them had families of their own.

In 1920, Elizabeth Cowan married William Olive, who interestingly was *another* Aboriginal man. Family oral history tells us that she lived with William for several years before they married, when Elizabeth was 65 years old, and William, 55 years old. In our family, he was endearingly known as 'Grandpa Olive' by my grandmother, her siblings and their children. Considering their ages, and the fact that they both are dressed so formally, I suspect the photograph we have of them together was taken on their wedding day.

Elizabeth died of 'senility' at the age of 91, in 1946. Knowing Aunty Pat grew up with Aunty Esmay in Grafton, and that both ladies were older than my father, I recently rang Aunty Pat to see if she had any memories of her great-grandmother Elizabeth. She said she was only a little girl when Elizabeth died, but Aunty Pat remembered seeing her grandmother Edith when she and Aunty Pat's mother, Doris, went to visit. Aunty Pat said her mother, Doris, loved Elizabeth very much, and often spoke of her. When Doris was hospitalised after a brutal domestic violence attack, it was her grandmother Elizabeth who took her in, nursed her back to health and then helped her start her new life away from her abusive husband.

Aunty Pat remembered that before she died, Elizabeth was cared for by Edith in a house that had a very long driveway, which was basically just a rough track that led to the road. She said, 'It's funny how you can't remember many things that happened when you are very young, but certain instances really stand out, and you never forget them. I remember when

Mum's grandmother [Elizabeth] died, there was a gate and a post with the letter box on it. After they removed her body from the house, the dog waited at that gate for her return. He just sat there and waited and waited. I remember my family had trouble getting the poor thing to come inside to eat and drink. I remember it so clearly.' Sadly, she added, 'But I don't know what ever happened to the dog.'

4

My mother's side of the family

'Darkie, you be a good boy and we'll get on fine, but if you are
a bad boy, this gun might go off and shoot you!'

SUPERINTENDENT IVINS (DEEBING CREEK ABORIGINES RESERVE)

Throughout our entire lives, my sisters and I observed that
whenever the opportunity presented itself, our mother, Rita
(Anderson) Bostock, gleefully told people that her grandfather, Sam Anderson, was a famous Aboriginal cricketer who
got Don Bradman out for a duck. When we had visits from
her sisters Aunty Ruby and Aunty Gwen, they just as proudly
announced the same. I could clearly see that they believed it
was true, but I have to admit that in my teens and young adulthood, I wondered if it was really true, or just a perpetuated
myth. Perhaps it was predestined that I was meant to become a
historian one day, because I remember always wanting to know
the origins of family stories. It wasn't until I was in my early
fifties that I actually found the evidence that proved this story
to be 'kind of' true. My great-grandfather Sam Anderson did
indeed 'get' the world-famous Australian cricketing legend
Sir Donald Bradman out for a duck, but as dismissals in cricket

are attributed to the bowler, I must clarify that Sam 'caught' Donald Bradman out for a duck. (It was Irvine's wicket.)

As a historian, there is no more thrilling moment than when, after years of searching, you *finally* find a piece of archival evidence that authenticates a story that you wholeheartedly believed in but could not previously prove. Sometimes a forensic investigation into the historical record can yield shocking or unexpected results, and sometimes archives can reveal information that can completely up-end your previously held ideas. It's a humbling experience when your search for irrefutable proof ends with results that force you to surrender your fixed belief. During my search to find out about the origins of my mother's family lines, some stories brought about deep introspection and reflection that ultimately changed my mind. Thankfully, the story that Sam Anderson's granddaughters so proudly told can be repeated by future generations, safe in the knowledge that it is a verifiable fact that Sam took that catch.

The early Andersons

Sam Anderson's oldest son was my grandfather Henry Anderson, and he and my grandmother Evelyn Solomon had three daughters, Ruby, Gwen and (my mother) Rita. Later, my grandfather had two sons, Kevin and Dennis, to a lovely Aboriginal woman whom Aunty Ruby named 'Mum Joyce'. My mother's sister Ruby was a well-known Aboriginal author, Ruby Langford Ginibi, and before she passed away in 2011, Aunty Ruby always encouraged me in my early years of history research. The story about Sam Anderson's role in the dismissal of Donald Bradman was one of the few pieces of information I ever knew about the Anderson side of the family until Aunty Ruby showed me a photograph that was taken in 1895 at

Deebing Creek Aborigines Reserve, near Ipswich, in south-east Queensland.[1] She told me that Sam was the boy seated on the far right with his arms crossed, and his 'full-blood' mother, Mary Jane, was standing behind him in a white dress, holding the baby. Until then, I had neither seen the Deebing Creek Aborigines Reserve photograph, nor known that Sam's mother's name was Mary Jane.

This photograph fascinated me. Taken when my great-grandparents were alive, it is very similar to another group photograph taken when my grandparents were living at Box Ridge Aborigines Reserve, near Coraki, in New South Wales. These are two of the most important photographs in this book because they visually make evident the government's Aborigines Protection Board practice of segregating Aboriginal people from white-settler communities, and from white society in general. Some Aboriginal people were rounded up and incarcerated on Aborigines reserves by force. Others had no choice but to go to these places because the colonisers denied them access to their traditional lands—lands that had provided Aboriginal people with sustenance for thousands upon thousands of years. Into the 1900s, and during times of crisis, Aboriginal people had to rely on missions and reserves to obtain government rations for their survival.

Gulf Country Man

Aborigines reserves were sometimes called 'Aborigines Stations' if the Aborigines Protection Board supplied a superintendent or manager. These managers seemed to have unlimited powers, and Aboriginal people were often at the mercy of their temperament. In the group photograph there is a white man reclining on the grass on the left. This is Thomas Ivins, the superintendent at Deebing Creek Aborigines Station. In an interview with one of his daughters, Doris Smith, she said her father was 'rather forceful and quick tempered, and a law unto himself', but she added that he was also generous and outgoing. She then re-told a story that speaks volumes about white fear of traditional Aborigines, as well as her father's power over the residents on the reserve:

> A native from the Gulf country in North Queensland was brought to the station. He was from a different tribe to other natives on the station and had speared, killed and eaten a white missionary. The authorities decided to bring him to Deebing Creek, and on his arrival, Mr Ivins had a good talk to him (with his Mauser pistol in his hand) and said to him, 'Darkie, you be a good boy and we will get on fine, but if you are a bad boy this gun might go off and shoot you.' Then he shot it up in the air, several shots in succession, which really frightened Darkie, and he said, 'Me be good boy, Boss, me be real good boy'—and he kept his word and never gave any trouble on the station. He was a real loner though and didn't mix much, preferring to wander about on his own, usually with a spear in his hand hoping to spear a fish or some native food, which he seemed to prefer. He wore only a loin cloth.[2]

I choose to call this man by the more dignified name of Gulf Country Man and, in my opinion, that part about him eating a white missionary has such a lurid 'rumour has it' vibe that I simply don't believe it. It is unknown why he killed the missionary (if he did at all). We don't know what the circumstances were that led to his arrest, so it is advisable to avoid an automatic 'blackfella bad/whitefella good' presumption, and to

100

consider that being a missionary, while humanitarian, does not automatically guarantee a life free from sin (as some historical records reveal).

When I see Gulf Country Man in my imagination, I see a traditional Aboriginal man who was forcefully taken over 2000 kilometres from his family and his Country. I see Gulf Country Man as a man who was trying to survive the 'old way'. He had the sacred knowledge of his Country. He knew where to find water, and how to hunt game and trap fish, and he knew the seasons and where to find specific bush food all year round. He knew how to 'read' nature, but Deebing Creek was not his Country. It must have seemed like a prison cell compared to the wide-open spaces that he would have known. He was on foreign land. I imagine him wandering around alone on the reserve, yearning to be on his home Country with his own family, and his own tribal group, and my heart weeps for him.

Mary Jane

Like Gulf Country Man, my great-great-grandmother, Mary Jane, was taken from her homeland and sent to be incarcerated at Deebing Creek Aborigines Station. Records in the Queensland State Archives reveal that Mary Jane was a Wakka-Wakka woman, originally from Esk in Queensland. Finding out that my great-great-grandmother Mary Jane came from Wakka-Wakka Country is important to me, because now I can remember her in connection with that land (rather than the Aborigines Reserve), and in some small way diminish the memory of her dispossession at Deebing Creek, a place that was far from her homelands. The baby that Mary Jane is holding in that photograph is very likely to be Sam's sister, Kathleen, because archival records reveal that there was about ten years age difference between them, and, judging the ages of the children in the photograph, that looks about right.[3]

It was 1998 when historian Maurice Ryan gave Aunty Ruby the copy of the Deebing Creek photograph, and Aunty Ruby wrote the foreword for his 2001 book *Dusky Legend: Biography of Sam Anderson, Aboriginal cricketer*. As soon as it was published, my mother Rita immediately bought four books, one for herself, and one for each of her three daughters. Inside was the same photograph with a caption that read 'Deebing Creek Mission. Residents of the Station circa 1895. Note on the extreme right, Mary Jane in the long white dress holding child. Sam is sitting in front, arms folded.' Much the same as my experience with Charmaine and the baptism records, I felt compelled to travel to meet Maurice Ryan. But instead of scalp tingles and goosebumps, this time it felt like an inner *knowing* that I should go.

I wasn't quite sure how to track him down, but examining my copy of his book, I read that it was published by Northern Rivers Press, so I gave them a call. Oddly, the phone call was answered with a casual 'Hello', and when I explained that I wanted to contact one of their authors called Maurice Ryan, the elderly voice at the other end of the phone quietly said, 'Speaking'. I was surprised to find him so quickly. I explained who I was and after talking to him for quite a while, I asked him if I could visit; he happily agreed. Depending on the traffic, Lismore is about two and a half hours' drive from my home in Brisbane, and a couple of days after we spoke on the phone, I set off for yet another road trip. This time I made sure that I had my laptop computer and portable scanner with me, in the hope that he would also be happy to share some of his research information.

Morrie Ryan

Over coffee and biscuits, I enjoyed talking to Mr Ryan, and he insisted I call him 'Morrie'. I asked him how his interest in Sam Anderson had come about, and he explained that he had often heard stories about the locally famous Aboriginal cricketer. Back in 1976, he was a senior lecturer at Southern Cross University, and he decided to set one of his students, Margaret Keller, the task of researching and writing about the life of Sam Anderson for an assignment. Northern Rivers Press was his own creation and Morrie was an enthusiastic self-published local history researcher who had written nine books before *Dusky Legend*. He was in his late 70s when I met him, and during his retirement years he continued to add his own collection of information about Sam Anderson to Margaret Keller's work. In 2001, when he published the book, he was 69.

I brought my copy of *Dusky Legend* with me, and as I flicked through the pages and asked him questions, I could see he was delighted that I showed so much interest in his work. He was also quite chuffed when I asked him to sign my book. Morrie told me that Mr Ivins' children grew up on Deebing Creek Aborigines Reserve and, in the 1970s, when they were quite elderly, Margaret Keller wrote them several letters to ask them about their memories of Sam Anderson.

Mrs Doris Smith, Thomas Ivins' daughter, clearly identified 'Sammy' and his mother Mary Jane from the group photograph.[4] Our family didn't have any photographs of Sam, so I was elated that his image was positively identified by someone who knew him, even though he was only a boy in the photograph. Morrie then got up from the table and said, 'I think I still have some of her papers here that you can have. Follow me.'

He took me to his study, which was adjacent to the kitchen and dining area, and while the rest of his house was tidy, his workspace was filled with an enormous amount of clutter. It looked like a hoarder's room. None of his desk could be seen under the piles of papers stacked on top, and the tallest piles of papers meandered up the walls on either side of his window, right up to the upper frame of the window, magically avoiding collapse. Piles of papers were pushed against the wall at floor level, some two or three piles deep, and the piles at the back went up the wall too. He didn't care how messy the room was, and neither did I. To me it was just a visual presentation of how serious he was about compiling history. I was just so grateful for what he did next.

Morrie shuffled files here and there, and opened the filing cabinet drawers to pull out papers. He looked at them, decided if they were useful to me, returned the papers that weren't, and dropped the 'useful' ones into my hands, before he turned away to look for more. 'Oh, this is good!' he said, dumping a manilla folder in my hands. 'Here, take that, and that'—more piles and drawers were searched—'and that.' By the time he finished, I was holding a large pile of papers in my hands. I sincerely thanked him and we went back to the dining-room. It would have taken too long to look closely at them at that moment, so while he put the kettle on, I picked up small sections of the messy mound of papers to straighten them up and place them in one neat pile to take home.

While doing that, I saw that he had given me the actual handwritten letters that Margaret Keller had written in 1976 to Thomas Ivins' daughter, Doris Smith. Surprised by his generosity, I asked him if he was sure that I should have them, and he said, 'Yes, yes, of course, they're about Sam Anderson, you can have them.' Just as I was about to put the last of the papers into my bag, I spotted a handwritten letter from Sir Donald Bradman. To be honest, I just *had* to ask, 'Are you sure about this one?' He looked at it and said, 'Oh—ah, no—I think I will keep that one.' Not realising I was holding my breath, I exhaled and asked him if he would allow me to scan it so I could have a copy, and he kindly replied, 'Yes, of course!'

Donald Bradman

Stapled to the Bradman letter was the original letter that Margaret Keller had sent to him, dated 18 April 1977, which read as follows:

Sir,

I shall be writing a book shortly in which I hope to mention the time that you visited Lismore with Alan Kippax's team to play the Tweed-Richmond side (15th September 1928).

A final year student at the College of Advanced Education, Lismore, I have been asked to collaborate with the Far North Coast Cricket Council and the Community Learning Unit in writing the life story of an Aboriginal cricketer, Sam Anderson, who died in 1959.

Over the years, a legend has grown up over Sam Anderson and the projected story has aroused considerable community interest. Indeed, there are those who feel that had Sam Anderson been a white man, he might have risen to become a cricket star, as he had a great natural ability.

Cricket has always been an important part of the lives of people here, and on that Saturday in 1928, the whole town was agog to see the Sydney players in action. The crowd was mightily disappointed that you were bowled Irvine, caught Anderson, for a duck, as it had hoped to see you bat.

As the years passed and your name became a byword in the name of cricket, the fact that Sam Anderson caught you out once has gained in intensity and it has become quite a 'feather in his cap' so to say. Oddly in the same match, Sam Anderson also was bowled and caught out for a duck.

Knowing that the people of the Northern Rivers District, who represent a truly devoted section of your admiring public, would be delighted to have from you a few words concerning this match, I decided to write to you about it . . .

The rest of the letter was cut off because my portable scanner had an A4 screen, and the original letter was typed on an old manual typewriter on foolscap paper.

Bradman's letter was on a much smaller page that was less than A4 sized, so I had that in its entirety. The paper was from a professionally printed stationery set, with a formal, personalised letterhead. On the top left-hand side, the words 'Sir Donald Bradman' were printed in upper-case letters, and, on the right-hand side, the address '2 Holden Street, Kensington Park, South Australia 5068' was also written in upper-case letters. His letter was dated 22 April 1977, and his handwriting was in blue pen, in a neat, cursive style. Bradman wrote:

You must think I am *Argus* to remember every facet of my career in such detail and I'm sorry I can't live up to that expectation. The truth is, and I hate having to admit it, that I can't remember a single incident about the match in question.

I'm very sorry that I can't help you, but such is the penalty of the passing of 49 years.

In *Dusky Legend*, Morrie wrote that, as with visits by earlier state sides, spectators packed the Lismore Recreation Ground. There was great excitement:

> Apart from the obvious attraction of the New South Wales captain, Alan Kippax, and his star-studded team, there was also the local champion, the dusky legend, Sam Anderson, whose exploits were already the stuff of legend in these parts. Spectactors came from near and far, by car, bus, train, river droghers, horseback and rowing boats. The crowd fell silent as Sam trudged off with a duck to his name, but they had some satisfaction when their hero Sam caught the rising star of Australian cricket, Bradman, first ball for a duck. Graham Smith, in his book *How It Seamed*, wrote: 'How many present would have realised when Sam caught Don, they had just witnessed the dismissal of one who was soon to be the world's greatest batsman.'[5]

Morrie transcribed the scorecards of both the Kippax XI and the Richmond–Tweed XI in his book, but it wasn't until I actually saw the original newspaper article that I truly believed the Anderson family story to be true. It's not that I didn't trust Morrie's research, but seeing the results officially recorded in the *Northern Star* newspaper (rather than seeing it in Morrie's little 90-page self-published book) completely erased any remaining doubt. The article, published on 17 September 1928, was titled, 'Narrow Win: Kippax Team's Visit: District Men Shape Well', and on one line of the scorecard were the words 'D. Bradman, c Anderson, b Irvine 0'.[6]

This section and the previous one have described my meeting with Morrie, and provide the evidence that upholds the truth of our family story. But I need to fill in a gap between Sam's departure from Deebing Creek and Sam taking that catch to reveal what happened during that time.

Morrie wrote in his book that Sam played cricket with local cricket clubs right up until the time he left Deebing Creek 'to escape the strict rules of the Native Affairs Department of Queensland'. In New South Wales, he went to Woodenbong, then on to Casino, where he worked at an abattoir. Many Richmond River towns had turned to dairying and, along with beef and timber industries, there were plenty of opportunities for rural workers.[7]

Cunningham Henderson

Sam gained employment on Cunningham Henderson's vast property called Main Camp. What started out as a small selection was built up to be one of the largest cattle stations on the Richmond River. The property comprised 70,000 acres (28,330 hectares) and carried approximately 7000 head of Hereford cattle. As revealed in the previous chapter, Henderson's opinion of interracial marriage was clear. He truly believed that the 'full-blood' Aborigine was 'vastly superior to the half caste' and he called 'half-caste' Aborigines 'outcasts'.

Historian Henry Reynolds has noted that in colonial print material, Aboriginal people were called 'myalls' and 'niggers' and 'gins' and 'piccaninies' and were never called men, women and children—because using these insulting names made Aboriginal people seem further removed from humanity.[8] Cunningham Henderson conceded there were three 'outcasts' who were exceptions to the rule, and he named my great-grandfather Sam Anderson as one of them. Henderson wrote about how he met Sam: 'He came to me looking for a job, and

I liked him on sight. He was a medium horseman, but a splendid man at other work. Everything he did showed capability and intelligence.'[9]

After working for Henderson for a fortnight, Sam asked him where he could find a cricket game, so Henderson sent him to his neighbour, Mr Yabsley, who was a keen cricketer with his own team called the 'Bungawalbyns'. Henderson said that the next time he saw Yabsley, his neighbour described Sam as the best county cricketer that he had ever seen, so Henderson decided to 'transfer him altogether'. Sam played against the best North Coast and New England teams for many years. He was generally a good bowler and fielder, an all-rounder, but he stood out as a batsman and wicketkeeper. Henderson said that 'with the addition of Anderson the Bungawalbyns won nearly all their matches. He knew every stroke and move in the game and was entirely without conceit. He was unfortunate in two things. He was a drinker and a half caste.'[10]

Aunty Ruby included excerpts of Cunningham Henderson's manuscript in her third book, *My Bundjalung People*, and to the above quote, she responded, 'That's right, my grandfather became a commodity that could be handed from one white man to another. Whoever could use him could have him!'[11] Aunty Ruby made it very clear that she thought that Henderson's effort to gain the trust of the local Aboriginal people was purely motivated by his need for workers. She added, 'it was to his advantage to win their respect because in return he received 60 years of Koori [Aboriginal] labour which he used to increase his own wealth. Let's face it, those early settlers could not have built up their empires without Aboriginal labour.'[12]

In my head, I can hear Aunty Ruby's voice saying this very angrily. Her first impression was right; it *was* to Henderson's advantage to win their respect, and he *was* motivated by his need for workers, for which he *did* receive many years of service. Henderson was pretty upfront about that, but I can see where Aunty Ruby's anger comes from. She had the impression that her grandfather was being exploited, but I didn't initially see it that way.

I thought that Sam had a degree of agency and there was reciprocity in action. Sam wanted to play cricket, and so Henderson transferred him to Yabsley, where he could still have a job, but also enjoy the sport that he was so gifted at playing. Henderson met Sam's needs, securing another job for him, and in return he received his neighbour's gratitude and guaranteed a winning streak for the Bungawalbyn cricket team. For Aboriginal people, just having a job at that time was a rare commodity. Henderson and Yabsley provided consistent, long-term work for Aboriginal workers and it is no surprise that Aboriginal employees stayed with them for many years.

Later, however, I realised that Aunty Ruby was right. Sam truly was being exploited by both the cricketers who wanted him to play for their team, and the cricketers from opposing teams. They both used Sam's alcohol addiction for their own ends. Morrie said that 'Behind every gum tree there was a bottle of rum or plonk for Sam's use, put there by his club or the opposition.' Sam's drinking problem was, of course, part of the legend surrounding him. Morrie was well aware that there was a dark side to the retelling of stories about Sam. 'If he drank a fraction of the amount attributed to him he would have been dead of cirrhosis of the liver long before he actually died. It was one of those aspects of his career where different storytellers vied with each other to try and cap the other's tale.' Morrie was at a loss as to why someone would try to bribe him by putting a bottle behind a tree, and I am at a loss to understand why people would intentionally contribute to another man's downfall for the sake of winning a game of sport.

It wasn't just about winning a random match here and there; it was about winning *all* of the matches. I have the original copy of a 1977 letter that Margaret Keller received from Mr M.J. Nolan. He was in a nursing home when he wrote of his many memories of Sam. He relayed how the 'arrangement' with Sam was more contractual than informal. 'Sam's retainer from Yabsley for the cricket season was 10 shillings for plonk if he scored 100 [runs and] no remuneration for less and possibly a gallon of beer for 50 if they won the match.'

Nolan said that when he came through Coraki in 1917, in uniform from the First World War, he was included in a challenge match on the Glebe Cricket Ground (Lismore/Casino turnoff). It was a 'Blacks versus Whites' match and the selectors remembered he had some luck as a bowler before his enlistment. Nolan wrote, 'The blacks won the toss and Alex James and Sam opened up, and when it got too dark to continue, Sam and Alex were about 300 not out. It was the only match I had ever played in which no wicket had fallen.' Publicans were not permitted to serve Aboriginal people alcohol in those days, but Nolan remembered another occasion when Sam was on his way to an important match and the licensee of the Empire Hotel at Woodburn said, '"If you score a 100, Sam, I'll give you a gallon." Sam asked for wine too, and after he scored 110 runs and took 10 wickets in the match, he collected his beer and wine and shared it with his team-mates.'

Morrie called the restriction of alcohol supply to Aboriginal people 'a pernicious rule which did several things; it led Aborigines to drinking horrible substitutes; it left Aborigines open to exploitation by unprincipled publicans, who would charge exorbitant prices or sell inferior liquor at a top price; and it left them open to shady characters who would trade in selling alcohol to the natives. So, the non-drinking rules at hotels had more harmful effects than the right to drink openly would have done.'[13] As a history researcher, I have found that there is a large number of examples of white Australian's patriarchal control over Aboriginal lives, and the following chapters of this book will reveal the shocking extent of that control.

To close this section on a lighter note, though, I would like to return one last time to Cunningham Henderson's manuscript, because it compellingly highlights all kinds of white Australian interactions with Aboriginal people, and they were not always negative. There are two particular stories narrated by Henderson that I would like to share.[14] The first is about an old Aboriginal man called 'Ding', who was considered a local identity in the country town of Coraki:

> A group of us were yarning in the Post Office at Coraki. An Aborigine called 'Ding' was passing on the other side of the street. Ding was a powerfully built man, and worked on a farm.
>
> One of our group said—'You just watch me take a rise out of that Abo.'
>
> In response to a call Ding came across, and this is what followed.
>
> 'Ding, don't you know there's a war on?'
> 'Yes, I know.'
> 'Then why don't you enlist?'
> 'Me enlist, what for?'
> 'Why, to go and fight for your country!'

'Fight for my country!' (scornfully) 'My country! You bloody white fellers took this country from us a long time ago.'

And he continued to walk.

The second story was about another local identity named 'Peel'. Henderson wrote fondly: 'About the town was an elderly black fellow named Peel. He had given up bush work, and did odd jobs about the town. He was a born comedian, and ready for a crack with anyone—the jolliest I ever saw. Everyone liked Peel.' Henderson wrote that one of the local shopkeepers shared this story with him:

Peel walked up to the drapery counter one morning, the shopkeeper standing by. The girl behind the counter knew him. Everyone did!

'Good morning Peel,—what can I do for you?'

'Mornin Miss. I want a pair of stockings for my granddaughter.'

He was shown a pair of cheap ones. Examining them, Peel said—'Something better than that, miss.'

A second pair were shown and rejected. As she tied up the box the girl remarked—'Now I know what you want, Peel. You want something right up to date.'

His eyes twinkling, Peel said—'No miss—up to the knee will do!'

I had to laugh. These two stories stayed with me well after I had finished reading them, and the more I thought about them, the more I asked myself why. I came to the conclusion that I held a lot of preconceived ideas, and because Aboriginal people were so subjugated in history, I assumed that they wouldn't dare speak back to whitefellas in the early days, let alone joke with them. I also thought that, given the circumstances, they would have avoided interactions with whitefellas. These kind of stories—like Henderson's ones about Ding, who was a feisty old fella, and Peel, who was 'ready for a crack with anyone'—are among my favourite finds, because they make me feel as though I have been transported back in time, and am invisibly observing what was happening in the town of Coraki in the early 1900s.

The early Solomon family

Tracing my mother's maternal line, the Solomon family, as far back as I could go in history led to a couple recorded as a 'full-blood' man called Solomon and a 'full-blood' woman called Ruby Morgan. Solomon and Ruby were the parents of a son called Octo Solomon and my great-grandmother Nellie Solomon. As I said earlier, I use the term 'full-blood' like this when an archival record has recorded the person as such. As an Aboriginal family history researcher, I do not find the term 'full-blood' offensive, because this non-Indigenous differentiation meant that I had found a traditional ancestor, one whom I see as a bridge back to our pre-colonisation ancestors on the continuum of Aboriginal history.

Unlike the displaced Andersons, the Solomon family were always on Country, at a location near the town of Kyogle, New South Wales. The Kyogle Aborigines Station was first recorded in the historical record as a pastoral lease called 'Runnymede'. Later, it became known as Runnymede Aborigines Reserve and/ or Runnymede Aborigines Home, before finally being known as Kyogle Aborigines Station.

ABO blood

My mother and her sisters only ever knew that their grand-mother's name was Nellie Solomon, but they did not know who their great-grandparents were. Unexpectedly, I managed to locate a record with a reference to Nellie Solomon at the Queensland State Archives. It was a very strange way to find out who the last set of my great-great-grandparents were. The reference was to a paper written by a man called Gilbert Phillips, B.Sc., from the Department of Physiology, University of Sydney, for the Australian National Research Association. The article, titled 'An introduction to the study of the iso-haem-agglutination reactions of the blood of Australian Aborigines', was published in the *Medical Journal of Australia* on 7 April 1928.[15]

Phillips travelled to the Runnymede (Kyogle) Aborigines Reserve/Station at the time that my great-grandmother Nellie Solomon lived there. He wanted to test the blood of 'full-blood' Aboriginal people and in his article he made sure to include information about the genealogy of the people whom he tested. Phillips outlined the process that he went through to ascertain that the people he tested were 'full-blood', and he wrote:

> This work was carried on at the expense of the Austra-lian National Research Council at Runnymede Aboriginal Station[,] South Kyogle, New South Wales. As no record of genealogy was kept on the station, I investigated the purity of my subjects in three ways;
> - By information supplied by the Manager of the Station.
> - By careful cross-examination of the subjects.
> - By the cross-examination of other people who had known the parents of each subject.[16]

I was curious about why Phillips was testing the blood of 'full-blood' Aboriginal people on the reserve. Along with the study done at Runnymede, I found that Phillips conducted another study at Barambah Aborigines Reserve, Queensland, now known as Cherbourg. I sent this study to the Aborigines Reserve museum called 'The Ration Shed', because in this study Phillips recorded the names and original Country of all the 55 Aboriginal people he tested. Incredibly, this record has the potential to inform 55 Aboriginal families of their ancestors' original home Country before they were incarcerated at Barambah.

I have to admit that I was suspicious of Phillips' motives. I thought, *Why on Earth did they want to test my ancestors' blood? Is this some kind of Darwinian* Origin of Species *investigation? Did they really think we had different blood?* I wanted to get to the bottom of what this was all about, but both articles contained a lot of complex medical jargon that I did not understand.

I decided to search for a haematologist who could explain it to me. Daringly, I sent an email to Associate Professor Dr Steven Lane, a clinical haematologist, who at that time was the head of the Cancer Program at the QIMR Berghofer Medical Research Institute. With the email, I attached both of Phillips' studies, and gave an explanation of who I was and what I was hoping to find out. To my delighted surprise, I received an immediate response.

Dr Lane took the time to read Phillips' studies and sent me an email in response to my questions:

This paper is interesting, but the research and ethical frameworks are quite outdated by today's standards ... the methods are outdated (no consent information provided, we would usually de-identify research subjects these days). Basically—the author was looking to see if Aboriginal Australian population blood types had distinct differences to Caucasian blood types. This is really important to know for purposes such as blood transfusion (incompatible blood can be fatal if administered). There were some differences identified (as one might expect). Groups I–IV are the groups we now speak of as AB, A, B, and O (ABO blood groups). The paper concludes that Aboriginal Australians have the same distribution of ABO groups as Caucasian Australians, although this is not specifically tested. Again, they don't identify the other antigens (sometimes rare, sometimes common) that cause the agglutination, but in the subsequent 100 years, these have been classified in detail.[17]

Reading this information, and seeing those three letters, A-B-O, which when put together read 'ABO', reminded me of when I was growing up in the 1970s. I remember being called ugly names during my early school years. One of the most common (and hurtful) racial slurs was the word 'Abo'. I was a sensitive kid, and I still inwardly wince whenever I hear it. It evokes all those childhood memories of being considered the 'other'. Of course, most kids were colourblind, but it's the times when mean kids were racist that you never forget.

I remember being teased for being an 'Abo' and asked if I had any witchetty grubs in my lunchbox. Calling Aboriginal people an 'Abo' was, in my experience and opinion, just as bad as calling an African American the 'n' word. I don't know what triggered my response, or how to describe it, but when I read Dr Lane's words where he said, 'Aboriginal Australians have the same distribution of ABO groups as Caucasian Australians' a chuckle escaped my lips.

Phillips and his delegating superiors were not being 'evolutionists'; they were genuinely investigating Aboriginal blood because if they did transfusions on Aboriginal people the results could have been fatal. I was very happy to find Phillips' studies, because I was able to know seven out of eight of my great-great-grandparents' names (Sam Anderson's white Australian father remains unknown). Additionally, Phillips recorded my great-grandmother Nellie Solomon's traditional name, Babunde. So, I now knew Nellie's traditional name as well as Mary Jane Anderson's traditional name, Bunjue.[18] Seriously, what are the odds of me finding an obscure archive written by an educated whitefella who visited my ancestors on an Aborigines reserve in 1928? It is beyond extraordinary to discover that he personally interviewed my great-grandmother Nellie to ask her about her pedigree, and recorded it in writing.[19] It was mind-blowing.

Subject VI.

Nellie Walker, *née* Solomons, aged thirty-two years, a female, legally married and a full-blooded aboriginal, was born at Roseberry Station, New South Wales. Her native name was Babundē. Her genealogy is as follows:

? Solomons· (full-blood)—Ruby Morgan (full-blood)

Albert Walker—Nellie Solomons
(half-caste)

Three children

The minute books

Like many other Aboriginal children, Nellie was removed from her family to be placed into domestic service. It appears that removing Aboriginal children from their families was one of the main goals of the Aborigines Protection Board.[20] It started in normal court proceedings under the *Neglected Children and Juvenile Offenders Act 1905*:

> A 'neglected' or 'uncontrollable' child may be apprehended and brought before a court which can release the child on probation, commit the child to an institution until the age of 18 years, or to the care of a willing person. A child in an institution may be apprenticed in accordance with the *Apprentices Act 1901*.[21]

The *Apprentices Act 1901* regulated apprentices' terms and conditions and provided for a minimum age of fourteen for apprentices. The *Aborigines Protection Act 1909* gave the Protection Board statutory powers in relation to all reserves. The Board's duties included that it provide for the custody, maintenance and education of Aboriginal children. The Board could apprentice 'the child of any aborigine or the neglected child of any person apparently having an admixture of aboriginal blood in his veins' subject to the Apprentices Act. The Protection Board was vested with the power to control all Aborigines reserves, and that included the power to remove people from them. Regulations 'could be made for the care, custody and education of Aborigines and prescribing the conditions on which certain children may be apprenticed under the Act'.[22]

The Aborigines Protection Board minutes below pertain to my great-grandmother Nellie, and I have formatted them the same way they appear in the actual minute books to show the perfunctory way in which the Board made major decisions about the lives of Aboriginal people.

9/11/1911

Indenture of Miss Nellie Solomon, Runnymede, to Mr E F E Edwards, Kyogle

APB Response: *Completed*

6/6/1912

Local Committee, Kyogle, re conduct of aboriginal girl Nellie Solomon, apprenticed to Mrs J C Edwards, of Roseberry Park, Kyogle

APB Response: *Cancellation of indenture approved, arrange for the girl to be sent to Sydney*

27/6/1912

Further reports re Aboriginal girl Nellie Solomon, apprenticed to Mrs Edwards Kyogle

APB Response: *Nellie Solomon to be allowed to remain with Mrs Edwards*

26/9/1912

Re: Aboriginal girl Nellie Solomon of Runnymede Home, apprenticed to Mr Edwards of Roseberry, Kyogle

APB Response: *Arrange for this girl to be sent to Sydney*

16/10/1912

Refusal of aboriginal girl Nellie Solomon (lately employed by Mrs Edwards of Kyogle) to come to Sydney, as directed by Board

APB Response: *Inform Local Committee a member of the Central Board will be visiting in the New Year; meanwhile endeavours might be made to obtain another place locally for the girl.*[23]

From the above entries, we can see that Nellie's conduct was cause for the Aborigines Protection Board to be concerned. Whether she just resisted being employed by (specifically) the Edwards family, or she resisted being indentured overall is unclear. The Board teetered between wanting to make her stay where she was or sending her to Sydney, I think as punishment, but it was seemingly powerless when she refused to go. Nellie was not the only young girl to resist relocation, and the Aborigines Protection Board minute books record other instances of Aboriginal girls refusing to go, but they were rare.

I speculate that Nellie and other girls of her time who were successful in staying on Country might have only achieved such a feat because the Board was still fumbling along trying to implement legislative changes to the Aborigines Protection Act. The Board wanted the power to remove Aboriginal children without having to prove 'neglect'. The *Aborigines Protection Amending Act 1915* removed that requirement, so children could be taken away without the court or anyone else obstructing its intentions.[24] Historian Heather Goodall stated that even though the legislation was not officially passed until 1915, the obsessive tenacity of Board members saw children removed as early as 1912.[25] Here we see my great-grandmother Nellie first being removed in 1911. Going by her age when she married, and counting back to 1911, she was fourteen years old.

Yes, Nellie!

There is a miraculous story to tell about how I found the records pertaining to my great-grandmother Nellie Solomon in the Aborigines Protection Board's minute books. It was the last day of a research trip to the New South Wales State Records archive in Western Sydney, and I was booked to fly home to Brisbane that evening. I had spent hours that morning meticulously photocopying all the school files from the 'Aborigines Only' schools on the missions and reserves where my grandparents lived as children. With that job done, I only had the afternoon hours for one final search of the archives before I had to catch two trains to get to Sydney airport in time for my flight home.

I had such a strong urge to find Nellie, and as time was dwindling away, that sense of urgency grew stronger. There was only one place left to look, so I turned my attention to the minute books. Knowing that she was born around 1897—and knowing that she was a teenager at a time when the Board was hell-bent on removing Aboriginal girls from their families—I felt certain that she would have been targeted by them for indenture as one of their so-called 'apprentices'. The pages of the Board's minute books were captured on microfilm reels to be viewed on the archive's old microfilm reader machines. A multitude of images of minute book pages could be contained on one reel of microfilm. Onto the machine I loaded a reel which covered the years I was interested in searching. The machine had large 'rewind', 'stop' and 'forward' buttons, like an old-style cassette player.

I was painstakingly reading the minute books page by page, and time was running out as I sat there scrolling through what seemed like endless pages of microfilm images. There were years and years of daily records to go through, and I became worried that I would have to make another research trip to Sydney, which I couldn't afford.

When I held the 'forward' button down, the machine would skip forward quickly—*ker-chunk ker-chunk ker-chunk*. Then I would stop, read the page, and skip forward again. Fear of missing something important would set in, and I would press the rewind button—*ker-chunk ker-chunk ker-chunk*—to go back, read the pages, and then move forward again. It was chaotic. I felt stress rising, and the next time I looked at the clock, I was shocked to see that I was within forty minutes of my set departure time. I *knew* Nellie was in these pages, I just knew it!

If I missed the train to Sydney Central, then I would miss the connecting train to the airport. Realising I needed to calm the heck down, I closed my eyes and began to do some slow, deep breathing. I remembered my Uncle Gerry telling me years ago that we can call on our Spirit guides and ancestors when we need help—so, with nothing to lose, I decided to give it a go. As I centred myself, I mentally put out a call. A feeling of calm descended upon me, as though they had casually dropped down from Heaven to surround me. I heard myself say, 'I feel like you have guided me to be here, like I am meant to find something. If that's true, help me now. Time is running out.'

I decided that I would continue to press the 'forward' button until I felt guided to stop. Opening my eyes, I located the big green button. I held it down, then I closed my eyes tightly and ordered my senses to focus as I continued: *ker-chunk ker-chunk ker-chunk*. Suddenly, almost automatically, my hand reached out and slammed down on the stop button. As I looked up at the screen my jaw dropped open. My hand had stopped the machine on the page that recorded the sentence, *Further reports re Aboriginal girl Nellie Solomon, apprenticed to Mrs Edwards Kyogle*.

I was gobsmacked! Stunned! This gave me a pinpoint on the timeline within which I could then move forward and back to locate more records about Nellie. I was beside myself. By this time my heart was thumping in my chest as I first went backwards page by page, and then forward page by page, until

I found the last record. A volcano of emotions rose up in me, and I was filled to the brim with molten pride as I read that this young Aboriginal girl, confronted with white government authorities (more than likely accompanied by a policeman), defiantly stood her ground and refused the order that would take her away from her home and her family. I felt a mass of emotions suddenly explode and I thumped my flat, open palm onto the tabletop, and shouted loudly, 'YES, NELLIE!!!'

To my horror, I realised I had smashed the silence of the archives reading room, and all eyes were on me. My hand was instantly stinging and swelling from the pain of hitting the table so hard, and as my eyes scanned the room from left to right, I saw several elderly (historical society) archive helpers with their white-cotton-gloved hands pause in the middle of turning yellowed pages. An old man glared at me in disgust. Everyone, including the younger archivists behind the help desk, was motionless as they stared at me. It was like God had pressed the pause button on this movie. But, over on the right-hand side, there sat a non-Indigenous woman, alone at a large table, papers spread out before her—and when her eyes met mine, she put down what she was holding and smiled at me with such loving kindness that I was taken aback.

There's an old saying that 'a picture is worth a thousand words'; and in that moment her look conveyed a thousand words. The energy of that smile swept over me like a warm hug, and it conveyed so much information that it felt as though I could telepathically read what she was thinking as she held my gaze. She could see that I am Aboriginal, and she knew enough about history to know that it was unusual to see an Aboriginal person finding good news in a history archive. She was happy for me, and there was an almost imperceptible nod of her head as she acknowledged me. I smiled back and responded with a similar nod.

As I went back to my research work, I was still charmed by this lovely exchange and I thought to myself, *I bet she's a historian*. State archives and historical society libraries can be places of powerful emotions.

While the search for information about Nellie elicited an exhilarated, joyful response, there have been countless times when I have found records so saddening, so shocking, and at times so infuriating, that they have caused streams of tears to pour down my cheeks. This chapter has only scratched the surface of the truth about Aboriginal history.

My friend Professor Peter Read named three major components of Aboriginal history as 'The Terrible Threesome'—the frontier killings, land theft and the Stolen Generations—and he added:

> Sooner or later our nation is going to have to confront the enormity of the managed reserve system which degraded, abused and humiliated Aboriginal people for 90 years after 1870. That's a story as big and as hurtful as the Stolen Generations themselves.[26]

The managed reserve system

The idea of allocating land as 'reserves' for Aboriginal people actually goes back to when the British abolished slave trading in 1833. The Anti-Slavery Society and other humanitarian groups turned their attention to the plight of Indigenous people and their living conditions throughout the British Empire.[27] As previously described, the Land Act of 1842 began to formalise the sale of land in the colony and, for the first time, Crown land was to be reserved for the use of Aboriginal people. This reflected British concern about Aboriginal people and their access and rights to land.[28] British secretary of state Earl Henry Grey argued that leases were 'not intended to deprive natives of their former right to hunt over these districts or to wander over them in search of subsistence in the manner in which they have been hithertofore accustomed'. Earl Grey also argued that 'Crown lease to pastoralists allowed only limited rights, and that much of the rights of possession remained reserved to the Crown'.[29] In late 1849, Governor Fitzroy and the Crown land commissioners supported restrictions on pastoral leases but were not keen on the creation of Aboriginal reserves in the squatting districts. Any form of recognition of Aboriginal rights to land was bitterly opposed by squatters.[30]

Nonetheless, the creation of Aborigines reserves went ahead; 35 reserves were created in 1850, but as they were only a small portion of once vast traditional lands, they offered little protection from the continuing violence, which threatened to cut off Aboriginal people's access to their land altogether. The discovery of gold in 1851 dramatically changed relations between Aboriginal people and pastoralists. White Australian workers abandoned their jobs in the gold rush, and squatters and pastoralists who only a few months prior attacked and murdered Aboriginal people, now coveted Aboriginal workers, whom they desperately needed to work as stockmen on their stations. Aunty Ruby immediately popped into my thoughts, and I imagined her standing behind me as I typed these words, then flicking the back of my head in exasperation and saying, 'See! I told you those early settlers could not have built up their empires without Aboriginal labour!'

For the first time, pastoralists began to offer reasonable conditions, cash wages and safe access to traditional lands, so the original reserves faded in significance as Aboriginal people returned to Country.[31] From the 1860s, fencing became more common, and cattle work only became available at set times for mustering. As a result, pastoralists only paid Aboriginal people for seasonal work, and during the off-season they were forced to live off bush tucker.[32] As mentioned in Chapter 2, it was after the gold rush that land was opened up with the Robertson Land Acts, and white settlers, like my great-great-grandfather Augustus John Bostock, could apply for 'free selection' of land under conditional purchases.

Digesting this information, I immediately thought about the sad faces of the Gumbaynggirr, Yaegl and Bundjalung people captured in the Lindt photographs, and imagined what they had seen in their lifetimes. Their traditional homelands were carved up by white settlers, their precious and sacred ceremonial sites trampled, and their crystal-clear springs and waterways muddied and fouled by hooved beasts. Newly erected fences must have been seen as puzzling, strange contraptions that scarred the landscape. I reflected on Toolbillibam's strong conviction that land should be left for him and his people to occupy, and imagined him standing powerless, silently witnessing the encroaching, destructive force of invasion. They had already been pushed onto the high country.

The distress of Aboriginal people caught in intensifying land changes and the increasing loss of traditional game caused missionaries at Maloga on the Murray River and at Warangesda on the Murrumbidgee River to appeal to the New South Wales Government for urgent benevolent aid for Aboriginal people, whom they described as 'impoverished and without any alternatives'.[33] In 1881, a chief protector of Aborigines, Mr George Thornton, was appointed and given a secretary and

a few hundred pounds of funds for the distribution of necessary aid. The following year, an inquiry was launched into the
workings of the two Aboriginal mission stations at Maloga and
Warangesda. The New South Wales Government, as a result of
the inquiry's report, decided to appoint a 'Board for the Protection of Aborigines' composed of five to seven members and it
was 'gazetted' (meaning it was published in the government
gazette and made official) in June of 1883.[34]

The Lands Department provided the Aborigines Protection Board with 'plans and particulars of twenty-five reserves
in different parts of the Colony, including a total area of
3500 acres [1400 hectares], which have been set apart for the use
of aborigines'.[35] The chief secretary approved that a 'Local Board
of Advice and Management' be appointed for each station and
these came to be known as the 'Local Board'. In May 1910, the
local boards officially ceased to exist and instead 'Local Committees' were created.[36] In towns near the reserves, the Aborigines
Protection Board appointed the local committees as local agents
for matters concerning the Aborigines reserves. These committees were usually comprised of a handful of upstanding town
citizens who reported to the Board's head office in Sydney.

It is interesting, yet sadly ill-informed, that residents of
Aborigines reserves thought that the reserve was 'granted' to
them 'for life'. This misunderstanding can be traced back
to Chief Protector Thornton's wording, describing Crown
land for the use of Aborigines as land 'grants' and implying a
more permanent process that just didn't exist. Unfortunately,
police and land officials such as local committees may have
explained reserve lands to Aboriginal people in this way—and
it led to Aboriginal people strongly believing that their reserve
officially *belonged* to them—but, as far as the New South

Wales Government was concerned, that certainly was not the case.[37]

With the depression in the 1890s and the following drought causing high Aboriginal unemployment in most areas, unemployed Aboriginal people had no choice but to apply to the Aborigines Protection Board's managers for support and to rely on the Board rations. This brought the Board's attention to the need for increased rations, and also the realisation that Aboriginal people were not disappearing as they had assumed. In their words, 'full-bloods' were certainly reducing in number, but there was a significant increase in the number of 'half-castes', 'quadroons' and 'octoroons'. White Australians at that time were so obsessed with the degrees of Indigenous peoples' Aboriginality that it was measured in fractions: *half-caste* meaning half Aboriginal; *quadroon* meaning one-quarter Aboriginal; and *octoroon* meaning one-eighth Aboriginal. In 1882, only 26.7 per cent of the Aboriginal population appeared to be of mixed European and Aboriginal descent—but by 1900 this proportion had risen to 55 per cent.

At this time, biology was seen as a powerful determinant of behaviour and character, and as social Darwinism was at its height, the increase of a racially distinct minority and any form of cultural assertiveness was viewed with fear and alarm. Board member Mr R. Scobie was even recorded as saying that Aboriginal people 'are an increasing danger, because although there are only a few full-blooded Aborigines left, there are 6,000 of the mixed-blood growing up. It is a danger to have people like that among us, looking upon our institutions with eyes different from ours.'[38]

The Aborigines Protection Board concluded that mixed-race Aboriginal people weren't separating themselves from the Aboriginal community, but were in fact self-identifying as Aboriginal people and living with their Aboriginal relatives, and were identified by whites as being Aboriginal. There was a strong desire by the Board to gain a legislative base and, by 1907, it had prepared a draft bill that convinced the government that it should have the power to control the access of Aboriginal people to alcohol, to decide who could and could not collect rations from the reserves, and to 'disperse' the Aboriginal population. Unlike the years of horrendous violence during the frontier wars, the word 'disperse', at this time in history, meant to eject or send Aboriginal people away from reserves.

As discussed in Chapter 3, what the Board wanted most of all was the power to remove all authority that Aboriginal parents had over their children and give it to the Board. It requested the power to stand *in loco parentis* (in place of the parents), and it emphatically argued to the premier that it was only when it gained such power over all Aboriginal children that they would be educated and indoctrinated into the habits of industry. The *Aborigines Protection Act 1909* gave the Aborigines Protection Board statutory power over all Aborigines reserves. This meant that officially documented, binding laws passed by the New South Wales Government granted Board officials the power to perform acts. But as much as the Board fought for control of all Aboriginal children, they only achieved the same power as the Children's Relief Department: to take control of children if, and only if, they were judged by the courts to be 'neglected'.

Another member of the Aborigines Protection Board, Robert Donaldson, was obsessed about removing Aboriginal children from their families. He found Aboriginal social and cultural life abhorrent and 'led a deputation to the Chief Secretary in May 1912 in which he pleaded that Aboriginal parenting and community life was so corrupting that the only hope for children and adolescents was to be taken away regardless of their own wishes or those of their relatives'. Donaldson's bloody-minded determination persuaded the New South Wales Government to amend the legislation, and he was assured that the Board would have all the powers it wanted.[39]

The Board's campaign for power *in loco parentis* became frenzied, and 'although it took until 1915 to pass the amending legislation, the Board began from 1912, to remove as many children as it could'. Also in 1915 (as soon the amending legislation was passed), Donaldson resigned from the Board and took up one of the positions as inspector to personally oversee the removal of Aboriginal children from their families. He fulfilled his job until 1929, conducting a relentless routine of travel around the state to select Aboriginal children for removal. It stands to reason that my ancestors and other Aboriginal people strenuously avoided Mr Robert Donaldson, the obsessed 'kid collector', who was the most feared and hated man in the state.[40]

The history books say that the removal of Aboriginal children in New South Wales began as early as 1912, up to three years earlier than legislation allowed, but my research revealed that my great-grandmother Nellie Solomon experienced removal as early as 1911.

5

Reserves and whitefellas

'Then all of a sudden the Board informed them that they are taking their land back again. And it proved that Aborigines had no rights whatsoever. And I think . . . I really think, that's what broke the spirit of the men who had done all that work, really for nothing.'

AUNTY GERALDINE BRIGGS, CUMMERAGUNJA ABORIGINES RESERVE

I have always been curious about the Aborigines reserves where my grandparents were born and lived, and I came across the emotional letter below during my search for information about Dunoon Aborigines Reserve, the place where my grandfather Henry Anderson was born. It was written by Mr Billy Robinson, an Aboriginal man who lived on the reserve, and it was sent to the Minister for Lands in 1922. The *Northern Star*, Lismore's local newspaper, published the extract below from Mr Robinson's letter. I consider this letter an exemplar of Aboriginal frustration and distress over the capricious, niggardly decisions made by the government's Aborigines Protection Board in regard to Aborigines reserve land. This was one of the first historical newspaper articles that I had come across at the beginning of my research

132

journey, and it provided a large amount of information to unpack.
What happened to the Aboriginal people at Dunoon happened to
other Aboriginal people all across New South Wales.

> We have seen your report regarding our reserve. You have
> ascertained that it is overgrown with lantana, and is harbour-
> ing noxious animals. The statements made to you regarding
> noxious animals supposed to be sheltering in our reserve are
> untrue. As for the lantana, it is being brushed and cleared every
> day. Had the police given us a decisive answer at first we would
> have had it cleared by now, but they caused delay and kept us
> back seven or eight weeks. No one consented to go to Runny-
> mede. We are all remaining here. There are 52 here now. You
> have proposed to allow us ten or twelve acres. So you intend to
> pack us in like sardines in a tin! The 52 here now are only part
> of the tribe—where are the remaining 30 or 40 going to live?
> How are 52 going to make a living on 10 or 12 acres as you
> propose they should do? This is our home for life granted to us
> by our old friends Messrs. Barrie, Hewitt, Garrard and Inspec-
> tor Evans, who informed us that no white man was to interfere
> with us. We are not willing for our reserve to be cut up because
> it is small enough already, and there will be trouble if another
> acre is taken. Two or three acres of it have already been taken
> for the soldier settlers. We are trying to get along with our crops
> and rebuild the houses ourselves. We are not asking the Protec-
> tion Board for help. If we are left alone we can do what requires
> doing ourselves—if we were only left alone in peace to earn our
> bread the same as the white man does.
>
> Mr Billy Robinson
Dunoon Aborigines Reserve
The Northern Star newspaper, August 1922[1]

When I first read this letter, I knew that 'Messrs' was an abbreviation of 'Messieurs', an old-fashioned term that was used as the plural of 'Mister'—but who were 'Misters' Barrie, Hewitt and Garrard, and Inspector Evans? Why were the people told to go to Runnymede (Kyogle)? Why did the reserve get 'cut up'? What were 'soldier settlers'? My initial intention at that stage of my research was to gain an understanding of my ancestors' lived experience on certain Aborigines reserves, but this newspaper article helped me to realise that I had to put the micro-study of reserves on hold for a while. There were bigger picture understandings to be learned first, and I had to find answers to questions raised about the Aborigines reserve space itself.

Whenever I closely examined photographs of large groups of Aboriginal people taken at reserves run by the New South Wales Government's Aborigines Protection Board, I could see that scattered among the Aboriginal residents were white Australian men and women (and sometimes children), and I was curious about who these white people were and why they were there.

As I delved deeper into reserve research, I noticed that the list of non-Indigenous people involved with Aborigines reserves was getting longer. There were Aborigines Protection Board officials; Protection Board managers or matrons; members of the Local Committee; the local police; the Department of Public Instruction (DPI) inspectors; teachers from the segregated schools for Aboriginal children; and the United Aborigines' Mission (UAM), or other denominations of Christian missionaries. Looking into the interactions between Indigenous and non-Indigenous people, I was struck by the absurdity of what was a common state of affairs across a number of Aborigines reserves in New South Wales.

White Australian townspeople furiously demanded that Aboriginal people be pushed out of towns and onto Aborigines reserves, and Aboriginal children be removed from their 'public' schools—but after Aboriginal people were forced on to reserves away from towns—it was those same white Australian townspeople who went out of their way to *go to* the reserves to control and interfere with Aboriginal people's lives. Billy Robinson's poignant words echoed in my mind: *If we were only left alone in peace we can do what requires doing ourselves—if we were only left alone in peace . . .*

I decided to look into Aborigines reserves where my family once lived. These were Dunoon Aborigines Reserve near Lismore, where my grandfather Henry Anderson was born; Nymboida Aborigines Reserve, where my grandmother Edith Cowan was born; Ukerebagh Island Aborigines Reserve, where my great-grandparents Gus and Lena Bostock were segregated from white Australians; and Box Ridge Aborigines Reserve/ Mission, where all four of my grandparents were married.

Although they were married at Box Ridge Mission, my mother's parents also lived at Kyogle Aborigines Reserve. As there were such large amounts of surprisingly detailed archives about Kyogle, and one particular Aborigines Protection Board manager, I have dealt separately with Kyogle reserve in the next chapter. Included in this chapter, before I move on to sections about Dunoon, Nymboida and Ukerebagh Island reserves and Box Ridge Mission, is a brief explanation of who the 'soldier settlers' were. Understanding both how Aborigines reserves were established in Australia, and who the 'soldier settlers' were is essential to understanding how the New South Wales Government disregarded Aboriginal peoples' basic needs in order to prioritise and accommodate white Australians.

The soldier settlers

When Billy Robinson said that *two or three acres of it [Dunoon reserve] have already been taken for the soldier settlers*, he was referring to the government's Returned Soldier Settlement Scheme, which was an expansion of the original Closer Settlement Scheme. Before I could know more about 'soldier settlers', I first needed to go way back in time to understand what the Closer Settlement Scheme was. Governor Lachlan Macquarie, the fifth governor of New South Wales (1810–1821), was principally opposed to large landholdings, which he believed discouraged genuine settlers. Generous allocation of land in Tasmania enabled Robert Bostock to become very wealthy, but in New South Wales, Governor Macquarie was against lavish land grants. He believed that the granting of large areas of land would hinder genuine settlers and force new settlers to go further out, hence the use of the words 'Closer Settlement'.

By the 1830s, the Closer Settlement Scheme had been superseded by the squatting era, when land grants by purpose or auction were introduced to raise government revenue. (That is how Joshua Bray purchased the Wolumban run.) A swing back to closer settlement came in the 1860s when the discoveries in the goldfields began to decrease.[2] When the First World War ended and soldiers began to return home, the New South Wales Government felt that it was only right that they were given a block of farming land as a just reward for their service and facing the terrors of war. The government expanded the Closer Settlement Scheme of 1905, enabling soldier settlers to select a small block of agricultural land in certain areas. It was not so much a generous offer on the government's part as it was a cheap solution to costly rehabilitation.

There were 154 Aboriginal men in New South Wales who had volunteered and fought overseas in the war, and like white Australian servicemen across the state, they expected to benefit from the soldier settler scheme, not just to secure a farm but, in some cases, to regain some of their own Country. But the promises of the soldier settler scheme turned out to be offered only to white soldiers. No discriminating laws or regulations were put in writing, but as applications were handled and ranked in dozens of local land offices, there was no soldier settler land for blackfellas. When the goal of closer settlement was coupled with the call to compensate the 'heroic diggers', the New South Wales Government found it almost impossible to deny the requests for reserve lands. Therefore, the Returned Serviceman's Settlement Scheme accelerated the demand to revoke existing Aborigines reserve lands.[2] That's what was happening at Dunoon Aborigines Reserve, and that is why Billy Robinson wrote in anguish, *So you intend to pack us in like sardines in a tin!*

Dunoon Aborigines Reserve

The Dunoon Aborigines Reserve was situated on the Lismore Tweed Road, about ten kilometres north of the country town of Lismore. It originally consisted of 420 acres (170 hectares) and became an official Aborigines reserve in 1903. It continued to exist as an Aborigines reserve for a little over three decades, until it was revoked in 1935.[4] These dates could be likened to being the dates of birth and death of Dunoon Aborigines Reserve. Sometime before June 1916, my great-grandparents decided to take their family far away from Dunoon and migrate south to Box Ridge Mission, near Coraki, where my grandfather (then five years old) was enrolled at the Coraki Aborigines Only School.[5]

There's a story to tell about why my great-grandparents moved to Box Ridge Mission. In 1914, when a Protection Board manager was employed at the previously unsupervised reserve at Dunoon, the reserve became a station, and this led to a series of conflicts between the Aborigines Protection Board manager, Mr Terry, and the Aboriginal residents. These conflicts were so great that Aboriginal people, including those who had been farming the land, moved off the reserve to unreserved vacant land closer to Lismore, vowing they would not remain under the Board's control.

This Aboriginal move was strategically clever, and happened at other Aborigines reserves run by the New South Wales Government's Aborigines Protection Board. It forced the sacking of reserve managers, because the Board couldn't justify paying a manager's wage when there were no Aboriginal people to 'manage'. A consequence of this was that the segregated 'Aborigines Only' school on the reserve also had to close, which it did in 1916.[6] It made sense that their son's education, and continuing conflict on the reserve, would be reason enough for my great-grandparents Sam and Mabel Anderson to uproot their whole family—but I wanted to know *exactly* what this manager could have done that would cause a whole community of Aboriginal people to vacate a reserve.

Mr Terry was employed by the Aborigines Protection Board to replace the schoolteacher, and when he arrived he told the people that he was a 'schoolteacher and a Christian manager'. In a letter to the local newspaper several years later, Aboriginal Dunoon resident Charlie Brown said with hindsight, 'if we had known he was a manager [from the Aborigines Protection Board] we would not have allowed him to enter our reserve'.[7] Mr Terry told the Aboriginal residents that if they performed any paid work outside of the reserve, then he (Terry) must receive their wages *for them* directly from their employers. Brown stated, 'Those that did not agree to that walked out of the reserve'. During my history journey, I have found several sources that record dishonest, sometimes ruthless actions of Aborigines Protection Board managers, and now I could add attempted extortion to the list. Brown wrote in his letter to a local newspaper:

> We don't understand why the Aborigines Protection Board gives these managers a job of looking after the aborigines when we are well and able to look after ourselves. We are honest and can work as well as the next one, so we don't understand why they allow the white man to make his living by the aborigines . . . We would like you to have more respect for aborigines. By them you are making your living.[8]

Aboriginal people returned to Dunoon in 1917 when it was clear that no manager was going to be reinstated, and Dunoon became a focus for migration from other reserves as Aboriginal people tried to escape the Board's interference. Despite the fact that the Board had leased much of the land to white Australians in 1917, the Aboriginal population grew substantially in 1919, and in 1922 even more had arrived, seeking refuge from managerial interference on Runnymede (Kyogle) and Cabbage Tree Island. To stop this movement, the Aborigines Protection Board decided to revoke the Dunoon Aborigines Reserve in May 1922. This act of spite was met with continuous and effective Aboriginal protest, expressed in the letters to the Board from Aboriginal people and white Australian supporters.[9] The protest at Dunoon embarrassed the government's Aborigines Protection Board because it was made public knowledge through letters being sent to the local newspapers.

In the same letter to the newspaper referred to above, Charlie Brown asked a simple question: 'Supposing you were working under a manager, how would you like him to receive your money from your boss where you were working?' When I read this, I was disgusted by the audacity of Terry. Brown poignantly described the effect of the harassment they experienced from white Australians, but he defiantly stood his ground:

> We know we have rich soil here, but ever since the home was appointed out for us we were never left alone by the whites. We are still in trouble. We don't know whether we are on our head or feet. The members of the P.P.U. [Primary Producer's Union] are trying to remove us. They have got as much chance as of getting water to run up hill.[10]

From 1917, the reserve was under the watchful gaze of white Australian individuals and groups like the Primary Producer's Union (PPU). The PPU were certainly not backward in coming forward, and they openly revealed that they were determined to have the land made available for soldier settlers.[11] It seems this was the first Dunoon Aboriginal people had ever heard about the potential revocation of their homes on the reserve, because they were shocked by what they saw in the newspaper. While the PPU were hell-bent on taking land from Dunoon Aboriginal people, the Municipal Council of Lismore was set on ejecting north Lismore Aboriginal people from the town.

The mayor, the Lismore council and the inspector of police wanted Aboriginal people out of their town entirely, so it was decided to close down the north Lismore house where they lived, and the inspector served verbal notice.[12] The north Lismore people who refused to return to Dunoon then had no choice but to go to land located at the back of the cemetery.[13]

Although the Aborigines Protection Board decided to disband the local committees when they appointed Mr H.L. Swindlehurst and Mr R.T. Donaldson as inspectors in 1915, a former Local Committee member, Mr James Barrie, went to check on Aboriginal people during the 1919 pneumonic influenza pandemic. Barrie found seven or eight Aboriginal people at the back of the cemetery at north Lismore in what he described as 'a humpy hardly fit for a decent dog in wet weather'. The people were reported as being hungry, and 'quaking with fear and wondering what was happening to their relatives at the hospital and what was to be their fate'.

Barrie argued with the police officer, saw that they finally received misplaced rations and then went out to check on the Aboriginal people at Dunoon. It was reported in the local newspaper that at the next Sunday church service, Mr Barrie told the whole congregation about 'the case of these unfortunates'. He believed that 'were it known, he was sure something could quickly be done to relieve these unfortunate creatures, and also the others at the Dunoon camp'.[14]

Emerging at the end of the First World War, the 'Spanish Flu' killed more than fifty million people worldwide. It appeared in Australia in 1919 and about 40 per cent of the population fell ill and around 15,000 died as the virus spread through Australia. Horrifically, some Aboriginal communities recorded a 50 per cent mortality rate.[15] Searching through local newspapers of the time, I found gut-wrenching stories about Aboriginal people's experience of the pandemic, but the saddest, most upsetting of all was written by a Christian missionary, who wrote to the local newspaper under the name 'Leslie Ogilvie, Evangelist'.

He explained that when the sickness broke out at Bean Tree Reserve, a van was sent to take the whole community to Stoney Gully Aborigines Reserve at Kyogle. Many people told him that healthy Aboriginal people who had not been within miles of sick ones were rounded up. Ogilvie said that 'a man or woman had only to have a black face to ensure being imprisoned in the compound'. It consisted of a few miserable huts in close proximity with each other. They were unlined, windowless, draughty and leaky. 'A cattle-breeder would not allow his prize bull to be housed in any one of them, and yet into these hovels one hundred and ten human beings were herded, "sick" and "well" being crowded together in such a way that there was no possibility of them escaping contagion.'

Wet weather came on and the disease rapidly spread. Ogilvie stated that 'Had the last two or three sick ones been quarantined in some suitable place, and the "contacts" in a separate place for a few days, as is done with white people, it is probable there would have been no death reports at all'. In the early stages of the quarantine, the flour supply was unfit to eat and only 50 pounds of meat [22.7 kilograms] per week was supplied to feed 110 people. The rest of the rations were correspondingly short. As a result of this, the people came dangerously close to breaking out of quarantine, and it was only through the intervention of a policeman who saw to the increase of the quality and quantity of rations that trouble was averted.

White townspeople were threatening to shoot any black found outside the compound, and these same people threatened to shoot the manager and the doctor for taking possession of the South Kyogle schoolhouse as a second hospital for the sick. Ogilvie added:

> The Government of this land pretends to protect and help these people . . . There are Christian men and women in this land who have long desired and worked to secure better conditions for the Australian aborigines, but they have been expecting the Government to do something. It is now generally admitted in this district that all that the Government had done, or is likely to do, will not improve the position, but rather the reverse. If the Government is allowed to put its hand on the movement it will be strangled by 'red tape' and whatever funds are voted for the benefit of the natives will be swamped in salaries to useless and incompetent officials . . . Judging by the stories told by many of the natives, and corroborated by white witnesses, these aborigines have been treated by a blundering officialdom in a callous and inhuman manner. Had any company of white people been treated in the same manner as the 'Kyogle blacks' the Government of this land would have been [sued] in thousands of pounds for damages.[16]

In April and July 1921, the Toolaroo PPU reported that the minister Mr George Nesbitt had presented the branch's request—that the Dunoon reserve be 'thrown open for lease'—to the Department of Lands. The Board advised that all the huts on the reserve were occupied, and the people were making improvements (e.g. clearing the lantana for future cultivation etc.). Additionally, the people had clearly stated their intention to make the reserve their permanent home.[17] But the Aboriginal people at Dunoon could not rest assured that they could live peacefully on the reserve.

In May 1922, another white Australian group had their eyes on the reserve, and this time it was the Terania Shire Council. They sent the shire clerk to report on the reserve and he found that nine weatherboard dwellings were in need of extensive repairs. The shire council decided to draw the attention of the Protection Board to the reserve by requiring the Board 'provide sanitary conditions to each of the dwellings on the reserve'.[18] After the shire council's complaints, the Board decided to demolish the buildings and remove the residents to Kyogle.[19] So, rather than fix the problems, the Board's immediate reaction was to close the reserve and relocate the people. Defiant, the people refused to leave. The following two letters, like the one at the beginning of this chapter, express the depths of despair and uncertainty Aboriginal people faced. In June 1922, a statement was issued under the pseudonym 'The Aborigines', which angrily and powerfully declared:

> We should like our neighbours around us to attend to their own affairs. It is through them that we are in trouble. Through their complaining and taking the bread out of our mouths we are remaining here. We will not be shifted. We have a few acres cleared and we want to know where we stand. When this reserve was given us we were told it was our home for life, and we are not going to leave it. When we first came here it was dense scrub. After years of hard work we have made our homes and envious people want to dispose us.[20]

A month later, Aboriginal man Albert Morthen wrote an angry letter to the local newspaper's editor about the Toolaroo PPU, the full text of which is reproduced below. His beseeching tone and emotions are evident:

Sir, - We object strongly to the action of the Toolaroo P.P.U. in trying to remove us from our homes on Dunoon Road, according to a report we saw in the paper of their last meeting. Are we harming anyone, or are we being pests to anyone in any way? Have we stolen anything belonging to any member of the Toolaroo branch of the P.P.U.? We want to know are you going to leave us alone? We do not agree with you in trying to get these five acres from us. You have got hundreds of acres of your own without interfering with our little bit. We ask you to show more respect for us and leave us alone before there is any trouble. We have stood it long enough. It would suit you better to look after your own cows and pigs instead of looking after us. Are you not satisfied with your own home and shelter? We have wives and children just the same as you have. When old friends saw us, camping under a ti-tree bark, they pitied us and told us they would get a home for us, which they did. They were the late Mr Barrie, Mr Hewitt, Mr Garrard, and Inspector Evans. They told us this was to be our home for life, and that no white man would interfere with us. We belong to the soil you are living on. There is no law to say that anything given to the aborigines shall be taken back, so we are remaining here for good.[21]

Nymboida Aborigines Reserve

My grandmother Edith Cowan was born at Nymboida Aborigines reserve in 1911, but no record exists of her birth. I remember being told by family that she was born at 'Nymboida mission' and later 'the mission moved to Box Ridge', near Coraki, but the reason for the move was unknown. Referring to a map, I could clearly see that Coraki is a considerable distance north of Nymboida, especially if the Aboriginal residents travelled by foot, horseback, or horse and sulky, and so the question of why the mission and my family members moved was added to the many questions to which I wanted to find answers.

Since the early 1880s, Aboriginal people had camped on a portion of the water reserve near the Nymboida River. By the mid-1890s, they were destitute and in need of the provision of rations and clothing from the Aborigines Protection Board. In 1903, the Grafton Land Board considered that the camping of Aboriginal people with their dogs on the water reserves was 'detrimental to depasturing of stock, and should be prevented'. By 1910, the Minister of Lands approved an area of 20 acres (a little over 8 hectares) on the left bank of Nymboida River for a reserve for Aboriginal people.[22] Four years later, complaints continued and the integrity of the water supply was added to the list of local residents' concerns. So, the member for Raleigh, on behalf of the South Grafton Municipal Council, wrote an application to the chief secretary to 'have the aborigines station removed from Nymboida, as the camping ground is within the area from which the Nymboida water supply is obtained for the towns of South Grafton and Grafton'.

The chief secretary informed him that it was not necessary to remove the station, but certain precautions would be 'adopted so far as the station is concerned in order to prevent pollution of the water supply'.[23] This begs the question of how Aboriginal people, who depended on the supply of water for survival, and had successfully camped there since the early 1880s, could possibly pollute the whole town of Grafton's water supply more than herds of travelling cattle. It is clear that the white Australians at Nymboida thought more of their cattle than Aboriginal people.

Not satisfied with the removal of Aboriginal people from

the vicinity of their stock, white Australians at Nymboida also wanted Aboriginal children removed from their public school. The townspeople signed a petition and sent it with a letter of objection to the Department of Public Instruction's district school inspector, Mr Henderson.[24] The Department of Public Instruction (DPI) was early terminology used to describe what we now know as the Education Department. It was a common occurrence for petitions to be sent to the district inspector, and it did not surprise Inspector Henderson. He wrote that the 'inclusion of aborigines at our ordinary public schools is an old trouble'. Henderson, as he had previously done at other places, recommended that the teacher at Nymboida Public School be instructed that he must not allow the Aboriginal children to attend the public school, and the Aboriginal parents should be informed that the minister would be prepared to consider an application to establish an 'Aborigines Only' school at Nymboida.[25]

All recommendations were approved and the Nymboida Aborigines School was officially completed in 1908.[26] Interestingly, in his report, Henderson stated that the local Aboriginal people 'have been here for years and are likely to remain' and the Nymboida area is 'looked upon as their home. If they go away for a short time, I am told, they invariably return.'[27] This observation contradicts the common white Australian belief that Aboriginal people were nomadic hunters and gathers, when in fact Aboriginal people tried to stay on their traditional lands, but were often forced to move by circumstances beyond their control.

A few years later, when my grandmother Edith Cowan was a small child, all the Nymboida Aboriginal people had left the Aborigines station. In 1913, according to the local newspaper, the Aborigines Protection Board appointed Mr Newnham as manager, and it was 'not long before all the blacks left the station'.[28] The hostility from the town's residents, the segregation of the children from the public school, and the Board's employment of a station manager increased tension between Aboriginal people and white Australians in Nymboida—but the critical reason for the mass exodus of Aboriginal people from the reserve was fear of child removal. In January 1915, a Grafton newspaper reported an incident at Nymboida that pinpoints the pivotal moment when Aboriginal people, including my family members, fled from Nymboida en masse.

The story of what happened at Nymboida is an account of why Aboriginal families were forced to run away from the government's Aborigines Protection Board. Running away in fear of government officials was not an uncommon experience in the lives of Aboriginal people during the years of the managed reserve system. The following is a transcript of a newspaper article called 'Darkies and Officialdom: Trouble on the Clarence', which was published in the *Richmond River Herald and Northern Districts Advertiser* on 2 February 1915. My grandmother was four years old when this happened, and I believe that my great-grandparents would have been involved in the urgent abandonment of the reserve. This newspaper article reveals genuine sympathy for Aboriginal people, but most importantly, the article reveals the heart-wrenching sadness and grief of the people:

There are a large number of blacks on the Nymboida Aborigines' Reserve. They are provided with houses and rations by the Government, it is maintained that the rations are not sufficient, and, that the blacks have to go forth to earn money from outside sources. A man and his wife—Jacky and Gracie

Lardner—work more or less regularly at the Nymboida Hotel. There is one son, Norman, aged seven, and a daughter, Janie MacDougall, aged 13, a half-caste, born before Lardner and Gracie were married. The school-teacher on the reserve (Mr Noonan) desired the Lardners live in a house on the reserve. They objected, on account of some of the tribe having died in the place, and remained in a gunyah of their own not far away. A lady inspector from Sydney, a Miss Lowe, was at Nymboida recently, and it is believed she made a report on the matter. However word came to the police to arrest the boy. (The girl, about whom it is possible there was some other cause for prompt removal from the camp, had left for the home of connections at a locality we will not mention at present.) A police officer went out from Grafton on Thursday and arrested Norman under the Neglected Children's Act as instructed. There was a great weeping and wailing from the tribe—it was heard nearly a mile away. The child was brought into Grafton but was discharged from the Grafton Children's Court, no evidence being forthcoming that the child was neglected in any way. He was clean and healthy-looking, and a splendid writer, and a regular attendant at the Nymboida School and also at Coutts Crossing when the family were there. The charge of having no fixed place of abode seems a ridiculous one to aim at nomadic people like the blacks. The police officer mentioned, we are informed, was also instructed to offer another 14-year-old (Jenny Layton) her fare and 'safe conduct' to the home near Cootamundra, but the girl refused to go and the mother to let her stir. Word of these doings fled like the wind, and we are informed that, at the end of last week, 24 aborigines left the home on Grafton Common (it is said they came to the Richmond) fearing that the report they had heard was true that the Government was out on a campaign having for its object the tearing away of the children from their parents. The affection the blacks have for their children is well known, and the sight of the whole of the Nymboida tribe calling at the police station to say 'good-bye' to Norman Lardner on the morning of his arrest will not soon be forgotten by those who saw it.[29]

The parents' decision to reject the suggestion by the manager, Mr Newnham (not Noonan), to live in a house was based on cultural reasons, and it resulted in Norman Lardner being labelled as 'neglected'. Days later, more scathing comments about the incident came from another non-Indigenous supporter, who had considerable knowledge and experience with Aboriginal people. This anonymous person wrote:

> The idea of trying to compel blacks to live in a house or hut where another aborigine had previously died reveals a lamentable ignorance of the feelings and customs of the natives. In bygone days it was quite the rule to destroy by fire the hut which had been the scene of a death, and in many cases the whole camp was shifted to another spot. The aborigine superstition is very strong on this point.[30]

I read in the Aborigines Protection Board's yearly report for 1912 that Miss Lowe was appointed as its new 'home-finder'. The report stated that the home-finder's duties consisted of visiting the camps and stations to 'induce' Aboriginal parents to allow their children to be apprenticed out, or (if they were too young) to consider sending them to Cootamundra Girls Home to undergo a course of training to 'fit them for situations'. This announcement goes on to state that once suitable homes are found for the girls, they are visited regularly by the home-finder, who sees they are properly treated and receive pocket money.[31]

The 'pocket money' received by indentured Aboriginal people was usually a sixpence, hence the name of a renowned documentary film on the subject, *Lousy Little Sixpence*. This 1983 documentary was produced by Alec Morgan and my uncle Gerry Bostock. The associate producer was my other uncle, Lester Bostock. *Lousy Little Sixpence* is held in very high esteem by Australian filmmakers, who consider it a landmark film.[32] (At the time of writing this book, this film can be seen on YouTube.) At the end of the 1970s and early 1980s, Uncle Gerry interviewed elderly Aboriginal people around my grandmother's age and asked them about their experience of being indentured. Violet Shea had to go and work for, and live with, white Australian strangers when she was just twelve years of age:

They used to wake me up at half-past five in the morning and I had to do everything, the washing, the ironing and the cooking, and I hardly knew how to cook but I pretty soon learned. I worked seven days a week, whatever had to be done in the house—I did. At Cameron's, Mr and Mrs Cameron's, it was one and six a week. A shilling into a trust fund with the AP Board and a sixpence a week pocket money for me, but I never ever, never ever got that sixpence, and different people have said to me 'Well, why didn't you ask for it?', but you— you just didn't do those things. If I'd have asked for it well they just probably would've said 'Well I'm putting it away for you'. Or something like that, but err, she dressed me, [pause], not well! I didn't wear a pair of shoes, oh, all the time I was with her. The children were always well dressed. Now these were missionaries, more or less, preaching the word of God to you. They drummed it into our ears, morning and night.[33]

Aunty Violet's account was added to Margaret Tucker's account of being indentured. Aunty Margaret and her two sisters were taken from their mother and sent to Cootamundra Girls Home to be trained as indentured servants for white Australians.[34] At the age of thirteen, Aunty Margaret was punished with physical abuse at Cootamundra Girls Home and, when interviewed at the age of 74, she said, 'I have marks on my body right now from the beltings I had'.[35] Three months later, after being indentured to a white Australian family, she was again punished with humiliating physical abuse.[36]

Historian Inara Walden wrote a scholarly paper called '"That Was Slavery Days": Aboriginal domestic servants in New South Wales in the twentieth century', and the use of the words 'Slavery Days' is not an exaggeration. Walden's research illuminates some interesting facts and figures about Aboriginal indenture. The Aborigines Protection Board called stolen Aboriginal children 'apprentices', but I refuse to use that term. In my opinion, the word 'indenture' is a word that more accurately describes how they were 'bound to service':

570 girls were apprenticed as wards under the (NSW) Protection Board between the 1910s and the 1930s. Over the course of three decades more than 1200 employers in city and country areas benefited from the services of these 570 girls. During any one year in the 1920s there would have been between 300 and 400 aboriginal girls apprenticed to white Australian homes. Aboriginal wards thus represented approximately 1.5% of the domestic workforce at this time.[37]

The Aborigines Protection Board's yearly report for 1912 glowingly reports that the appointment of Miss Lowe was well justified because, since having started her job, Miss Lowe brought an enormous credit to the Board's trust account that year of £493 1s 8d, as opposed to the £322 8s 8d achieved at the end of the previous year.[38] There is no doubt that Miss Lowe was zealous in the execution of her job.[39]

Ukerebagh Island Aborigines Reserve

Gus and Lena Bostock, my great-grandparents, were at one time quite literally 'on the Tweed' when they lived on Ukerebagh Island Aborigines Reserve, located at the confluence of the Tweed River and Terranora Creek, south of Tweed Heads. We know from family oral history that they lived on the Aborigines reserve on the island and later moved across the river to live on the southern bank of the Tweed River. The story of Ukerebagh Island can be likened to other stories about the plight of Aboriginal people who, like Gus and Lena, were pushed to live on the margins of white society.

Information about Ukerebagh Island Aborigines Reserve was quite hard to find. Ukerebagh reserve is listed in the Aborigines Protection Board yearly reports for 1940, 1941, 1943 and 1944, but there is no information about it. I was, however, able to retrieve some information about Ukerebagh from a study done by heritage consultant Megan Goulding. She examined the significance of Ukerebagh Island to local Aboriginal people in order to establish its suitability to be declared an 'Aboriginal Place' under the *National Parks and Wildlife Act 1974* (NSW). The results were published in 2005 and it is the most comprehensive information I could find about Ukerebagh Island.[40] The island was gazetted as a reserve 'generally for use of Aborigines' on 4 February 1927, and the reserve was revoked on 26 October 1951. A large portion of the island is uninhabitable mangrove swamp.[41]

It was a general practice of the Aborigines Protection Board to move Aboriginal people away from European population centres, and even though it officially became a reserve in 1927, Aboriginal people were forced onto Ukerebagh Island in the early 1920s.[42] As with other Aborigines reserves, people survived on rations of tea, flour and sugar that were limited to certain amounts per adult and child. The people had to supplement the meagre Board rations with more traditional food resources nearby such as fish, mud crabs, oysters, ukeres (another word for pippies), wallabies, birds and lizards.[43] Goulding interviewed Elders (Tosie Terare, George Browning, Rosalie Browning and Robert Corowa) and they explained that this continued until the 1930s, when the men obtained work wherever they could in farm labouring, chipping bananas, cane cutting, bean picking and commercial fishing. During the Great Depression of the 1930s, men's work was rationed to two days a week, for it had to be shared equally among many.[44]

Ukerebagh Island was isolated. The nature of the island made it difficult for people to access work and school and, aside from a precarious, often-flooded handmade rock wall used as stepping stones on the south-east edge of the island, the only access to the mainland was via boat. Goulding added oral histories of local Aboriginal people, and Aunty Joyce Summers said that 'going back a long time ago', she asked Uncle Toesy Trent why everybody left:

How come all the people moved off Ukerebagh Island? He said, 'when the war came they had all their boats towed up the river'. Now yous might remember that. Towed all the boats up the river and tied them up, apparently so the Japanese couldn't get hold of it and do damage. I don't know what damage they was supposed to do. But the people didn't have any way of going shopping, getting the kids to school or anything, you know, so they had to leave the island. So, it was around about that time that we left. So, I don't remember, sort of, my childhood on that island because we sort of had to leave there.[45]

My father's cousin Aunty Joyce Frater, the oldest surviving grandchild of Gus and Lena Bostock, told me the same story. Senator Neville Bonner, the first Aboriginal person to be sworn in to the Australian Parliament (on 17 August 1971), was born 'on a government blanket laid over the hard ground' at Ukerebagh Island on 28 March 1922.[46] As my family's oral history reveals, my great-grandmother Lena acted as a midwife for his mother, Julia, when he came into the world under the island's well-known palm tree. I remember an older family member saying with pride, 'It was Granny Bostock who brought Neville Bonner into the world.'

In 1975, Senator Bonner spoke about Ukerebagh Island in a speech to the Australian Senate, and he was very emotional about the island and the treatment of Aboriginal people from the Tweed River area:

You came, you saw and you conquered as you proclaimed in those days that our land was your land. The white people of that era herded my parents and grandparents and their contemporaries on to Ukerebagh Island to live and die in the blacks camp there . . . but equally as many people lived, and I stand here this evening, Australia, as your ghost, your conscience, your demand to right what was wrong on Ukerebagh Island 53 years ago.

Senator Bonner's research revealed that Ukerebagh Island was actually declared a water reserve on 24 December 1861, and Aboriginal people were 'herded' there long before its gazettal as an Aborigines reserve in 1927. Bonner said that the people did not want to move to the mainland because they wanted to live there, but authorities threatened that if parents did not send their children to school, then they would be gaoled and their children taken away.[47]

Government officials made cursory contact with the welfare department and asked if the department required the island for an Aborigines reserve. When the answer was no, because Aboriginal people were not living there, the reserve was gazetted and reserved from sale for future public requirements. In effect, the Australian Government forced Aboriginal people onto the island to segregate them from white society, then many years after they were settled, in a wartime panic, they confiscated their boats; they threatened child removal if the children did not attend school, and then when the people moved off the island, they proclaimed their intention to revoke the Ukerebagh Island Aborigines reserve on the basis that there were no people living there.

All of this was done without consulting with Aboriginal people and without ascertaining why they had left the island in the first place. Even after adjusting to being confined on a reserve, making a new life there, and eventually setting down roots at Ukerebagh Island, my great-grandparents and other Aboriginal people were forced to leave.

Box Ridge Mission

The events that led to the segregation of Aboriginal people from the town of Nymboida were remarkably similar to those that occurred at Box Ridge Mission, near Coraki, on the Richmond River. In March 1907, Mr Henderson was also the district inspector for Coraki and, as happened at Nymboida, he was presented with a petition from the townspeople calling for the exclusion of Aboriginal children from the local 'public' school.[48] This petition brought about the erection of a segregated school for Aboriginal children, but not straight away. A year later, Aboriginal children were still excluded from the town school. Henderson informed the DPI that there were about fifteen school-age children in total.

In the town of Coraki, the members of the Local Committee for the nearby Box Ridge Mission were William Nolan, Herbert Hunt, J.T. Olive and Reverend A. Stanley Homersham. This Local Committee was not at all trusted in the way that the Dunoon Aboriginal people trusted their Local Committee. It played a role in carrying out the Protection Board's goals, not for child removal but for the indenture of Aboriginal children. Archival documents reveal that Reverend Homersham was given the job of sending the secretary of the Protection Board a letter informing him of the names and ages of the children to be enrolled at the proposed Coraki Aborigines School.[49] The list mentioned seventeen children, whose ages ranged from five to thirteen years old.

At five years old, my grandfather Henry Anderson was one of the youngest on the list. The oldest child on the list was my father's grandaunt.[50] I found a letter written by Reverend Homersham to the Aborigines Protection Board to bring their attention to Aunty _____ (name withheld). He wrote:

The President—[Alderman] Nolan undertook to make enquiries as to finding a suitable situation for _____ and to report at the next meeting (Nov 6th) the result of the enquiries will be communicated to the Board . . . The committee realises that the Board's policy in the removal of likely girls to the Cootamundra Home might be very beneficial in some instances. Yours Sincerely, A. Stanley Homersham.[51]

By 'finding a suitable situation', he meant finding a suitable place where Aunty _____ could be indentured as a domestic servant for white Australians. Aunty _____ was only thirteen years old. Two days later, Reverend Homersham requested that forms setting out the conditions of her 'apprenticeship' be sent to the committee by the office of the Protection Board.[52] I couldn't find any records that informed me whether Aunty _____ actually was indentured, but I do know that Aunty _____ married my great-grandfather's brother at Box Ridge, and upon her death, was buried at Coraki cemetery in 1969.

Almost all the BDMs I have collected over the years have my female ancestors' occupations recorded as *domestic*, and my male ancestors' occupations recorded as *labourer*. There were a variety of locations for Aboriginal work opportunities, such as pastoral stations, the timber industry, abattoirs, dairies, laundries etc., but in general I found that Aboriginal women usually worked indoors as domestic servants, and Aboriginal men usually worked outdoors doing hard physical work as labourers, whatever the setting.

The 'Cootamundra Home' was officially called the Cootamundra Domestic Training Home for Aboriginal Girls. In 1910, the Board purchased the old Cootamundra Hospital, which they converted into an institution to confine the girls, having been empowered to remove them. The renovations were much more expensive than anticipated, so—forced to choose between coming up with urgent funds or abandoning its goals—the Aborigines Protection Board decided that it would sacrifice Aboriginal land to fund its programs to take Aboriginal children away from their families.

This was a momentous decision that they deceitfully decided not to publicise. Up until 1910, the annual reports for the Aborigines Protection Board often repeated the same stirring humanitarian plea for the security of Aboriginal land:

> the land already available to this unfortunate race is so limited that every attempt on the part of Europeans to acquire these reserves for settlement purposes should be strongly resisted.

But in 1911, there was silence. The Board not only dumped its earlier defence of Aboriginal land, it began to lease out Aborigines reserve lands for its own revenue.[53]

In 1924, the Board built Kinchela Boys Home, which became infamous after a police investigation uncovered sustained cruelty against the young boys held there by a series of drunken and sadistic superintendents. It was a frightening place where boys removed from their families were subject to abuse and loneliness, and were taught to forget their Aboriginality.[54]

In contrast, Aboriginal children who grew up on Box Ridge Mission near Coraki—those who were either too young for indenture, or miraculously managed to avoid incarceration at Cootamundra or Kinchela—lived relatively peaceful lives on the mission. Box Ridge Aborigines Reserve was called a 'mission' because it didn't have an Aborigines Protection Board manager, and Christian missionaries ministered to the people there. The missionaries were determined to ensure that Aboriginal people were exposed to all aspects of 'civilised' and Christian culture.[55]

The photographs in this book of the Box Ridge Mission and the missionaries come from the private collection of the personal items belonging to UAM missionaries Mrs Alma Smith and her daughter Mrs Alva Atkins.[56] I used to search the internet regularly in the hope of finding new information, and one night I happened to find a link to the newly catalogued collection at the Mitchell Library (in Sydney) almost as soon as it was uploaded.

The missionaries lived in the town of Coraki and went out to the mission daily to organise regular church services for the Aboriginal adults, provide religious instruction and Sunday schools for Aboriginal children, and conduct services for christenings, weddings and funerals. Beyond religious ministering, they tried to make life happier for Aboriginal people; for example, organising clothes for children and organising pre-Christmas celebrations that they called 'Christmas Trees', which were Christmas parties that included festivities and donated gifts.

In 1916, after my great-grandparents left Dunoon Aborigines Reserve, my five-year-old grandfather Henry was enrolled at Box Ridge Aborigines School, and his teacher was Miss Green. After Miss Green left, a Scottish woman named Mrs Helen Mitchell was hired as a temporary teacher, but she remained on at the school until her departure in 1930. Mrs Mitchell was a hard worker who treated Aboriginal people with kindness and compassion. In the historical archives, numerous documents reveal that she went above and beyond the call of her duties as the schoolteacher on the mission.

In 1931, Mrs Mitchell was replaced by Mrs Irene English, who was employed as the matron-teacher and remained there until 1936. She was well liked by the Aboriginal people at Box Ridge Mission. A newspaper article glowingly reported that the people at Box Ridge Mission threw her a gala farewell party and presented her with gifts when she left to begin a new job as a district inspector with the Aborigines Welfare Board (the new name for the former Aborigines Protection Board).[57] Following Mrs English's departure, Mrs Ella Hiscocks was employed as the new matron at Box Ridge. Mrs Hiscocks was the matron when my mother Rita and her two sisters, Ruby and Gwen, were young girls living on the mission in the early 1940s. In the next chapter, I divulge the circumstances that caused my grandfather Henry Anderson to swiftly steal his daughters from Box Ridge Mission and never return.

Mrs Hiscocks left Box Ridge in 1945 to become the matron of Cootamundra Girls Home. Her position was meant to be only temporary, but she stayed for twenty years and retired as the home's longest-serving matron. Historian Anna Cole described Mrs Hiscocks as 'a functionary of the Board' who 'played her own part in a long-standing and systematic government attempt to break down and assimilate Aboriginal children into white society, a strategy in a wider battle against Aboriginal culture and identity'.[58]

Two very surprising discoveries that I made during the course of my research confirmed that the missionaries were not exempt from the government's assimilationist agenda. I came across two separate newspaper articles reporting that both my grandmothers, Edith Bostock (née Cowan) and Evelyn Anderson (née Solomon), had lovely weddings on the mission that would have been very hard to achieve without considerable help from the missionaries and others. At my grandmother Evelyn's wedding to Henry Anderson, the local paper reported that:

> Mrs English presented the bride with a beautiful wedding cake. During the afternoon the scholars of the reserve school entertained the company with yodelling solos and duets, also numerous selections on the gum leaves. The church was tastefully decorated by friends of the bride.[59]

The wedding of my other grandmother, Edith Bostock, was a great deal more elaborate than Henry and Evelyn's. Closely re-reading the newspaper article below brought my attention to the wording and tone of this piece of writing. Newspaper articles written by men at the time were quite obviously masculine, and I seriously doubt that a male, white Australian newspaper reporter would be asked to report on a blackfella's wedding at the local mission. The details in the following narration of the wedding confirm that the author would have had to have been present at the whole of the wedding. Newspaper articles written about social events at Box Ridge Mission have a decidedly feminine tone.

This article details the wedding party, the parents, the organist 'Mrs Roy Cowan, Aunt of the bride', the helpers, the Methodist clergyman officiating, the hymn sung, and the presence of Matron English—the only women left to write the article were the missionaries. Therefore, I am certain that one of the missionaries (likely Mrs Smith) would have written this article:

> A large and interested gathering filled the little church on the Coraki Aborigines' Reserve on Tuesday afternoon on the

occasion of the marriage of Norman Augustus Bostock, son of Mr and Mrs Augustus Bostock of Eungella, Tweed River, to Edith Irene, daughter of Mr and Mrs J. T. Cowan, of Coraki. The bride, who was given away by her father, wore a gown of white morocain, with veil and coronet of orange blossoms, and carried a sheath of white flowers. She was attended by Miss Florrie Kahn as bridesmaid, the latter wearing pink silk rayon, with pink hat to tone, and carrying a bouquet of pink rosebuds, carnations and blue cornflowers, tied with blue and pink streamers. The church was prettily decorated for the occasion, a special feature being the floral arch and bell, the latter opening at the close of the ceremony and showering the happy couple with rose petals. Mrs Roy Cowan, Aunt of the bride, presided at the organ, and played a verse of the hymn, 'All People That On Earth Do Dwell', which the congregation sang as the bridal party entered the Church. The Church decorations were the work of Mrs Geo[rge]. Breckenridge and Miss Hannah Breckenridge, friends of the bride. Mr L.A. Thompson (Methodist) tied the nuptial knot, and Mr Harold Yuke was best man. After the ceremony, the happy couple and guests adjourned to the bride's home where a splendid wedding breakfast had been prepared, and where the customary toasts were honoured, speeches made, and solos rendered by several of the natives. Matron English was responsible for most of the arrangements, making bouquets, preparing breakfasts etc. Many cameras were in evidence after the register had been signed, and numerous snaps were taken of the bridal party. The future home of the newlyweds will be at Eungella, Tweed River.[60]

Reading between the lines, I see these newspaper articles as a kind of presentation of achievement. It is as though the

163

missionaries were saying, 'Look at our good work! Look at what we have managed to achieve! See how we have civilised them!' Everything I've read shows that the UAM missionaries were zealous in their work and their beliefs. The following quote is from the UAM's own newspaper, called *The Australian Aborigines Advocate*:

> We have to praise the dear Lord for graciously supplying our needs in many ways, and thus enabling us to carry on His Work on the Reserve in spite of many discouragements, looking unto Him that loved us and made us Priests, intensely we desire the salvation of our people around us.[61]

To find out that the weddings of both sets of my grandparents were detailed in local newspaper articles was an extraordinarily surprising discovery, but nothing prepared me for the shock of being in the grand reading room of the Mitchell Library in Sydney and discovering that among the missionaries' personal collection was a photograph of my grandmother, uncle, aunt and father. UAM missionary Mrs Alma Smith's collection contained photographs that my grandmother had sent to her of my father and his siblings at various times in their childhood. It also contained an address book that belonged to Mrs Smith, and in its pages she had recorded a number of addresses of my grandmother.

This address book proves that Mrs Smith maintained contact with my grandmother decades after the latter left the mission to begin married life.[62] It is tangible evidence of an obvious affection between these two very different women, and at first I thought it was sweet. But the more I thought about the missionaries, the more unsettled I became. Here was a religious group who, while teaching and preaching the tenets of Christianity, found nothing wrong with being actively involved in separating Aboriginal babies and young children from their mothers and families.

Young Aboriginal children that the Aborigines Protection Board deemed neglected and removed from their families— those who were babies, or too young to be incarcerated at the Protection Board's institutions—were taken to the UAM's children's home at Bomaderry. The UAM organisation supported and perpetuated the removal of Aboriginal children from their families by providing the Aborigines Protection Board with a repository to deposit them into. I deliberately use the word 'repository' because it was a receptacle to hold Aboriginal infants and children, deposited for safe keeping. If the missionaries did not provide the Bomaderry Children's Home, then the Aborigines Protection Board would not have been as successful and efficient as it was in carrying out its child removal agenda. The Bomaderry Children's Home was like an orphanage that 'grew them up' to an age where they were ripe for institutionalised training at Cootamundra Girls Home, or Kinchela Boys Home, in readiness for their inevitable indenture.

Broken families and aspirations crushed

An article in the UAM's *Australian Aborigines Advocate* said, 'The Aborigines Protection Board deemed it wise to take away twelve of our bigger boys, and in their place have sent a similar number of girls and younger lads'. The article went on to say, 'Several boys were placed in situations, and so far as we have been able to learn, have and are giving satisfaction.' The author wrote that 'the same can be said for most of the girls' and then expressed their dissatisfaction by cryptically adding 'but one or two, yielding to the influence brought upon them by white associates, have not rendered as good an account of themselves as could have been wished'.[63]

Yielding to the influence brought upon them by white associates. I know there could have been a number of reasons why a missionary would think that some girls had *not rendered as good an account of themselves as could have been wished*, but what if the missionary was hinting in an indirect, socially acceptable way that those girls had sexual liaisons with white men? Did these poor girls come home from indenture pregnant, later to give birth to fair-skinned children? *Yielding?* That terminology sounds accusatory and appears to blame the girls for 'yielding', as though it was their choice to fail to render as 'good an account of themselves as wished'. What if it wasn't? Girls who turned fourteen years old were supposed to be 'apprenticed' as domestic workers up to the age of eighteen, but these ages were not strictly adhered to at the beginning and the end of the term of indenture. Let's not forget that in *Lousy Little Sixpence*, Aunty Violet told us that she was indentured at twelve years of age.[64]

Research findings reveal that many young Aboriginal girls suffered sexual abuse within the New South Wales Government's Aborigines Protection Board's indenture system. I wondered how the missionaries would have felt if their twelve- to fourteen-year-old daughters were taken away from them by government officials (most times accompanied by the police) and sent far away, with no protection, vulnerable to any male predator in the city or at remote farmhouses on rural properties?

In 1927, Fred Maynard, the leader of the Australian Aboriginal Progressive Association (AAPA), the first all-Aboriginal activist group, wrote to a young Aboriginal girl who was sexually abused while indentured, and his anguish and anger is palpable:

My heart is filled with regret and disgust. First because you were taken down by those who were supposed to be your help and guide through life. What a wicked conception, what a fallacy. Under the so-called pretence and administration of the Board, governmental control etc. I say deliberately. The whole damnable thing has got to stop and by God['s] help it shall, make no mistake. No doubt, they are trying to exterminate the Noble and Ancient Race of sunny Australia. Away with the damnable insulting methods. Give us a hand, stand by your own Native Aboriginal Officers and fight for liberty and freedom for yourself and our children.[65]

While reading the research done by historians Heather Goodall and Victoria Haskins, I was stunned by their statements about the Aborigines Protection Board's cold, premeditated intentions in regard to Aboriginal girls' indenture. Goodall said:

The Board stated quite openly in its reports and minutes that it intended to reduce the birthrate of the Aboriginal population by taking adolescent girls away from their communities. Then it intended that the young people taken in this way would never be allowed to return to their homes or to any other Aboriginal community. The 'apprenticeship' policy was aimed quite explicitly at reducing the numbers of identifying Aboriginal people in the State.[66]

Haskins' investigation delved more deeply into the exploitation of young Aboriginal women in domestic service, and she came to the shocking conclusion that:

The NSW Aborigines Protection Board colluded in, condoned and indeed encouraged the systematic sexual abuse and impregnation of young Aboriginal women in domestic apprenticeships with, I contend, the ultimate aim of eradicating the Aboriginal population.[67]

Haskins' husband, Aboriginal historian John Maynard, is the grandson of AAPA leader Fred Maynard. His meticulous research has brought to light the resistance and organised action of an all-Aboriginal group who 'tried valiantly to alter what it considered to be deliberate and detrimental government policies and actions that had serious and severe repercussions for Aboriginal people'.[68] Not only were Aboriginal families torn apart by child removal policies, another 'severe repercussion' was that the government's Aborigines Protection Board systematically separated Aboriginal families from their children, and continuously crushed Aboriginal aspirations for personal sovereignty, future security and independence.

When I think of the uncertainty created by the New South Wales Government's policies, the old biblical saying 'one hand giveth while the other taketh away' immediately comes to mind. Even when Aboriginal people who were removed to Aborigines reserves accepted these places as their 'new' homes—and worked for a secure future for their families—there were no guarantees that the New South Wales Government wouldn't change its mind and revoke the reserve lands—or that white Australian townspeople wouldn't demand Aboriginal people give up their homes for soldier settlers. The goalposts were constantly being moved further away. White Australians coveted Aboriginal-held lands, and shifts in Lands Department policy added to an escalation of demands for Aborigines reserve lands. The department endorsed most white applications for revocation.

It did not matter that Aboriginal people had done years of back-breaking work to clear the land for their families to physically and existentially put down roots. When the demands of white Australians for Aboriginal land became louder and more determined, the New South Wales Government often gave in to them. Dunoon is a prime example of the New South Wales Government's appropriation of Aborigines reserve lands to accommodate white Australians. In a little less than two decades, the Dunoon reserve was cut down from 420 acres (170 hectares) in 1903 to 10–12 acres (4–5 hectares) by 1922.[69]

In *Lousy Little Sixpence*, Aunty Geraldine Briggs, from Cummeragunja Aborigines Reserve, explained:

> A lot of the men were very keen on having farms of their own, and they sent a petition to the Board asking for land, and they were given so much land down near the river, and they were very enthusiastically cleaning it up, and chopping all the trees down and they planted crops. As a child I remember that vividly, it was really something to see this wheat grown by our own people. Then all of a sudden the Board informed them that they are taking their land back again. And it proved that Aborigines had no rights whatsoever. And I think that's what broke the spirit of the men who had done all that work, really for nothing.[70]

6

The Destruction Board

'They discovered that it was my mother lying under a tree in the tall grass moaning, she couldn't cry anymore you know ... but we were already on our own ... we might have been in Cootamundra by then ... I often wonder how many other children were taken like that, just like animals, because our hearts were absolutely broken.'

AUNTY MARGARET TUCKER, ONE OF THE STOLEN GENERATIONS

In 1934, Mr Joseph Percival Howard was employed as the new manager of Kyogle Aborigines station. He was instructed to use 'any reasonable means' to end the disputes between Aboriginal people and the townspeople of Lismore. The Board wanted to centralise a large number of separate Aboriginal communities and move the people to Kyogle and Woodenbong Aborigines reserves. In 1934 when the townspeople's protests were revived in Lismore, Frank Roberts Snr, an Aboriginal Christian lay preacher, wrote an accurate account of what happened to Aboriginal people at Tuncester, just outside of Lismore, New South Wales. Historian Heather Goodall has inserted the dates of actual Protection Board archives into Frank Robert's letter below:

Howard on his first visit to Tuncester, stopped his first visit to Tuncester, stopped the rations completely, starved the inhabitants, acting on instructions by his Board [12 September 1934; 16 November 1934]. He then attempted to bluff the people, saying that the Aborigines Protection Board is forcing them to another reserve and if they don't comply with his instructions he, or his Board, would take the children away from their parents [16 November 1934]. Next step was to demolish the school at Tuncester [5 February 1936] and remove it to another settlement 52 miles away [Woodenbong, 6 May 1936]. The result is now the thirty-five children without a school. Words cannot express what is scandalous treatment by the Destruction Board.[1]

'Destruction Board' was an appropriate way to describe the New South Wales Government's Aborigines Protection Board and its shocking treatment of Aboriginal people throughout many decades of last century. From the moment that Aborigines Reserve Manager Mr J.P. Howard was employed by the Board, he proved to be a conscientious worker and acted quickly to carry out the wishes of the Aborigines Protection Board. He was also the informant on my great-grandmother Nellie (Solomon) Walker's marriage and death certificates, and my great-grandmother Mabel Anderson's death certificate.

My mother often said, 'I was born at Stoney Gully', but when I found her birth certificate, I was confused, because it recorded that she was born at Kyogle, New South Wales. Later, I came to learn that Stoney Gully was the name of the land near Kyogle where the Aborigines reserve was situated. Prior to it being named 'Kyogle Aborigines Reserve Station', it was called 'Runnymede', which was the name of the first non-Indigenous property a pastoral lease of 128,000 acres (51,800 hectares) taken up by Ward Stephens in 1842. It's likely that Stoney Gully was the Aboriginal name of the place that later became known as Kyogle Aborigines Reserve. At any rate, older Aboriginal people called it by that name. My grandfather Henry Anderson met my grandmother Evelyn Solomon there, and it is where my mother Rita and one of her older sisters, Aunty Gwen, were born.

But Aunty Ruby, their oldest sister, was born at Box Ridge Aborigines reserve on 2 January 1934, and in September that year, her parents (my grandparents) were married on the mission. Several years ago, I was introduced to a very old Aboriginal man at a cultural event. He was a Bundjalung Elder and his name was Gilbert King. As soon as we met, he asked me, 'Who's your mob?', so I told him that my father's parents were Norman and Edith Bostock and my mother's parents were Henry and Evelyn Anderson. His face immediately lit up and he excitedly told me that he knew Henry and 'Eve-lyn'. Almost shouting, he said, 'I went to their wedding! I was there!' He tried to laugh, but it caused him to wheeze and he had to catch his breath as he told me that my Aunty Ruby was just a baby then, and 'Your grandmother Eve-lyn had to stop the service halfway through because Ruby was screaming so bloody loud that she had to give her some titty to shut her up!'

I bet Aunty Ruby would've loved to hear that story. When she was a child, Uncle Sam Anderson called her 'the Big Noise' because she was always singing as loud as she could. Later in life, after she became Ruby Langford Ginibi (the well-known author of five books), she was as publicly outspoken as she had always been privately.

My mother's Anderson side of the family is the focus of this chapter because there were a large number of Aborigines

Protection Board archives about my great-grandparents Sam and Mabel Anderson, and my grandparents Henry and Evelyn Anderson. Although these records span just a decade from my grandparents' wedding in 1934 through to 1944, they reveal the extent of the mind-blowing control and surveillance that my family members (and certainly other Aboriginal people) suffered at the hands of the Aborigines Protection Board. I am astounded not only by the copious records on my ancestors' lives, but also the revealing content of the correspondence written by the Kyogle Aborigines Protection Board manager, J.P. Howard.

J.P. Howard became the new manager of the Kyogle Aborigines Reserve in 1934, the same year that Aunty Ruby was born and my grandparents married.[2] Several years later, he became the manager of the Cabbage Tree Island Aborigines Station. He was a prolific writer of letters to the Aborigines Protection Board, so much so that I have a collection of his observations about my grandparents and my great-grandparents. Howard is revealed to be a person who took his job very seriously, and his devotion to carrying out the wishes of his employer bordered on fawning ingratiation. He must have spent a great deal of his time at his desk writing letters to the Board, dotting his *i*'s and crossing his *t*'s and, as a family history researcher, I am so pleased that he was such a consummate letter writer. Not only do his letters provide incredible insight into the everyday experiences of Aboriginal people, along with the archives, they provide detailed information about the bureaucratic workings of the Aborigines Protection Board.

In the previous chapter, I used a number of newspaper articles to capture the exact words of Aboriginal people in history, as a means of ensuring that their thoughts (and their voices) are heard in the present. This chapter, however, uses a large number of archives to capture the exact words of a white Australian manager of an Aborigines reserve and those of the Aborigines Protection Board officials to ensure that their thoughts (and also their voices) are equally heard in the present.

To use a photographic analogy to describe my research of this period in Aboriginal history, I felt like a photographer adjusting the focus on the lens. I have 'zoomed in' with a microcosmic focus on the individuals and the reserve/mission space—and then I have 'zoomed out' to capture the macrocosmic bureaucracy of the Australian Government's Aborigines Protection Board (which, in 1940, became the Aborigines Welfare Board). Viewing the broader scope of history, I would say that Aboriginal resistance was ramping up during this time, not only on the political front (with Aboriginal freedom fighters like William Cooper, Bill Ferguson, Pearl Gibbs, Jack Patten and Fred Maynard), but also 'on the ground', in the everyday lives of Aboriginal people and families.

J.P. Howard

J.P. Howard's interpretation of the Aborigines Protection Board's instruction to 'use any reasonable means' created furious confrontations between Aboriginal people and the Board. The people at Baryulgil were refused rations and instructed to move to Woodenbong. Both the Tuncester and Baryulgil people refused to move, even though 29 of their children were being denied access to education. These two communities were still standing their ground against Howard in 1938, until the Protection Board decided that it was best to amalgamate Woodenbong and Kyogle reserves, which they did in 1940, a year after my mother was born there. The number of students in both cases would have been enough to justify the establishment of an Education Department school for the children, but at this time the Education Department was still denying its responsibility for the education of Aboriginal people. The universal segregation of Aboriginal children from public schools in northern New South Wales, the refusal to establish a school at Baryulgil, and the removal of the Tuncester School can only be seen for what it was—a deliberate measure to enforce the Board's confinement aims—and J.P. Howard was determined to carry out the wishes of the Aborigines Protection Board at all costs.[3]

Howard was in a position of authority over Aboriginal people, and he took his job so seriously that the needs of the people became secondary to the eagerness with which he presented himself to the Board. He used whatever means he had at hand. Frank Roberts said he tried to 'bluff the people' by saying he or his Board would take away their children if they didn't comply. Howard resorted to using lies to cajole parents into allowing their children to be removed.

In Alec Morgan and my Uncle Gerry Bostock's film *Lousy Little Sixpence*, Aboriginal Elder Florence Caldwell said that during a visit by Inspector Donaldson (the kid collector), Donaldson chose the girls to be taken from their families for indenture. Shortly after that, Howard came to see her parents, armed with police officers. In the interview, she told Uncle Gerry and Alec Morgan:

> They asked my mother if she'd agree to send me down to Sydney. He [Howard] told me that I'd have a lot of pretty frocks and I'd be going to parties, and all that kind of thing, and I knew he was telling lies. Even at that age I wasn't stupid.[4]

In this instance, Howard tried a cajoling tone, but with my great-grandmother Mabel Anderson, he commanded that she 'get them out' [for indenture] and if she didn't 'the Board would'.[5] Violet Shea also spoke of Howard coming to her family home with police officers in tow. Speaking sadly, in a soft voice, she said:

> One day the Manager came over to our island, Ulgundahi Island, and told me that I was to go and work for them. He wasn't living on the island, because there was too much flooding for them. So, anyway I went along with it, because you just didn't, well you just couldn't do anything about it, you just had to go. When I got over there, I was told I was to work for them, and I was only twelve years of age.[6]

On 19 September 1937, my great-grandmother Mabel Anderson died, at the age of 48, on the Kyogle Aborigines Station. Her death certificate records that she was buried at the Kyogle Cemetery and Howard was the undertaker.[7] She left behind her husband (my great-grandfather), Sam Anderson, and their children, (my grandfather) Henry, aged 26; Sam Jnr, aged 22; Bob, aged 21; Kate, aged 19; Eileen, aged 18; and her mid-life surprise baby, Phyllis, who was three months short of her seventh birthday. Under the *Deserted Wives and Children Act 1901* (NSW), on 17 August 1938, my great-grandfather Sam Anderson was charged with a 'Maintenance Order for the payment of support for his daughter Phyllis of 10/- [10 shillings] weekly with the first payment to be made on the 24th August 1938 to Mr J. P. Howard'. Custody of Phyllis was 'granted to the Aborigines Protection Board' and Howard doggedly pursued my great-grandfather Sam Anderson for maintenance payments for Phyllis.[8]

A few months later, Howard wrote an astonishing letter to the Aborigines Protection Board about my family members. It was a detailed summary of the Anderson family's major events from December 1930 to March 1939. As a family member, I frowned at Howard's nasty comments about my ancestors, but they didn't cause me any pain or embarrassment. We all knew Sam had an alcohol problem. It was known through family oral history and I have found it recorded in random newspaper articles. It was also documented in Maurice Ryan's biography of Sam, as I have mentioned. Not surprisingly, as a history researcher I devoured every word of Howard's letter and 'read between the lines' to pull out every nuance and revelation. I have included parts of this letter here. It was written by Howard at Kyogle Aborigines Station, and was dated 6 March 1939:

Phyllis Anderson was born at Coraki on [her birthdate]. The family was transferred here in 1931 on account of continual quarrelling of the parents, due chiefly to the father's drunkenness . . . The mother was also a very hard person to reason with . . . There was further trouble in 1935 when two daughters were ready for service, and when told if she did not get them out—the Board would, she left the Station.

The family lived more or less a nomadic life from then on, chiefly between McLean, C.T. Island [Cabbage Tree Island] and Coraki. They eventually drifted apart, practically only the youngest, Phyllis, being with her mother. The latter took seriously ill and went to hospital. Phyllis being left in the care of relatives at C.T. Island. Later Mrs Anderson returned here a physical wreck, to reside with a married son [Henry]. She asked for Phyllis to be returned here . . . [The manager of CTI] was communicated with and he was of opinion that it would be to the child's advantage to come here, and arranged a transfer. The mother died shortly afterwards, and Phyllis was left in the care of her married brother [Henry] and well looked after.

In September last year there was trouble in this family owing to the wife's [Evelyn's] immoral relations with another man. An inquiry was held and the matter settled, but she fancied people were talking about her and persuaded her husband to go away for a change. They left in October, leaving Phyllis with a cousin here [Kyogle] . . . this arrangement was not very satisfactory, but was not interfered with as word kept coming of Anderson's intended return.

In December, an adult brother of Phyllis' [Uncle Bob Anderson] came from Cabbage T. Is. to see if he could take Phyllis away for the holidays. He was told that a court order was taken against his father on August 17th . . . Also that the child had been made a ward of the Board and committed to the care of the Station, so that I could not give any permission without referring the matter to Head Office. He said he would take her at once. He was asked to sign the attached paper [not found with this letter] . . . Inquiries have been made re the girls return here, on account of the above order . . . A separate brief report re maintenance of this child is enclosed. J.P.H.[9]

I assume that the missionaries asked my great-grand-parents to leave Box Ridge Mission because of Sam's drinking and their (Sam and Mabel's) quarrelling. Perhaps they thought that a male station manager would be better able to positively influence Sam? At the time that they moved to Kyogle, my grandfather Henry was unmarried and twenty years old, Sam Jnr was sixteen and Bob was fifteen.

I am so proud that Mabel refused to allow her daughters, Kate (then seventeen) and Eileen (then sixteen), to be indentured. They had been lucky to have avoided it up until then; most were taken at a much younger age. Like Violet Shea and her parents, a lot of Aboriginal people did not have the power to refuse, especially when Howard brought police officers with him. In *Lousy Little Sixpence*, another Aboriginal Elder, Margaret Tucker, explained what happened when the Board and the police came to remove her and her sisters from their mother:

> The children at the school would stand on the desk and look out the window when a motor car . . . came for us with a police man in the car, and it was a Mrs Hill who was teaching us and she sent two boys to run like mad, must have been about a three quarters of a mile over the river to tell my mother. Anyway she must have ran all the way back because she still had her apron on, and she put her arms around the three of us and she said, 'You're not taking them', and he said, 'Well then, I'll have to use this', he said, patting the case with the handcuffs in it. But we in our childish imagination, we thought it was a gun . . . and we both yelled in together, 'We'll go, we'll go Mum, we'll go!' . . . and er, he was very kind, he tried to be very kind, and my mother said, 'Well I'm going too' and she still had her apron on, and went twenty-five miles to Deniliquin, and we weren't there very long when the car took us then to Finley and on the train to Cootamundra. Well I heard years later how my mother cried and cried, and she had nowhere to go, so she went out into the bush . . . and my older Aunt and them said as they were coming past . . . on the outskirts of Deniliquin . . . they heard this moaning like an

animal you know, and they stopped the buggy and went over to see, and they discovered that it was my mother lying under a tree and in the tall grass, moaning, she couldn't cry anymore you know, and they had to care for her and look after her . . . but we all were already on our own . . . we all might have been in Cootamundra by then, you know by train. But I often wonder how many other children were taken like that, just like animals, because our hearts were absolutely broken.[10]

Mabel must have got away before Howard had the chance to organise a police visit. I am also proud of Uncle Bob. I often close my eyes and imagine what historical scenarios may have looked like in real life. In Howard's letter about my family members, when he said, 'I could not give any permission without referring the matter to Head Office'—and when Uncle Bob said 'he would take her at once'—the picture that came to mind was one of an angry confrontation, with Uncle Bob fiercely and defiantly taking Phyllis anyway. We'll never know what Uncle Bob actually said, but the fact remains that he completely rejected the authority of Howard and the Protection Board.

Both of these stories about my great-grandmother Mabel and my granduncle Bob are evidence of my family members' personal power and their contempt for the Protection Board's attempts to control them. I think it's so important that stories of this kind about our empowered ancestors reach all generations of Aboriginal people.

When Mabel became ill, Phyllis was at Cabbage Tree Island, probably in the care of her older sister Kate or her older brother Bob, who also lived on the island. Even as ill as Mabel was, knowing she was a 'physical wreck', and hearing Mabel's request to have Phyllis brought to Kyogle, Howard couldn't make the decision on his own to reunite the ailing mother with her youngest child. He always sought approval at every turn. After Uncle Bob collected Phyllis and took her to Cabbage Tree Island for the Christmas holidays, Phyllis ended up staying there with her older sister Kate.

Despite Phyllis being with her family members, Howard took the Protection Board's custody of Phyllis seriously and he wanted to keep his 'ward' under his supervision at Kyogle, so he planned to place Phyllis with a married couple there until my grandparents returned. However, in April 1939, an Aborigines Protection Board inspector, Mrs English, overrode the maintenance order and recommended that Phyllis live at Cabbage Tree Island under the care of her married sister Kate.[11]

What's interesting to note here is that the inspector, Mrs English, a mere employee of the Aborigines Protection Board, had the power to override the maintenance order issued by the special magistrate of the Children's Court (under the Deserted Wives and Children Act).[12] Also interesting is a later letter from Howard which reveals that Aunty Kate refused to return Phyllis to Kyogle after the holidays, and that it was because she wrote directly to Mrs English that Phyllis was allowed to stay. This is an example of another calculated form of resistance, as Aunty Kate rejected Howard's authority and his demands to send Phyllis back to Kyogle, then went behind his back to a higher authority to ensure that Phyllis live with her.[13] Howard was such a stickler for rules and regulations that he must have felt frustrated in being overruled by Mrs English, and annoyed by the Board's lack of support for his justifiable (in his view) standpoint.

In fact, all of the first half of 1939 was a tough time for Howard, and between the lines of his detailed letters, I could sense his frustration. Howard wanted to solve the problem of overcrowding on the reserve, and he bravely took the initiative to approach my grandfather Henry Anderson and two Aboriginal brothers about a project to build some more huts. He suggested to the Board that Henry and the brothers could go ahead and build one hut as a trial, and if the job was done well enough, they would get the contract for the other two.[14] There was a delay when the Protection Board didn't respond with approval straight away, so the older of the brothers forced the issue by giving Howard an ultimatum that if he did not employ him straight away, he had a long contract of work lined up in Coraki.[15]

As mentioned earlier, Howard found it extremely difficult to make a decision without first gaining the Board's approval, but his accounts ledger shows that immediately after the ultimatum, he commenced paying the older brother.[16] With Howard having been forced to make a decision on the spot, the extraordinary wording of his ensuing letter to the Board clearly reveals that he was almost prostrate in his apologetic explanation of the reasons he employed the men without their prior consent:

Feeling that the men could do a good job, anxious to prove that much could be saved in labour costs, also realising that the feelings of the men were touch and go that they would not do the work, it being so hard to instil reason into their stubbornness, added to the uncertainty of getting other labour and so having the job again postponed indefinitely, as well as the fact that the timber would deteriorate on the ground, and probably a quantity disappear, I told them they would be given a trial of one hut, to start forthwith, and that further work should be subject to approval after inspection ... Approval

for this action is respectfully requested, as under the circumstances, an immediate decision was felt to be necessary. Could
arrangements please be made for the remittance of 55/- per
week, as the men will expect weekly payments?'[17]

Whether the older brother really had other paying work lined
up at Coraki or whether he was deliberately hastening a financial commitment from Howard is unknown. I suspect the latter,
and I wouldn't be surprised if my grandfather Henry's friend
winked at him and gave him a 'thumbs up' behind Howard's
back. This man's defiance and his disrespect of Howard, of his
role as manager and of the Protection Board was made very
clear later that year. The older brother was left in charge during
Howard's frequent absences to perform his duties, and he began
grumbling about pay and inciting others. On 26 November 1939,
Howard wrote:

This was a constant worry. As time went on he adopted a
cheeky attitude toward me showing off to the men. To save
a row, and the stoppage of men, this was ignored or passed
off . . . The next move was to induce the women to complain
that the school was being neglected, and whenever the Matron
(Mrs Howard) or I had occasion to speak to them about untidy
homes, or misbehaviour of children, it was always blamed
in a spiteful way on the lack of schooling . . . At such times
as it was necessary for me to remain on the job all day, or
on manual days, the girls would be placed in the care of the
Matron, for domestic training, and the boys go with me to
take lessons in carpentry. This was looked upon as neglect of
school and working the children for our own benefit . . . [One
day] I left [the older brother] to drive in the pegs and nails on

the boards and Anderson mixing cement . . . on my return I had found that the framework had been nailed 18" short, a most obvious error, especially as boards were cut to size. When pointed out, in quite a nice way, he said, *'That's with you going riding about instead of getting on with your work.'* I pretended not to hear him, but when he came to the office to collect his pay I asked him why it was he spoke in such a cheeky way so often? He said he had to for the pay he got and for other reasons. When asked the reasons he refused to state them, said he was keeping them 'til someone else came along. I told him I was quite able to listen to any complaint, but in any case he must speak properly to the Manager.[18]

This kind of openly aggressive resistance was very different from the more passive resistance I had seen in archives from earlier decades. Here we see an Aboriginal man scornfully ridiculing a Protection Board manager face to face. When Howard first made the proposal of the project to the Board he was very positive about the older brother's carpentry skill, stating that compared to his brother, he was 'a much superior workman, and a very reliable man' and he paid him a higher wage than the other men because of his experience and skill.[19] This information, and the fact that the boards were cut to size, would appear to indicate that the older brother (and perhaps my grandfather Henry, too) had deliberately nailed the boards short just to torment Howard. He also used the Aborigines Protection Board's policy against Howard, accusing *him* of neglect when he took the Aboriginal children out of school for the 'manual days' (indenture training days) and of working the children for the Board's benefit. Howard chose to 'save a row', 'ignore and pass off' and 'pretend not to hear', but the man's 'cheeky

In 2013 I saw an episode of *Australian Story* about the J.W. Lindt collection of photographs called 'Australian Aboriginals'. One of them shows two women with the tips of their left-hand pinky fingers removed. Among the other images I was to find an ancestor. (Held by the Grafton Regional Gallery)

In the early 1870s, Lindt also photographed Mary Ann of Ulmarra, who has since been identified as Mary Ann Cowan. The facial similarity between Mary Ann and my grandmother, Edith Cowan, is apparent.

My great-grandmother Lena Bostock (left) surrounded by grandchildren. *Left to right:* Lester, George, Lindsay, Gerry and a local boy. Her son Norman married Edith (Nan, right) in 1933.

Edith's grandmother, Elizabeth Cowan (left), with William Olive, her second husband. Her first husband, Jonathan Cowan, was Mary Ann's brother. Because they are dressed so formally, I suspect the photograph was taken on their wedding day in 1920. Another photo (right) shows Grandpa Olive with Jack Cowan, Edith's brother (c. 1930).

Aunty Lilly, Augustus (Gus) Bostock's firstborn, identified the tall, bearded man standing by himself behind the fish crates in this photo, taken on the Tweed River, as her grandfather, A.J. Bostock. A group of women and children can be seen standing nearby to the left; one of them may be One My, his wife. (Courtesy of Michael Aird)

Residents of Deebing Creek Aborigines Reserve in 1895. The boy seated on the far right with his arms crossed is my great-grandfather Sam Anderson. His 'full-blood' mother, Mary Jane, is standing behind him, holding baby Kathleen. The white man reclining on the left is Thomas Ivins, Superintendent. (State Library of Queensland)

ALAN KIPPAX'S XI. v. RICHMOND-TWEED XI.

Visiting and local representative cricketers who took part in Saturday's big match at the Recreation Ground, Lismore :—
Standing.—J. J. Moss (umpire), S. Anderson, T. Rummery, S. Irvine, C. Haynom, R. Wotherspoon, L. Benaud, C. Nicholls (Kippax XI.), F. Armstrong, F. Smezde, C. Trumper (Kippax (XI.), C. Amies, A. Wood (umpire).
Sitting.—C. Callaway, E. Rofe, H. Moore, E. L. Waddy, Archie Jackson, Alan Kippax (capt.), C. Halpin Richmond-Tweed (capt.), R. Bradman, E. R. Bubb (manager), S. Josslyn, W. Bassett.

One family story is that Sam caught Bradman out for a duck. In this match photo, Sam is second from left, back row, and Don Bradman is fourth from right, front row.

My grandmother Edith Cowan was born on Nymboida Aborigines Reserve in 1911.

Group shot from Box Ridge Aborigines Reserve, near Coraki. All four of my grandparents were married at this mission.

Christmas being celebrated at Box Ridge. The missionaries organised pre-Christmas celebrations that they called 'Christmas Trees'.

Mrs Helen Mitchell with some of the children she was employed to teach at Box Ridge until 1930. She was very kind and worked hard for the advancement of Aboriginal people.

The bridesmaid on the left of this photo is my grandmother Edith. She later celebrated her own wedding at Box Ridge in 1933, wearing 'a gown of white morocain, with veil and coronet of orange blossoms'.

Runnymede or Stoney Gully, later also called Kyogle Aborigines Station. My grandmother Evelyn Solomon's maternal family line originates here.

J.P. Howard wrote on the back of this photo from the Howard family album, '126 natives attended Sunday Service'. (Courtesy of the Howard family)

Boys working in the fields. The Aborigines Protection Board did not provide enough funds to feed the people at Kyogle Aborigines Station, so J.P. Howard taught the children how to grow vegetables. (Courtesy of the Howard family)

Young Aboriginal children that the Aborigines Protection Board deemed neglected were taken to the United Aborigines' Mission's children's home at Bomaderry.

The Bostock kids in the early 1940s. *Left to right:* Lindsay, Lester, George and Phemie.

The photo that Nan sent to Alma Smith, a UAM missionary (c. 1945).
Left to right: Aunty Phemie, Uncle Lester and Nan (Edith). The little boy
at the front is my dad, George. (Mitchell Library, SLNSW)

My father with the Albion Boys in the late
1950s. My father grew up in suburban Brisbane
but moved to Sydney soon after these photos
were taken.

My mother, Rita, and Gwen at an All Blacks Football Club Dance at Waterloo Town Hall (c. 1954–55) (left) and Edith and Rita dressed up for a wedding (c. 1960) (right).

Rita perched on the family car in Redfern in the late 1950s.

My Aunty Ruby (Anderson) Langford and Harold Cowan, Edith's brother, in the early 1960s.

Edith at Tranby College, Glebe (in the late 1960s or early 1970s). She was employed there as a cook.

Uncle Gerry and my dad, George, in uniform in 1961.

The three brothers—Gerry, George and Lindsay—all served in the Vietnam War. Lester, my dad's oldest brother, did not serve in the military.

My cousin Pearl, Aunty Ruby's daughter, dancing with Prime Minister John Gorton at the Foundation for Aboriginal Affairs debutantes' ball, Sydney Town Hall, July 1968. (Anna Clements/APA/ SLNSW)

ASIO surveillance photos of Uncle Gerry departing from Sydney airport for China on an Aboriginal delegation to China in 1972 (left). Delegates were also covertly photographed at Sydney airport on their return (right). (ASIO File: Bostock, Gerald Leon)

Uncle Gerry's play *Here Comes the Nigger* was performed in 1975 at the Black Theatre in Redfern. Marcia Langton, Kevin Smith and Bryan Brown were all members of the cast.

"What is colour
What is blue and what is white
Can colour be distinguished
In the darkness of night?"

G. L. BOSTOCK

HERE COMES THE NIGGER!

Lousy Little Sixpence interviewed members of the Stolen Generations and opened in 1983. My uncles Gerry and Lester were both involved in the film's production.

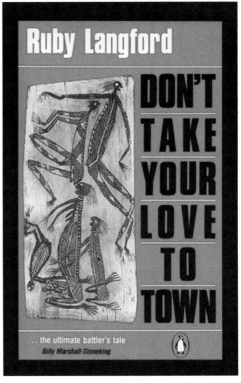

Aunty Ruby's first book, *Don't Take Your Love to Town*, was published in 1988 as part of her mission to provide non-Indigenous readers with an Aboriginal perspective on Australian history.

My father with his mother, Nan/Edith, in 1969 on his return from Vietnam.
HMAS *Sydney* is in the background.

Me and Nan in the late 1990s. It is one of the last photos I have with her.

attitude' and criticism of his absence from his work clearly got under Howard's skin.

In addition to pressure from the workers, Howard also experienced stress over the white townspeople's interest in what he was doing on the reserve. In May 1939, Howard wrote a report to the Board on the progress of the building of the next two huts on the reserve. The new buildings were right on the main road and drew people's attention. Some people called in to inspect the buildings and others stopped him in town to ask questions. Howard said that 'when told it is the natives work, our voracity is doubted'. A contractor asked Howard why he had not called for tenders to 'give the white man their due'. He responded that he thought the Aboriginal men should be given a trial. The contractor then said that he had seen the work and admitted it was a very good job, but in a veiled threat, he told Howard that he thought he was not giving white tradesmen a fair deal, and he would make further inquiries about it.

This information held my interest because I realised it added to a growing number of historical records that expose the antagonism and resentment of white Australians towards Aboriginal people possessing things of value. Usually, it was Aboriginal land that was most coveted, but this time it was paid work. If my mother were alive today, she would say the contractor was a 'dog in the manger'. Attributed as an Aesop moral fable, the old-fashioned 'dog in the manger' story is basically about being mean-spirited and spitefully wanting to keep something for oneself, especially to prevent others from having it. There is enough historical evidence to support the notion that, in those times, Aboriginal success attracted jealous and greedy scrutiny. I have no doubt that Howard included this exchange in his report as a means of forewarning the Board of the possibility of backlash from the white townspeople.

Another inclusion in this report that sent an interesting message to the Board was Howard's final paragraph. The Country Women's Association, well known as Australia's largest rural advocacy group, were a self-funded, non-partisan, non-religious organisation. They were passionate advocates of country women and their families, and they worked tirelessly to ensure vigorous representation to all levels of government on issues that impacted their communities. It was no secret that they were a politically powerful group, and Howard mentioning them in the closing of his report was, in my opinion, a calculated effort to justify his actions, and minimise the Board's disapproval. He informed the Board that:

> A motion was moved at the C.W. Association meeting this month that the government be asked to provide better housing for Aborigines. This is for the Conference agenda. Mrs Howard was present and took the opportunity of explaining that the Board was already doing this as fast as finances would permit, and invited the ladies to come out and inspect the building now erected. Several promised to do so.

'Protection' to 'Welfare' Board

The New South Wales Government's Aborigines Protection Board exercised control over Aboriginal people by way of the *Aborigines Protection Act 1909* and its various official amendments in 1915, 1918, 1936, 1940 and 1943. The amendment in 1940 saw the transition of the Aborigines *Protection* Board to the Aborigines *Welfare* Board.[20] The Commonwealth of Australia held a conference in Canberra in 1937 where representatives of all the nation's state and territory Aborigines Protection authorities came together to discuss policy.[21] In November that year, New South Wales Labor member Mark Davidson MLA wanted to continue the momentum of the Canberra conference, so he moved in the Legislative Assembly that a select committee inquire into and report on the general administration of the Aborigines Protection Board.

Ashlen Francisco, an Indigenous historian, has researched the history of the Aborigines Protection Board before and after its transition to the Aborigines Welfare Board and she told me that the select committee inquiry was the most controversial of political events leading up to the amendment in 1943 'because of its systematic detailing of the failure of the Board's Administration':

> The inquiry uncovered a Board, whose power was wielded by managers and inspectors, that comprehended and managed inhumane policies that perpetuated Aboriginal people into a cycle of disadvantage, dominated by political handballing and racial profiling. The inquiry was jeopardised by a lack of a quorum on numerous occasions and the committee was disbanded when government was reformed in 1938.[22]

Due to the inability of the select committee to produce a report, the Public Service Board published *Aborigines Protection: Report of the Public Service Board* on 16 August 1938. An exhaustive survey of Aborigines Protection Board activities—including administration at head office and the conduct of its stations, reserves and homes—was carried out. A final report, containing important recommendations, was printed on 4 April 1940 and presented to the House of Representatives during the passage of a bill to amend the Aborigines Protection Act. These recommendations included the reconstitution of the Aborigines Protection Board to become the Aborigines Welfare Board. As well, they included a reorganisation of staffing, including separation of the roles of managers and teachers; the appointment (if possible) of fully qualified teachers; increased production of crops to augment Aboriginal people's diet; additional funds for improving housing; and a policy to gradually assimilate 'suitable' Aboriginal families into the general community. Other recommendations covered issues such as health, hygiene, education and training, the issuing of food and clothing, and the administration of family endowment.

Assimilation

While the Protection Board was happy for Aboriginal people to demonstrate economic independence, and until 1936 refused to have anything to do with people who were not living on reserves, the new Welfare Board was resolved to intervene in the lives of Aboriginal people at the most fundamental levels, no matter where they lived or how successful they had been in escaping the Board's influence.[23] Amendments to the Aborigines Protection Act that were passed in 1936 gave the Board substantial new powers and allowed them, for the first time, to confine Aboriginal people against their will. Aboriginal people called it 'the Dog Act', because they could be penned up and shifted around just like animals.

It was the definitive example of the surrender by the New South Wales Government's Aborigines Protection Board to the demands of white townspeople who had, for many years, been calling for the permanent removal and confinement of local Aboriginal people. That led to Aboriginal people facing incredibly crowded and insanitary conditions on reserves and stations, and from 1930 to 1936, the Board simply had no funds to improve accommodation, water supply and other infrastructure. So, according to the Board, the solution was to take more control over adult Aboriginal people and force them to conform to white expectations. The Board were intent on changing Aboriginal people and insisted that in the end, they would no longer identify or be identified as Aboriginal, and could finally be 'dispersed' and removed from reliance on the government ration books.[24]

Determined to erase all evidence of cultural identity, the Board was unrelenting in its belief that Aboriginal people's commitment to their own communities was an undesirable obstacle to 'progress' and 'successful assimilation'. After the Aborigines Protection Board became the Aborigines Welfare Board, the decision was made to direct money away from enhancing the infrastructure of a small number of reserve stations and instead expand their network by deploying district welfare officers. These new welfare officers would be posted to towns that had seen a rapid growth of the Aboriginal population, and there they would coax Aboriginal people to 'keep in constant contact with them'.

Aboriginal people went to live in these towns not only to gain work, but often quite explicitly to escape Welfare Board control. The welfare officers were placed in towns that the Board felt were the most 'troublesome', and they were ordered to keep those Aboriginal people who lived privately in towns and houses under the same kind of constant observation as those who lived on the managed reserves. The Board's specific goal was to 'assist and guide' Aboriginal people towards successful assimilation. It was simply expected that Aboriginal people would accept the values and behaviour of the dominant European culture. The Welfare Board insisted that Aboriginal people not only earn an independent living, but that they show the Board they could save money in a bank account. Aboriginal people had to demonstrate that they were avoiding contact with other Aboriginal people, refusing to participate in community-oriented activities like sharing resources with kinsfolk, and were not travelling to visit their relatives and their home Country. Over and over again, the Board's reports criticised Aboriginal people for being among their own kind and clinging together in groups.

To achieve their assimilation aims, the Aborigines Welfare Board implemented a crude 'carrot and stick' incentive to try to modify the behaviour of Aboriginal people: if they could convince the welfare officers that they had cut themselves off entirely from their culture, family and land, they would be rewarded with an 'Exemption Certificate'.[25] The Board said that the reward of an Exemption Certificate would make it easier for them to achieve the benefits of access for their children to public schools and to Commonwealth pensions and unemployment benefits. It would be more likely that Aboriginal children would be safe from removal, and economic security would be a little closer. The Board promised that an Exemption Certificate, and faithful attention to the welfare officers' 'guidance', would make Aboriginal families eligible for a house in town.

The houses offered status, but the offer of a 'respectable' dwelling was not without conditions. The aim was to use them to modify Aboriginal people's behaviour. The houses were to be inspected constantly to make sure that Aboriginal people made a proper commitment to the appearance of 'stability'. The houses were to be peppered throughout white communities and surrounded on all sides by white residents so there would be no

Aboriginal neighbours. The 'assimilation' of families could then be under the scrutiny and judgement of the families' all-white neighbours as well as from the Board's welfare officers. For Aboriginal people the offer was intensely attractive, but not because of the white aspirations of 'status' or 'respectability'.

Aboriginal people were impoverished and desperate for security. How could they be otherwise, given their historical experiences? Every shift in the economy, every racist decision of the Aborigines Protection Board made it harder for them to stay in the town or on the land where they had previously reached some foothold, however tenuous, with the settler colonials. The dispersals and dispossessions of the 1920s, the constant threat of child removal and the enforced concentrations of the 1930s had each caused fear-filled recurrences of reluctant migrations. Even when people only had to go to the next town to seek asylum within their Country, they usually found only temporary residence, often in less secure conditions than those they had been forced to leave. So, when the Welfare Board announced that if Aboriginal families could demonstrate that they would live in 'conformity to the standards of white people', this was indeed a sweet-looking carrot.

A house in a town was almost an impossible dream for Aboriginal people. Most Aboriginal families who tried to rent were confronted with an invisible, unspoken alliance between white landlords, real estate agents and local councils. Of course, sometimes slums would be on offer, but most of the time there was a peculiar absence of any rental accommodation whenever Aboriginal people applied. Aboriginal people renting accommodation in towns was a challenge for white rural townspeople who wanted to exclude them, and the Welfare Board underestimated the depth of the commitment white townspeople had for segregation in both public and residential spaces. Since the 1880s, segregation was an endeavour that required purposeful intent.

Keeping Aboriginal children from so-called 'public' schools was just the most formal of such exclusions. Hospitals had been closed to Aboriginal people, too, and many Aboriginal mothers remember the humiliation and discomfort of giving birth in a makeshift area at the back of the main building, or on the hospital verandah. The enjoyment of leisure activities was strictly segregated, with picture shows, swimming pools and tennis courts usually closed to Aboriginal people—even Aboriginal football teams were excluded from the local competitions under the insulting grounds of 'health risks'. Some examples of this 'petty apartheid' were bizarre.

At Murrin Bridge, the white townspeople demanded that the manager of a nearby reserve only bring Aboriginal people in to shop for no more than two hours, so that they would not use the town's 'amenities'. Otherwise, they demanded, the Welfare Board would have to build a 'Blacks Only' toilet block, which was to also provide seating so that Aboriginal people would only be allowed to rest in the same strictly limited area. As late as the 1950s, the townspeople of Lake Cargelligo tried to preserve the 'Whites Only' public toilet. On a broader scale, the exclusion of Aboriginal people from the 'real town' meant they could always be defined as 'outsiders' and always be denied access in accordance with the wishes of the 'real citizens'.[26]

The newly formed Aborigines Welfare Board's program of assimilation had a seven-point plan: to inculcate the habit of self-help; keep Aboriginal people occupied; deal with the youth; apprentice the talented; select families to be removed from stations and assimilated into the white community; find employment far away from the reserves; and encourage local white people to become interested in Aboriginal matters. Historian Peter Read has said that these proposals were little more than 'a refinement of the older continuing policy of dispersal' and there was 'nothing particularly new', apart from the proposal to move families into town.

The Board focused its efforts on the 'managed stations' that had government-appointed managers, in areas where some services, like accommodation for families and education for Aboriginal children, were denied to Aboriginal people in the local towns. The managed stations were to act as 're-education stations' for 'unassimilated families', who would gradually be transferred to conventional housing in town under the strict surveillance of the Aborigines Welfare Board.[27] One of the most surprising archival documents I have collected over the years is a letter written by Aborigines Protection/Welfare Board manager J.P. Howard about assimilation. In this letter, it is clear that he took the government's assimilation agenda very seriously and was frustrated by the Aboriginal people under his management on two grounds—Aboriginal people's habit of sharing what they had with the whole mob, and the fact that there were not enough Aboriginal people with skin 'light enough' to be 'suitable' for merging into the white community.

MEMORANDUM
FROM: The Manager, Aboriginal Station, Kyogle.
DATE: 8-4-40.
SUBJECT: Merging of light Aborigines into white community.

If managers could please be informed something of the circumstances under which the people are to be merged into white population it would enable a better idea to be formed as to suitability etc. A man named [name supplied] at [location supplied] was telling me recently that he had tried to live as a white man for a considerable time, but he had not made a success of it, so he went back to [Aborigines reserve station].

Others I have known make similar attempts, and their downfall has been the fact that as soon as they get a house elsewhere their friends and relations would visit them until numbers grew to large proportions and they would stay as long as they were fed, thus impoverishing the original family. This will be the biggest trouble while all Aborigines are free to wander at will. A loafer will always make a place where he can get free keep. [The man] said he was always willing to make another try anytime if he could be given a start in the way of support until his crops were harvested. He admitted, however that the overcrowding and the eating out of house and home by other natives would cripple him, and he had no power to stop them coming, the Board would need to help him by Police supervision to keep the visitors away.

The only man on the station with anything approaching the necessary qualifications for such a move is Henry Anderson. He is light in colour, and his three young daughters lighter than he is, though their mother is darker. Another handicap is getting a whole family light enough.

Anderson . . . is good at any farmwork, and very dependable . . . A habit the people have acquired here now is, as soon as a number of them come home with cheques after a contract they must visit another Station, or the beach, and all their money goes in one day's outing, mainly in the hire of conveyances. They all go, and the few of them who have money pay for the lot. Only a week ago they hired a lorry, and 50 odd of them went to Beaudesert.[28]

The first time I read this letter I stared at the page in utter amazement and was shocked by the unabashed racism. It was like he was lamenting, 'Oh, if only they were whiter! If only they weren't so brown and black!' What I found confronting was my personal realisation that Howard's criteria for the 'suitability' of Aboriginal people to live in Australian society was in complete alignment with that of the New South Wales Government. Both parties (and white society in general) truly believed that if Aboriginal people were going to make it in this world, then they were expected to 'live as a white man'—and that meant living as individual or married members of society, providing for your 'nuclear' family only, and depositing any excess wealth in bank accounts for future prosperity. That whole way of thinking was diametrically opposed to Aboriginal ways of Knowing and Being. As I re-read the last paragraph of this letter, I was filled with an enormous sense of pride.

I laughed, because in my mind's eye it conjured up a picture of this great big mob of happy, smiling blackfellas laughing as they piled all the kids, men, women and the old Aunties and Uncles on to a big old flatbed farmer's truck, or some other 'conveyance'. I imagined their eyes twinkling with joyous anticipation at connecting with the Beaudesert mob, or taking the kids to the beach and, better yet, leaving behind their life of exclusion, poverty and oppression on the government reserve enclosure. I imagined the wind in their hair, and the pure joy of being able to escape, even just for one day. But, most of all, I admired their sense of compassion and brotherhood; clearly there was no reluctance to share all that they had for the greater good of all, even if it was just a temporary pleasure trip. For Aboriginal people, it was all about culturally maintaining connection with kin and Country in the north, and showing all their children a culture and life outside of their isolated mission or reserve existence.

Resistance ramped up

By examining the lives of my great-grandparents and grand-parents, I can see that there is evidence here of a broader shift in the power of Aboriginal people, with some of the attempts by the Aborigines Protection/Welfare Board to control them being thwarted and even outright rejected by regular, non-political family members 'on the ground' in everyday life. When J.P. Howard tried to remove my great-grandmother Mabel's daughters in 1935, Mabel was so heroic. Although suffering from a severe long-term illness before her death in 1937, she was able to get five-year-old Phyllis and her two older daughters away from the reach of Howard, the Protection Board and the police before she died at the young age of 48.

I am purely speculating here, but I would not be surprised if 'push came to shove' when Uncle Bob was told by Howard that Phyllis was a 'Ward of the Board and committed to the care of this Station'. Bob took her away immediately and Howard was powerless to stop him. A less confrontational but no less effective form of resistance came from Aunty Kate, who went behind Howard's back to gain custody of nine-year-old Phyllis from a higher Aborigines Protection Board authority.[29]

My grandfather's friend—the older brother—demonstrated resistance that was targeted at Howard. He was defiant, made snide comments, undermined Howard's authority, openly criticised him and, I suspect, tormented him.[30] I believe that my grandfather Henry was a more passive man, but even he had his limits. Fed up with the volumes of bureaucratic paperwork and the struggle over child endowment after my grandmother

Evelyn had deserted the family—compounded by terrible neglect of his children at Box Ridge Mission—he and Uncle Ernie Ord organised the pre-planned 'kidnap' of his three daughters, Ruby, Gwen and my mother Rita, from Box Ridge Mission. Like his mother, Mabel, Henry completely rejected the Board's plans for his children and moved them to a place where they were free from the fear of child removal, and under the loving care of Uncle Sam and Aunt Nell, while Henry worked all over Bundjalung Country to support his children.

Without doubt, one of the greatest examples of injustice in Australian history is the Aborigines Protection/Welfare Board's hypocrisy. The Aborigines Protection/Welfare Board accused Aboriginal parents of neglect, as a means to justify child removal, thereby *causing* the most heart-wrenching pain and suffering ever to be experienced by parents and children—yet the Board's appalling neglect of Aboriginal people had occurred time and time again, decade after decade, since the Board's formation. Is it any wonder then that, like the political freedom fighters of the time, regular, ordinary Aboriginal people were ramping up resistance and were even outright rejecting the authority of the New South Wales Government's 'Destruction Board'?

7

Control of Aboriginal lives

'I wish to notify you that I have taken my children away from
Coraki [Aborigines reserve] ... they were being ill-treated ...
they were neglected ... I don't want to hear any more
about it.'

HENRY ANDERSON (MY GRANDFATHER)

Family endowment payments for all Aboriginal people in New
South Wales were managed by the Aborigines Protection Board,
then the Aborigines Welfare Board, and administered through
its managers and police. These employees and police minions of
the Welfare Board issued orders for food, clothing, etc. as needed
by the Aboriginal people concerned. In certain cases, where 'it
was considered by the Commissioner, and on the recommendation of the Aborigines Protection Board', exceptions could be
made to this strict rule and payments could be made directly
to the Aboriginal person in cash. By 1938, there was a total
of 646 'Endowees', of whom 449 were paid by way of 'order of
goods'.[1] So, approximately 70 per cent of family endowment
payments to Aboriginal people were controlled and managed
by Aborigines Welfare Board bureaucrats. Archival documents

from my grandmother Evelyn's and my grandfather Henry's Aborigines Protection/Welfare Board files explicitly reveal the true extent of the New South Wales Government's control over Aboriginal lives.

The earliest record I have about my grandmother Evelyn Anderson and her child endowment is her account balance as at 31 July 1938, which was £3/1/8.[2] My mother was born on 11 May 1939, and although Howard had written to the Protection Board with a claim for the extra child way back in May, by September that year my grandmother Evelyn had still not received an adjustment to the account for her youngest child (my mother), who was over four months old.[3] This was just one example of the many stressful delays that my grandparents Henry and Evelyn Anderson, and other Aboriginal people, had to endure to receive family endowment.

As mentioned above, there were two ways Aboriginal people could receive endowment payments. They were either made directly to the recipient as a cash cheque or the recipient was instead given endowment cards where debits (otherwise known as endowment orders) were recorded. When my grandparents had to move to other country towns for short-term contract work, the bureaucratic red tape that the Aborigines Protection Board had in place meant that they had to survive long periods of time without the sometimes critical assistance of endowment payments.

Any Aborigines Welfare Board endowment card is interesting to a historian, but when you know that the one you are holding belonged to your grandmother, it feels like she has been instantly plucked out of an invisible past and made visible. My grandmother Evelyn's card shows the cost of purchases from the 'Owl Stores' and 'Biggs & Sons' at Kyogle. When I zoomed in to take a closer look, I saw that the date of the last purchase on this card was 10 May 1940. This was the day before my mother's first birthday, and Aunty Gwen and Aunty Ruby were three and six respectively.

I immediately imagined Evelyn walking into these stores, selecting items and then taking them to the counter to have the cost of the items written up by the storekeeper. The town of Kyogle was 9.5 kilometres from the Aboriginal reserve, so I wondered how she and other Aboriginal people got there. Did they walk, or did Howard take a group of Aboriginal people from the reserve into town all at once? How were they received at Kyogle? Did the townspeople, like the people at Murrin Bridge, demand that they keep their visits short so that they didn't use the town's 'amenities'? Was it galling for my grandmother to have to present her government card to some random whitefella for validation?

The deeper I delved into the archives, the more I learned about exactly how the family endowment payments were administered by the New South Wales Government, and what that system looked like for my ancestors and other Aboriginal people in history.

From Howard's letters, we know that my grandparents Henry and Evelyn remained in Kyogle after my mother's birth. A year later they were living in Casino. On *27 September 1940*, a man named James Rayner sent a letter to the newly named Aborigines 'Welfare' Board championing the case of my grandmother Evelyn, whose endowment was sent to Woodenbong, but Evelyn was residing in Casino 'doing casual work'. He insisted that she receive direct payment there. It is unclear who Rayner was, but I suspect he was a white Australian employer, because in the same letter he also champions another Aboriginal lady, who was also employed as a casual worker.[4]

No. A.P.B. 104 13. Name *Anderson, Evelyn.* 99

PARTICULARS OF ENDOWMENT.

Total amount of Endowment approved £ *13* : — : — from *5 : 4 : 1939*

Amount due to *16 : 5 : 1939* £ *1 : 10 : —*

Balance of ... ... £ *11 : 10 : —* payable in

23 fortnightly instalments of £ *— : 10 : —*

Husband's Name *Henry*

Names of Endowed Children : x *Ruby* ?

Gwen

From May 1st

1 Ration = 2/- wkly.

All payments received from H.O.

The strictest care must be exercised that Accounts are not overdrawn.
Endowment orders should not be issued in excess of the amount of credit available at date of issue.

4841 3.50 T. H. TENNANT, ACTING GOVT. PRINTER.

Date. 1940:	Order No	Firm on which Order issued.	Value of Order Issued. £	s.	d.	Credits and Fortnightly Instalments. £	s.	d.	Balance. £	s.	d.	Date A/c for'd to A. P. Bd.
		Brought forward										
Apl. 12		Balance - Credit	5	16	3				5	16	3	
" 3/24		A.P.B. Rations		10					5	6	3	
" 18th	75469	Owl Stores		5	4				5	0	11	
" 23rd	75465	S. Michael	2	10	0				2	10	11	
May 3rd	A.33332	Owl Stores		10	0				2	0	11	
" 3rd	A.33333	Biggar Son		7	6				1	13	5	
" 4th	A.33335	Owl Stores	1	0	0					13	5	
						Carried forward 15						
						11379						

In response, on *19 November 1940* the Welfare Board then requested that the police constable at Casino fill out a form about my grandmother and send it to them. It was common practice at the time for the Board to send forms to Aboriginal reserve station managers, teachers or matrons at Aborigines reserve schools, and local police constables to complete and send them back to the Board before direct payment would be approved. Officially, the standard form was titled 'Report on Application for Direct Payment of Family Endowment', but to me they are *character assessment* forms, because white Australian people in positions of power reported their opinion on the character of family endowment recipients to the Aborigines Welfare Board. The descriptors to report on were: 'Aboriginal caste' (e.g. HC = 'half-caste' or FB = 'full blood'), 'Thrift', 'Sobriety', 'Whether addicted to Gambling', 'Morality', 'Police convictions (if any)', 'Associates' and 'Good worker, or otherwise'. My grandmother Evelyn's *character assessment* form for Direct Payment can be seen below.

On *21 November 1940*, Constable Charles M. Ryan of Casino Police Station filled out the Aborigines Welfare Board Application for Direct Payment form. Constable Ryan reported that my grandmother was 'a half-caste aborigine and resides at Casino? She is of good character, strictly sober and of good morals. Is a good worker and cares for her children well, keeps her home clean and does not gamble.' He recommended that 'she be granted the usual allowance for her children and that the money be paid direct to her'.

The judgements of these people determined whether an Aboriginal person could be trusted with cash. This form was stamped as having been noted by the Aborigines Welfare Board on *28 November 1940*.[5]

ABORIGINES WELFARE BOARD.
ABORIGINES PROTECTION BOARD.—FAMILY ENDOWMENT.

REPORT ON APPLICATION for Direct Payment of Family Endowment by

No. APB........................ Full Name ....Evelyn Anderson.....

Address ....Casino.

	Wife.	Husband.
Aboriginal Caste	Half Caste	Half Caste.
Thrift	Good	Good.
Sobriety	Good	Good
Whether addicted to Gambling ..	No	No.
Morality	Good	Good
Police convictions (if any) ..	Nil	Nil
Associates	Other aborinals	Other aboriginals.
Good worker, or otherwise	Good Worker	Good worker.

GENERAL REPORT.

Nature of Home ....4 roomed weather board.... Is it kept clean?....Yes.
                        cottage

Do children attend School regularly?..One child of school age.attends regularly.

Do children appear well clad and nourished?....Yes.

Is home building kept in decent state of repair?....Yes.

What has been previous experience of expenditure of endowment moneys when paid direct?
Any monies received by the applicant has always been spent in clothing t
children and food for them.

If direct payment granted, could the parents be entrusted with the expenditure of a possible large

sum of money wholly in the interests of the children and without extravagance?....Yes.

GENERAL REMARKS AND RECOMMENDATION.

The applicant is a half caste aborigine and resides at Casino?she is of
good character,strictly sober and of good morals.Is a good worker and
cares for her children well,keeps her home clean and does not gamble.
I recommend that she be granted the usual allowance for her children an
that the money be paid direct to her

Register noted

DIRECT PAYMENT APPROVED.

28 NOV 1940

SUPERINTENDENT.
28 NOV 1940

(Signed) ....*Charles M. Ryan*....
Constable 1st Class.
Casino.

Date.... 21/11/40   Police Station....

In the course of my research, I was dumbfounded to learn
that the members of the Aborigines Protection/Welfare Board
were not employed full time for this role. The Board usually
consisted of high-ranking public servants. In 1938, they were the

Commissioner of Police, the Undersecretary Chief Secretary's Department, Chief Inspector of Schools Department of Public Instruction, the Director General of Public Health, and the Metropolitan Superintendent of Police. These extremely busy men only met once a month on all matters relating to Aboriginal people.[6] This further explained why it took four months for Evelyn to finally receive approval for a direct payment of the endowment that she so desperately needed.

Returning to the initial request by Mr Rayner on *27 September 1940* that my grandmother be paid endowment by direct payment, I found out that this application was finally approved on *14 February 1941*.[7] It took the Board over four months to give approval for Evelyn to receive direct payment of her endowment, but there was further bureaucratic delay. After Evelyn's direct payment of endowment was approved, she still had to wait to actually receive it. The Board required that she send her endowment card to their head office in Sydney for checking. This meant that she could not go to the stores for food, because she did not have her endowment card. She was a mother of three small children who only worked casually doing laundry—and then my grandfather Henry became very ill and could not work.

My grandmother Evelyn was in such dire straits that she had to present herself at the police station to beg for food relief to survive the delay that the Board's bureaucratic bungling and breathtaking incompetence had forced her to endure. I know this because, in a letter dated *24 February 1941*, Casino Police Constable McKinnon wrote to his senior sergeant, Sergeant Madelin, then to the Board, informing them that:

> Whilst Mrs Anderson was waiting for a decision to be made concerning her endowment, and owing to the sickness of

her husband, she applied for and was granted Food Relief at this station to the value of £11/0/6, and a Christmas grant of £1/4/6.[8]

Much later I found that some archive pages were stuck together, and that this was actually the *second* time that she needed urgent help. She had also received food relief on 30 November 1940. The Aborigines Welfare Board's management of endowment for Aboriginal people, whether intentionally or not, became a controlling, drip-feeding mechanism.

Around April 1942, Henry and Evelyn left Casino for the Woodburn area, as Henry had secured a job in forestry. When they were in Casino, Evelyn reignited her affair with Eddie Webb. He was the man that Howard was referring to when he wrote in his 1939 letter that 'there was trouble in this family owing to the wife's immoral relations with another man'. Sadly, she left my mother and her sisters behind, taking baby George with her. It turned out that Henry was not George's father. Constable Ryan stated in his letter to the Board that:

Mr Anderson has sent his three children to the aborigines Reserve Coraki, where they are being cared for by people named _____. It is evident that Mrs Anderson has deserted her children, and has no real home for them. Perhaps this matter could be brought under the notice of the Aborigines Welfare Board.[9]

My grandfather Henry had no choice but to leave my mother and her sisters in the care of others at Box Ridge Mission because he needed to find work to support them. The surveillance that Henry experienced before Evelyn had left him was mild compared to what he experienced afterward as a single parent. Every time he changed jobs or moved for work, he had to resubmit requests for direct payment of endowment. An illuminating way to show the extent of this surveillance is to simply list the dates of the back and forth correspondence of the Aborigines Welfare Board, the deputy commissioner of the Child Endowment's Office, the managers of reserves, the police and other correspondence relating to Henry Anderson, most of them requiring *character assessment* forms and/or action of some sort, causing excruciating delays. In 1942 alone, such correspondence was sent on 12 May, 10, 15, 17 and 20 June, 8, 10, 13, 24, 28 and 31 July, 14 August, an undated letter (but between these two letters), 2 September, 3 and 20 October, and 2 and 29 December.[10]

My mother and her sisters were three, five and seven years old and Henry left them with a married couple at Box Ridge Mission. (As these people have descendants, I will refer to them as the girls' temporary 'foster mother' and 'foster father'.) The Board's chairman sent instructions to the Casino police to ask the Kyogle police to inform the foster mother to apply for child endowment.[11] Sergeant Taylor of Coraki police also wrote a letter recommending that she be paid endowment. Constable Thomas in Coraki received this instruction and completed a *character assessment* form for the foster mother, which he returned to the Board on 15 June, recommending that she be paid child endowment for the Anderson children.[12] This was the beginning of tension between Henry and the foster parents that lasted for over two years.

There are 37 letters on file about my grandfather Henry from the time Evelyn left him to the time he removed his daughters from the mission. They date from 12 May 1942 to

30 October 1944, which was the date of the letter Henry wrote stating he had taken the girls from Box Ridge Mission. These letters went back and forth from Aborigines Welfare Board officials to the police, to the matron at Box Ridge Mission, Mrs Hiscocks. Henry applied for endowment but was knocked back. Mrs Hiscocks championed the foster mother and accused Henry of not sending any money to her. Henry subsequently wrote a furious letter stating that he had paid maintenance apart from 'a bout of malaria fever and being unable to work for a short time'. He added: 'I have started work again, and that woman will be paid £3 per week and if it aint enough to keep three children I don't know what will.'[13]

In September 1944, the Aborigines Welfare Board received a typed letter (written by Mrs Hiscocks) signed by the foster mother requesting that my grandfather be made to support his children and alerting them that Henry was working as a truck driver for the Bonalbo Timber Company Ltd.[14] The Board became suspicious after that and sent a copy of Henry's letter to Mrs Hiscocks, asking for an account of dates and sums of money that the foster mother had received for maintenance, but she could not produce one. Mrs Hiscocks wrote that the foster mother 'has no records of amounts paid, so cannot furnish information required', but she continued to be fierce in her determination to see that Henry pay more money.[15]

The Board knew that Mrs Hiscocks had written the September letter, because Acting Secretary Mr Mullins opened with, 'In connection with the letter of the 12th of September received from Mrs _____, and apparently prepared by you for her signature'.[16] My grandfather Henry had had enough of Box Ridge Mission and the false accusations of the deceitful foster mother and Mrs Hiscocks, so he removed my mother and her sisters from the reserve and took them to live with Aunt Nell and Uncle Sam Anderson. In October, he wrote the Aborigines Welfare Board the following letter:

> I wish to notify you that I have taken my children away from Coraki as they were being ill-treated and were doing women's work such as scrub floors, and so forth. So I would like you to get my wife to come straight up and get the children if she wishes. I have them with my brother in Bonalbo. I have been supporting them wholly and souly and the money that was paid to Mrs _____ was not spent on my children. They were neglected, they seem to have lost their manners, so I've never heard anything about me taking them away. Matter of fact I don't want to hear any more about it because I have them in a private home where they are being well looked after.

Henry Anderson, c/o Post Office, Bonalbo.[17]

The Bonalbo police were notified and a whole round of *character assessment* forms and surveillance began at Bonalbo. Henry's brother, Uncle Sam Anderson Jnr, lived with his wife, Nell, so I imagine Uncle Sam got Henry his job. A *character assessment* form was sent to the Bonalbo police and Constable Burgess recommended that Henry receive direct payment. As seen in the opening of this chapter, the constable stated that 'Sam Anderson [Jnr] is employed by the Bonalbo Timber Company and is a good worker. He lives more or less like a white man and is well respected'.[18]

My Aunty Ruby wrote about how poorly she, Aunty Gwen and my mother Rita were treated (after their mother had left them) when they lived at Box Ridge Mission. As a young child, my mother once fell on a sharp 'squaring axe' and needed several stitches, but Aunty Ruby stated that 'they didn't even take her to the doctor'. I have vivid memories of my mother's gaping, open, elongated scar on the underside of her forearm that went from just below her wrist and extended almost to her elbow. Aunty Ruby also said:

> One afternoon I was sent to stoke the fire. It was down to the coals so I put chips on and brambles and fanned it with a piece of cardboard. It still wasn't lit so I poured kero on and the rings were still on top of it and it blew up in my face with a loud boom. I was in pain for weeks, I had no eyebrows and all my face was blistered. They didn't take me to the doctor. Not long after that some kind person must have got word to Dad about the way we were being treated. He came in the truck and packed our things. Uncle Ernie was the only one who knew we weren't coming back. He helped us into the truck and kissed us goodbye then walked away from us with his head down crying.[19]

I remember Aunty Ruby telling me that the way my grandfather Henry removed them from the reserve was done like a covert operation to avoid surveillance. Henry tricked Mrs Hiscocks and others to believe that he was just visiting the reserve to take the girls out for a picnic that day, and only Uncle Ernie (his dearest friend and distant relative) knew the truth. Fed up with the way his children were being treated, Henry removed them from Box Ridge Mission and never returned.

I have lost count of the number of times that historical documents have caused me to become quite sad. As I read Constable

Ryan's report to the Aborigines Welfare Board stating that my grandmother Evelyn Anderson had deserted her family in March 1942, my heart wept for my mother, who, I realised, was only two months short of her third birthday.[20] She and her sisters were on the mission at Box Ridge until October 1944, so Mum was five years and five months old when she left to go and live with Uncle Sam and Aunt Nell. The earliest photograph we have of my mother is believed to have been taken at Box Ridge. Aunty Gwen and Mum—the smallest girl, with a bow in her hair—are sitting between two bigger girls, and I suspect this was not long after she and her sisters arrived at the mission. All that my mother remembered of Box Ridge Mission was the accident where she fell on the axe, but she constantly spoke of her love for Uncle Sam and Aunt Nell, and her memories of her time with them were joyously retold over and over again.

Over the years, I had witnessed several reunions of my mother and aunts, and when they got together they would shout over the top of one another to be the first to tell all the stories of the mischief they got into as children. It was the happy stories they wanted to tell. I never heard my mother Rita or her sister Aunty Gwen speak of their lives before moving to live with their Aunt Nell and Uncle Sam. Perhaps it was because they were so young. Only Aunty Ruby had memories of mission life at Box Ridge, and I have no doubt that if my grandfather Henry were alive today, he would have countless things to say about his memories of the mind-numbing government surveillance he experienced during those times.

I thought that the harassment Henry received from the Aborigines Welfare Board would have dissolved after he had removed his girls from the mission in 1944, but that was not the case. Probably the most frustrating archives I have collected during my research are the ones that reveal the true extent of the control the Aborigines Welfare Board had over the lives of Aboriginal people, and this was maintained by way of the vital child endowment payments. Wherever there were family endowment payments, there was control. After Henry removed the girls from the mission, there was copious correspondence between the Aborigines Welfare Board and the police about family endowment payments that should have been paid directly to Henry.

GENERAL REMARKS AND RECOMMENDATION.

Anderson's wife deserted him three years ago and until recently his three daughters were cared for by a woman named _____ at Coraki. Anderson considered they were not being properly treated so he brought them to Bonalbo and placed them in the care of his brother and sister-in-law, Mr and Mrs Sam Anderson. Sam Anderson is employed by the Bonalbo Timber Company and is a good worker. He lives more or less like a white man and is well respected. I recommend direct payment of family endowment in this case.

(Signed) W.E. Burgess,
Constable 1st Class, No. 3879
Police Station: Bonalbo
9/11/44

As I sorted through the archival documents and placed them into chronological order, I had difficulty understanding why the Board kept asking the police at Bonalbo to fill out and send in direct payment/*character assessment* forms. It was

211

confusing, because even after they had completed the forms and sent them in, they were still being asked to do so again. Then I realised that on the attached cover letters, I had only seen the typed initials, name and word 'S.L. Anderson, Chairman', and had not looked past the name to see what followed. After the Board chairman's typed name and title was the small word *'per'* followed by scribbled initials. It seems that S.L. Anderson was the official chairman of the Board, but other Aborigines Welfare Board staff were initialling letters on his behalf.

The fact that letters were being initialled by others raises the possibility of miscommunication, and that letters were not going to the people they should have. On top of that confusion, there were different hierarchical roles involved at the top of the Aborigines Welfare Board. There was the superintendent, A.W.G. Liscombe (who initialled his name as 'A.W.G.'); the acting secretary, Mr Mullins (who initialled as 'J.M.'); and the chairman, S. L. Anderson, who rarely seemed to sign letters at all.

There were even more delays to Henry receiving direct payment when the Aborigines Welfare Board's acting secretary reported his case to the deputy commissioner of Child Endowment. A classic saying comes to mind when I think about the Aborigines Welfare Board and its flunkies, and the Department of Social Services, Child Endowment Branch: 'the left hand didn't know what the right hand was doing'. Whether it was to administer a cash book or direct payment, the bureaucratic systems in place were compounded by dual management of family endowment payments. Each department created its own paperwork, and this worked *against* rather than *for* the prompt payment of much-needed funds for Aboriginal family survival.

The papers in my grandfather Henry's file provide a telling example of what I am talking about. As shown above,

Constable W.E. Burgess wrote Henry's *character assessment* form on 9 November 1944, and on it there were stamps of approval by the acting secretary on 14 November and the superintendent on 20 November 1944, yet the correspondence dragged on and on. This was because on 24 November 1944, the acting secretary of the Aborigines Welfare Board wrote to the deputy commissioner of Child Endowment:

> Subject—Child Endowment—Henry Anderson—Bonalbo. It has been reported to this office that the children of Henry Anderson, previously cared for by _____ of Coraki, are now under the control of their father at Bonalbo. He has placed them in the care of Mr and Mrs Sam Anderson. It is recommended that endowment in respect of these children be paid direct to Henry Anderson. Mullins AWB Acting Secretary.

The deputy commissioner of Child Endowment responded on the *30 November 1944* by asking for the Aborigines Welfare Board to have Henry fill out another form:

> Re: Henry Anderson Bonalbo Ref No. A43/702. In reply to your communication of the 24th November, 1944, I would be glad if you would have the above named person complete the enclosed endowment form in respect of his children under the age of 16 years and have same returned to this office as soon as possible. F. Pogson, Deputy Commissioner, Child Endowment.

On 8 December 1944, Acting Secretary Mullins, on behalf of the chairman of the Aborigines Welfare Board, sent the following letter to 'The Officer in Charge, Police, Bonalbo':

The attached form should be completed by the above named person in respect of his children under the age of 16 years and returned direct to the Deputy Commissioner of Child Endowment, 52 Carrington Street, Sydney. S.L. Anderson, Chairman . . . *Per J.M.*

The attached form that was sent to the Bonalbo police was not the Welfare Board's *character assessment* form, but a different one from the deputy commissioner of Child Endowment, so that is why my grandfather Henry had to go to the Bonalbo Police Station to sign it, but the form did not get sent back to the deputy commissioner of Child Endowment until 10 January 1945. Henry being away for long periods of time working on the land and the public servants' Christmas break were probably the reasons for the delay.

There are no records from then until 8 May 1945, when the Aborigines Welfare Board sent a *character assessment* form for the police at Bonalbo to fill out. Constable Upward stated: 'Home complies favorably with normal Australian standards. Monies paid directly—in this case it appears to be quite satisfactory. Recommend that direct payment continue until time for the next review.' There was only one form sent by the Aborigines Welfare Board in 1946, which was sent on 4 February to the Bonalbo police, who responded on 12 February. In 1947, another *character assessment* form was sent and received on 5 February and 13 February, respectively, with the Bonalbo police stating that:

Anderson is a good clean half-caste aborigine. Although not living with his wife, the children are well cared for by his sister-in-law, Mrs Sam Anderson, with whom the applicant resides. All monies are spent in the welfare of the children who are well clothed and nourished, and attend school regularly. Under the circumstances I recommend that endowment monies be paid direct to the Applicant.

It's fair to say that most of the interactions between my family members and the Welfare Board were either negative or controlling, but in the archival records, I came across records detailing the kindness of a welfare officer, Mr L. Austen, who was employed by the Board to look after the Casino District. Records reveal that my grandmother Evelyn Anderson left her husband and three daughters in March 1942, but in December 1946 there was seemingly an attempt at reconciliation.

On 7 December 1946, the Aborigines Welfare Board issued a rail pass to Evelyn to enable her to return to her husband in Casino.[21] While Henry was away working during the week, on Friday 13 December, Evelyn went to see Mr Austen, telling him that she had 'made up' with Henry, and asking him for a rail warrant to travel to Sydney to retrieve 'some clothes etcetera'. He dutifully sent a telegram to the Board's head office in Sydney and awaited instructions. He also sent a telegram to Henry and arranged for him to come in and see him on Saturday 14 December, as Henry was away on weekdays.

According to Austen, on Saturday 14 December Henry met with him and told him that he thought they had made up, but Evelyn had taken Friday afternoon's express train to Sydney. Then, confusingly, on Monday 16 December, Austen received a telegram from the Board in Sydney informing him that my grandmother Evelyn 'Returned to Sydney, with Webb, [but] now applies for pass return Casino to resume with husband, confirm whether husband agreeable and will pay cost pass'.[22]

I spent a fair bit of time shuffling through these archives, because none of this made sense to me. What on earth was happening here? My grandmother had run away from Casino, and arrived in Sydney with her lover, but then, almost immediately, wanted to return to Casino to go back to her husband and is asking for him to send her the train fare? I was baffled, and doubled-checked the archive's dates and information to see if I had made any mistakes. Henry ended up returning to Austen's office, saying he had received a telegram (informing him that Evelyn wanted him to send her the train fare to return to Casino), but he told Austen he couldn't afford the ticket. So, Henry asked Austen if the Board would pay for a pass, and he would reimburse them after Christmas.

Mr Austen sent another telegram to the Board in Sydney, stating that Henry desired reconciliation with Evelyn and the fare would be reimbursed later, writing 'see my report'.[23] In that report, Austen appealed for the Board to help Henry. He explained that Henry wanted a reconciliation but did not have enough money. What spare money he had needed to go towards an operation for kidney stones, which he had put off to support his children. If Evelyn came home, he could get the operation done. Until then, he had to keep working because his daughter Ruby was starting high school the following year and needed clothes. The way Austen wrote this report shows his kindness and compassion, a kindness and compassion that I certainly didn't expect from the Aborigines Welfare Board:

I may say that Henry does not look at all well, and I think this is a case where the Board might help to draw the wife and husband together again, so that Evelyn can look after the children at Bonalbo. I told Henry Anderson to wire Evelyn to go and see you on Tuesday afternoon, and discuss the matter with you. I know that Evelyn's past is not all it should be, but I think this is a genuine attempt at reconciliation and for the children's sake we should do all in our power to help.[24]

I closely examined this rail pass application and the accompanying declaration that is *allegedly* signed by my grandmother Evelyn. Intuitively I felt an inner *knowing* that something was not quite right here, so I crosschecked this handwriting with old letters I have that were written by Evelyn when she was 23 years old. My grandmother Evelyn's writing was not as confident as the writing on this form, and she had poor grammar skills at that age. Aboriginal people who were raised on missions and reserve stations were truly lucky if they received a decent education. That's backed up by the old Aunties in *A Lousy Little Sixpence*, who said that they were self-taught. In the only sample of her handwriting that I have, my grandmother Evelyn used phrases like 'and she tell me' and 'the last time they was here'.[25] Judging by her writing, I do not think she was capable of writing the formal, well-written words and sentences on this application form. The following sentence raised my suspicions: 'I wish to return to my husband and children with whom I have been separated. I am anxious to make a fresh start in caring for them.'

'I wish to' . . . 'with whom I have been separated' . . . 'I am anxious'? I'm a former schoolteacher, and having examined my grandmother's writing and grammar capabilities, I do not believe that she wrote these words. As a historian, I have found that the most amazing discoveries can be made when you slip into what I call 'detective mode', and you examine and cross-examine archives looking for clues to solve the mysteries

ABORIGINES WELFARE BOARD

NEW SOUTH WALES.

A 3530

18 DEC 1946

Application for Money Advance, Rail Warrant, etc.

I, *Susan Ellen Evelyn Anderson* , the undersigned,
(Name in full.)

residing at *33 Beaumont St Waterloo* , request—

(Strike out the part that does not apply.)

(a) an advance of
(State amount.)

(b) the issue of a Rail Warrant for a ~~return~~ single journey from *Sydney*

to *Casino*

at a cost of £ *2 : 16 : 11*.

The above request is submitted for the following reason—

I wish to return to my husband and
children from whom I have been seperated
I am anxious to make a fresh start in
caring for them.

I hereby declare that ~~I~~ *my husband Henry Anderson c/o c/o + Austin* will undertake to refund to the Aborigines Welfare Board *Welfare*

(Strike out the part that does not apply.) within *2 Month* months, the ~~amount of the Advance~~ cost of the Rail Warrant such payment to be *Office*
made in the following manner— *Casino*

Refund to be made to Mr Austin by 3
Instalments

(Signature) *S.E.E. Anderson*

(Date) *16/12/46.*

WITNESS *I English*
Abor. Welfare Board

(Date) *16. 12. 1946.*

Space reserved for Head Office Use.

Conditional fare approved
Jan
17. 12. 46.
Vehr X 58981 issued

1679 3.46

of history. I found that when I compared the writing on the rail pass application with the handwritten letter that my grandmother wrote, Evelyn's writing was very 'young' in comparison to the fluid writing on the rail pass application. The handwriting samples simply did not match. The rail pass application records the Welfare Board inspector Mrs I. English as a witness on the form, which raised my suspicions that she was in fact the one who filled out this form and, indeed, signed Evelyn's name. This would make it the second record that I have found where a female white Australian Government employee has deceitfully written letters for an Aboriginal person. (The first was when Mrs Hiscocks wrote and signed a letter in the foster mother's name so the latter could collect Henry's endowment payments.)

I returned to my archive collection to locate the pages of Mrs English's diary to see if I could find anything else. I cite below two comments from Mrs English's diary relating to indentured Aboriginal girls.

Diary for Week Ending *12th January 1945*
Name of Officer *I. English* Position *Inspector*
~~Aboriginal Station~~ *Head Office*

Monday—Head Office—attended to general welfare matters—. . . interviewed _____ who had absconded from her home at Clifton Gardens. Remained with girl until employer came for her at 6pm.

Wednesday—Head Office—attended to general welfare matters—. . . 10am To Bellevue Hill visit _____ conferring with employer. _____ proved very difficult to manage, was violent & stubborn—visited _____ while at Bellevue Hill. Returned to H.O.[26]

Monday's diary entries paint a very different picture of Mrs English to the one that I described earlier (in Chapter 5) as a woman who 'was well liked by the Aboriginal people at Box Ridge Mission'. Let us remember that it was Mrs English who presented the bride, my grandmother Evelyn, 'with a beautiful wedding cake'.[27] She was also the person responsible for all the arrangements of my other grandmother Edith's wedding (making bouquets, preparing the breakfasts, etc.), yet on this Monday in Sydney, Mrs English waited with an indentured Aboriginal girl who had run away from her employer to make sure she returned to them.[28]

In historian Victoria Haskins book *One Bright Spot*, a young indentured Aboriginal woman wrote a letter to sympathetic white supporters and told the story of how she was kept in servitude even after her term of 'apprenticeship' had expired. She wrote, 'I won't [*sic*] to go home where I came from . . . and Mrs English doing her best to keep me under them but the first train I can get home I am going home and they are not going to stop me I tell you.'[29] We do not know the reason why the Aboriginal girl had absconded from her employment, but I cannot help but ask the question, what if her reason for running away was sexual abuse? Haskins stated:

> There is no doubt that the Board knew of the high rates of pregnancies to girls in service and was aware of cases of alleged sexual abuse and rape. The Board's own records (which we may consider an underestimation) show more than 10% of the young women in service gave birth and the rate was notably higher among those who worked in Sydney, where the figure came closer to one in five.[30]

Evelyn had deserted her family, the first diary entry described a girl who had absconded from her indenture, and the second diary entry described a girl who was 'very difficult to manage'. These young ladies were obviously unhappy, but I think that according to Mrs English, these were defiant young Aboriginal girls who were not where they *should* be or behaving as they *should* have, according to the Aborigines Welfare Board.

Given that Evelyn almost immediately abandoned Henry and the girls again to return to Eddie Webb, I am certain that Mrs English filled out this form for the rail pass reimbursement. I also think it was Mrs English who sent the telegram to Mr Austen on Monday (16 December) that said Evelyn 'now applies pass return Casino to resume with husband, confirm whether husband agreeable and will pay cost pass'. I believe it was Mrs English who sent the telegram to Henry on 16 December informing him that Evelyn wanted him to send her the train fare to return to Casino. She was making sure that the fare would be paid so that she would not have to account for it. I believe that Mrs English was using coercion, threats and possibly force against my grandmother Evelyn. Perhaps the police *helped* her to put Evelyn on the train, as the police had *helped* Howard remove Aboriginal girls from their families.

In his dealings with my grandfather and other Aboriginal people, Mr Austen's report about Henry, and his diary entries, show that he practised care for Aboriginal people that went above and beyond his duties and responsibilities. About my grandfather Henry Anderson, Austen explained:

> I had to lend him a couple of pounds personally for him to get himself and his children back to Bonalbo where he has a home. I shall see him in a few weeks and arrange for the return of the

cost of the pass. I am of opinion that Evelyn must be having an affair with someone in Sydney. Perhaps you could contact her and find out what her future intentions are.[31]

Also on the same day, 16 January 1947, Austen was sent a terse letter from Mr Liscombe, the Welfare Board superintendent, reminding him of his December report and that the rail pass was issued on the understanding that Henry would pay him (Austen) back £2/16/11.[32] The letter demands to know what Austen is going to do about it. The superintendent's determination to recover the money is outlined in letters that follow, but a handwritten letter from Henry on 23 January 1947, addressed to 'Whom it May Concern' at the Aborigines Welfare Board, sheds light on further details about my grandmother Evelyn's latest desertion of her husband and children.

Henry stated that, three weeks prior, Evelyn had made the trip to Casino and he had taken the children 'down to her to look after'. He also wrote that he agreed to give her an allowance of three pounds a week and the use of the endowment for upkeep of the children, and had also given her four pounds for a week's allowance. Henry then said, 'and with that she left the kids with friends and took off back to Sydney'. When he found out she was gone, he took the children back to Bonalbo where they were living with Uncle Sam and Aunt Nell, and wrote, 'so I would like the Welfare Board to recover that four pounds off her or take Police Action against her for recovery of same. Her address is 33 Beaumont Street Waterloo or 44 Walker Street Redfern'.[33] The Board superintendent informed him on 3 February 1947 that they would not take such action, but would bring the matter to his wife's attention. However, the debt still stood.[34]

The Board's response to this letter, on 5 February, was to request that the Bonalbo police constable fill out yet another *character assessment* form for direct payment.[35] This time, the constable on duty was Constable Flowers and, not surprisingly, he wrote a good *character assessment* for Henry Anderson, dated 13 February 1947:

> Anderson is a good class half-caste aborigine—Although not living with his wife, the children are well cared for by his sister-in-law Mrs Sam Anderson, with whom the applicant resides. All monies are spent in the welfare of the children who are well clothed and nourished, and attend school regularly. Under the circumstances I recommend that endowment monies be paid direct to the applicant.[36]

What does being 'a good half-caste Aborigine' imply? Or, for that matter, what values are involved in being 'a good Aborigine', 'a good breadwinner', or 'a good husband'? Historian Ann McGrath asked these questions and explored the notion of 'a good husband' in her book *Illicit Love*. In Queensland, white protectors saw themselves as 'fathers of the bride' to all Aboriginal women in their care; they exercised authority over interracial marriage and approved or disapproved choices. When they assessed a white man's suitability to marry an Aboriginal woman, they applied 'eugenicist thinking and contemporary values around the constitution of a good husband'. McGrath wrote that:

> As captives to their own protectionist rhetoric, the protectors had to apply a fair test as to whether a man applying for a marriage permit matched up to their criteria for a 'suitable' husband ... defining anticipated duties and behaviours of

a good husband was especially challenging. Ideal husbandly attributes of the time included home ownership and settling down to a sedentary lifestyle, yet transient frontier zones had little substantial housing and highly mobile work patterns.[37]

Similarly, Aboriginal breadwinners lived in 'transient zones' with 'highly mobile work patterns' but had little hope of 'substantial housing'. Reviewing what was written on all the *character assessment* forms about Henry and other family members, we can see that the New South Wales protectors valued sobriety; thrift; no association with gambling, or other 'unsuitable' Aborigines; clean and tidy residences; well-clothed and well-cared for children, attendance of children at school; and generally good and moral behaviour as accorded with white social ideals. Therefore Evelyn deserting her husband and children to run away with her lover would have been seen as shocking, immoral behaviour. Henry's stubborn refusal to pay for the rail pass would also have been seen as indecent.

The Aborigines Welfare Board did end up bringing to Evelyn's attention the money that Henry owed them. I found out that after a large amount of correspondence back and forth, Evelyn visited the Board three years later and pointed out that the payment of the rail warrant was the responsibility of her husband, Mr Henry Anderson, of 22 Great Buckingham Street, Redfern. She produced a telegram from Henry dated 16 December 1946 in which he asked her to proceed to the Welfare Board and pick up a pass that *he* had arranged for her. It appears that she, as well as Henry, was refusing to pay the Welfare Board for the rail pass. The correspondence about the Board's stubborn determination to recoup the £2/16/11 my grandfather owed them beggars beliefs. The letters begin on 10 February 1947 and end on 10 April 1951.

In the middle of that timeframe, in 1949, Henry and his two oldest daughters left Bonalbo and moved to Sydney.[38] My mother stayed with Uncle Sam and Aunt Nell, as she was still in school. I am unsure when my grandfather Henry began his de facto relationship with an Aboriginal woman called Joyce Morris; although they never married, they lived together until his death, and they had two sons. Aunty Ruby called her 'Mum Joyce' and the name just stuck. Uncle Dennis was born in 1950, and Uncle Kevin was born a year later, in 1951. That was the same year that the Aborigines Welfare Board finally gave up on chasing Henry for the rail pass money that he stubbornly refused to pay. The government's Aborigines Welfare Board administration staff were incredibly efficient when it came to chasing money from Aboriginal people, but incredibly incompetent when it came to distributing it.

Henry, his new family, and Ruby and Gwen lived in a one-bedroom flat in Great Buckingham Street, Redfern. Ruby and Gwenny 'shared a three-quarter bed on the balcony and at the other end was a kitchenette'. The main room had a fold-out table, a big bed and double bunks for the boys, and a wardrobe. Mum Joyce looked after Henry, and after he left his job at Warragamba Dam, he finally had a home and a family again.[39]

His next job was at Henderson Federal Springs, and here he experienced something that most white people took for granted. For the first time in his life, at the age of 38, Henry experienced the certainty of permanent full-time work—he worked at the same place for ten whole years.[40]

During the time in Redfern, Aunty Ruby became pregnant with her first child, and she and the baby's father, Sam Griffen, left the city to go and live in the country with Sam's mother in Coonabarabran until the baby was born. Aunty Ruby said that (by becoming an unwed mother) she did not want to bring shame on her father, but he was more upset about her leaving and did not want her to go.[41]

Aunty Ruby gave birth to her first son, William Henry, my cousin Billy, in October 1951.[42] With baby Billy in her arms, Aunty Ruby ran into her cousin, Aunty Shirley (whose nickname was 'Midge'), in Casino. Aunt Nell and Uncle Sam had two daughters, Midge and Judy, and when Ruby, Gwenny and Rita went to live with Aunt Nell and Uncle Sam, the five cousins lived like sisters. Aunty Midge told Aunty Ruby that my grandfather Henry and Mum Joyce were in town for her wedding to Uncle Doug. Aunty Ruby did not tell her father that she was pregnant again with my cousin Pearl (who was born in Casino in December 1952), but she did tell him that she was going to live with Aunty Midge and Uncle Doug while Sam got work at the sawmill in Woodenbong.[43] Later, after Billy fell very ill, Sam and Aunty Ruby left the country to go back to Sydney, but when they were living in a Housing Commission flat, things did not work out, and Aunty Ruby and the kids moved back to Great Buckingham Street in 1954.[44]

That year, Aunt Nell was very unwell in Toowoomba Hospital and not expected to live, so my grandfather Henry gave Aunty Ruby the bus fare to go and visit Aunt Nell and Uncle Sam. It was the first time Aunty Ruby had seen her sister (my mother) Rita in the five years since she had left home. Mum was still in high school. When Aunt Nell passed away, my grandfather Henry took my mum to live with him, Mum Joyce and the boys at Great Buckingham Street. Uncle Sam was devastated that not only had he lost his beloved wife Nell, he also lost his darling Rita. This was the beginning of Mum's life in the big city.

The move from the country to the big city dramatically changed my family's lives for the better. I feel compelled to repeat that Henry was 38 years old when he experienced job certainty for the first time in his life, and with that came a better standard of living and prosperity. Better yet, he was finally free from the slave masters, the Aborigines Protection/Welfare Board, and its oppressive control.

There can be no doubt that the greatest difference between Sam Anderson Jnr's happy and secure life and Henry Anderson's stress-filled life was the profoundly opposite degree of white Australian interference in their lives. The Australian Government, rather than providing Aboriginal people with the same kind of support that white Australian citizens enjoyed, created a structurally racist drip-feeding of funds for Aboriginal people. While the Aborigines Welfare Board broadcast that its assimilation policy was to disperse Aboriginal families into anonymity, what it actually did was create a system that perpetuated government control and surveillance, making it very difficult for Aboriginal people to be truly autonomous.

I firmly believe that the reason Sam lived as happily as he did was because of two factors that transpired side by side. Firstly, the townspeople of Bonalbo did not appear to be racist. The police constable reported that Uncle Sam was 'well respected' by the townspeople; they were not pushed out of town because they were blackfellas; their children were not segregated from the public school; and the timber mill workers did not stop Uncle Sam from working alongside them. The second reason I'm certain that Uncle Sam was much happier than his brother was because he severed the Board's links to him by living a self-sufficient lifestyle. He lived far away from any Aboriginal reserve and had a well-paying *permanent* job that provided security for his family in a town that accepted him—therefore he had no need of the government's rations, family endowment or an exemption certificate. Sam was successful without having to surrender his Indigeneity, discontinue his culture or disassociate from his beloved family.

All things considered, the government's Aborigines Protection Board and Aborigines Welfare Board were parasites in the true sense of the word. Each was an organism that lived off another organism, in this case another *race*, Aboriginal people being the hosts. The Aborigines Protection Board and, later, the Aborigines Welfare Board lived on the nutriment of controlling Aboriginal people. Publicly, the New South Wales Government and its Board trumpeted their assimilation agenda as a means of inclusion—an intention to bring Aboriginal people into Australian society once and for all—but it was strictly on their terms. That 'inclusion' was conditional on Aboriginal dislocation and separation from Country and kin—and systems were put in place to make sure that Aboriginal people were placed under the continued control and surveillance of the Board. These systems fed the parasite's life force, but Uncle Sam starved it of its nutriment. He completely negated the need for the Aborigines Protection Board and Aborigines Welfare Board to control his life. Uncle Sam was truly free.

8

Redfern was a powerhouse

'It was hard to find work [in Brisbane]. I read in the paper that there was a lot of work in Sydney so I came down, landed here in the morning and walked into a handbag factory by eleven o'clock.'

AUNTY EUPHEMIA ('PHEMIE') BOSTOCK

My grandfather Henry, like many other Aboriginal people, had finally turned his back on the government, and its oppressive control and surveillance, and migrated south to the inner-city suburbs of Sydney. There was an industrial boom occurring in Australia, and by the late 1940s, contrary to the popular rhetoric about Australia 'riding on the sheep's back', more Australians were working in industries than in farms or mines.[1] The factories needed a multitude of workers and didn't care about the colour of their skin, so Sydney attracted many Aboriginal people, who instantly found work.

By 1955, thanks to his steady job, my grandfather Henry Anderson had been living in Redfern at Great Buckingham Street for approximately five years with Mum Joyce, their two sons, Uncles Dennis and Kevin, and his daughter Aunty Gwen.

As already mentioned in the previous chapter, when Aunt Nell Anderson died in Toowoomba in 1954, Henry went there to collect my mother Rita and take her back to Sydney 'so she could get work'.[2] From the age of fifteen, she worked as a seamstress at various clothing factories (like the Effco Stubbies Factory), using the big, high-powered industrial sewing machines.[3] In her first book, Aunty Ruby described their early years in Redfern, and Aboriginal community life in general, as being very social.

The family used to go and watch the All Blacks football games, and on Friday and Saturday nights, 'everyone met at the picture theatre in Lawson Street'. In summer, the Aboriginal population of Redfern would sometimes hire buses on a Sunday to go to the national park to picnic and swim. This reminded me of the same community spirit that existed on the mission. Just like the fun-filled excursions Aboriginal people in the country went on to get away from the mission, Aboriginal people in the city organised big days out for the whole community too. Some nights, the All Blacks held dances and presentation balls in Redfern and Waterloo Town Hall.[4] My Aunty Gwen proudly remembers the night that she won the 'Belle of the Ball' title at one of the Aboriginal socials. Old photographs reveal that my mother Rita and my grandmother Evelyn were also present that night, and this surprised me.

I naturally assumed that the sisters had never associated with their mother as young adults, because they certainly did not do so in my lifetime. Aunty Ruby had a lot of forgiveness in her heart, and she reconciled with her mother after they moved to Redfern, and later she called Evelyn 'Mum'. Aunty Ruby also said that eventually Henry and Evelyn 'treated each other as friends and visited and ate meals together'.[5] My mother, however, always referred to her mother as 'Old Evelyn' and was very vocal about hating her. I told Dad I was surprised to see them at the same social event, and Dad said that my mother did actually try to reconcile with Evelyn for a while. He told me that Evelyn helped Dad and Mum find a flat after Henry died. Sadly, their reconciliation was short lived.

I only ever saw my grandmother Evelyn once in my entire life, when I was about seven or eight years old. Dad was driving us through Redfern in our old Holden Belmont and Mum was in the passenger seat. My three sisters and I were sitting on the red vinyl back seat. Suddenly, and violently, Dad swerved a hard right over to the wrong side of the road and pulled up tight against the gutter, parking in the opposite direction to the oncoming traffic. He told us to wind the windows down. My mother gasped out loud when she realised what he was doing and immediately turned her head to the left, looking away from Dad's side of the car. She was furious, and did not say a word.

Dad called out, 'Evelyn! Evelyn!', and with that an older Aboriginal woman came rushing over to our car. Dad said, 'These are your granddaughters'—and she burst into tears; she reached in through the car window and tried to touch each of our faces and squeeze our hands, all the while saying over and over, 'Oh babies! Oh my babies! Oh babies!' My mother refused to turn her head even to look at her. She just stared out the window in a white-hot rage, with every muscle in her body as hard as steel. As a child in the 1970s, I was bewildered, but as a mature-aged adult in the 2010s, I found myself blinking back the tears. By that time, I had learned that there was much more to the story of Henry and Evelyn, and I grieved at never having known my grandmother.

Sometimes old photographs can be the only tangible link with the past that family members have. My family Elders did not collect historical information from books, archives, government documents and files in the way that I have, so photographs were always treasured, coveted and jealously guarded. Photographs are our primary sources, and the telling of personal and emotional stories connected with photographs of ancestors perpetuate our oral histories. For that reason, photographic collections are also our personal archives, and when they are crosschecked or combined with other archives, they can build on what we know about the time and place that the image was taken. An innocent photograph of Mum sitting on a car in Redfern captured glimpses of the inner-city terraces of Redfern housing at that time. When my grandfather Henry and Mum Joyce lived in a one-bedroom flat in Great Buckingham Street, Aunty Gwen and Mum shared a space on the balcony that would have been like the closed-in balconies seen on the terraced houses in the photograph.

Former Aboriginal activist Professor Gary Foley said, 'One thing everybody there had in common was that we were all poor. Redfern was regarded by the rest of Sydney I suppose as the slums, and despite there being some fairly dodgy landlords, it was a place where Aboriginal people could actually get somewhere to stay.'[6] Uncle Lester said, 'There was cheap housing in Redfern and it was close to the railway station, and just a short walk into the main part of the city.'[7]

My grandparents Henry and Evelyn were bound to run into each other in Redfern. Henry worked at the Henderson's Federal Spring Factory at O'Riordan Street and would have had to walk right past Beaumont Street, where Evelyn lived with her second husband, Eddie Webb. Henry worked for

Henderson's for ten years. His job was near a furnace, where he would roll eyes in springs; cars would drive in to have their springs changed. In 1954, Henry had a heart attack and was in St Vincent's Hospital on his back for two months while the doctors dissolved a clot in his heart valve. He was very conscious that his boys were still very young and he had to provide for them. He could not afford to be out of work, so once he was out of hospital, Henderson's sent home a small machine with the metal for making small springs, and sometimes at night Henry would sit up and roll springs.[8] This was a conspicuously kind gesture towards an Aboriginal worker by a white Australian employer that needs to be acknowledged.

In 1956, Aunty Gwen married a shearer called Ronald Griffen, and she and Uncle Ronny moved back to country New South Wales. Aunty Ruby was also in country New South Wales, when she read a newspaper article in the *Northern Star* stating that their grandfather, my great-grandfather, Sam Anderson Snr, was found dead in a drovers shack.[9] In February 1960, a year after Sam Anderson Snr died, his son Henry Anderson also passed away. No record of my grandfather Henry's birth was ever found, but, in her book, Aunty Ruby wrote that he died at the age of 44. This was based on the information supplied by my mother Rita, who was nineteen years old when she was the official 'informant' on his death certificate.

Something didn't ring true here, so I went back to the early Box Ridge School archives; there I found a record that indicated Henry began school at Box Ridge Aborigines Reserve in 1916, when he was five years old. That makes his year of birth 1911. Doing the maths, I concluded that if Henry died in 1960 at the age of 44, then that would make his birth year 1916, the same year that he is listed as being a *five year old* at

Box Ridge Aborigines Only School. I asked my mother Rita why his age at death was recorded as 44 when he was actually 49, and she said: 'Oh, I didn't know how old he really was! I was only nineteen when he died. He always lied about his age and told me he was 44 every time I asked him! There was never any birth certificate, so when they asked me I just told them he was 44.'

Aunty Ruby took Henry Anderson's and Sam Anderson Snr's death certificates at face value too, but I have learned that it is only when you crosscheck sources (particularly BDMs) with other sources that you can get closer to the truth. When grandfather Henry died, my mother Rita was nearing twenty years old and living with Henry, Mum Joyce, Uncle Dennis and Uncle Kevin in a two-bedroom terrace in Phillip Street, Alexandria. Mum Joyce and the boys moved to Wilson Street, and my mother Rita moved in with her then boyfriend, my father, George Bostock.[10]

My parents never really seemed certain about when they got together. From my research, I know that Mum's father, Henry Anderson, grew up on Box Ridge Mission alongside Dad's mother, Edith (Cowan) Bostock, and that both sets of my grandparents were married a year apart at Box Ridge Mission. Dad grew up calling the Andersons 'Uncle Henry and Aunty Evelyn'—just the same as Mum grew up calling the Bostocks 'Uncle Norman and Aunty Edi'. The Andersons left the country for Sydney, and the Bostock family eventually ended up moving to Brisbane. I have a vague memory of Mum once saying that she and Uncle Sam Anderson visited Uncle Norman and Aunty Edi Bostock in Brisbane after Aunt Nell died. It was so strange to hear Mum address her father-in-law and mother-in-law as 'Uncle' and 'Aunty'.

Brisbane and the Boathouse

The Bostock family lived in a suburb of Brisbane called Moorooka, in a shanty town where the poor Indigenous and non-Indigenous lived, before the family moved to a Housing Commission house at Acacia Ridge. Dad was, by his own definition, 'a young knockabout'. He and his siblings went to the rock'n'roll dances at the Boathouse. Similar to the social functions in Redfern, the Boathouse dances were organised by Aboriginal people for Aboriginal people. The dances were also a focal point of significant social change in the lives of many Aboriginal people, driven by a new, fledgling independence.[11]

The O'Connor Boathouse was a two-storey Queenslander-style building situated on the northern bank of the Brisbane River. The lower level stored boats for the local rowing club and on the upper level was a large hall surrounded by a wide verandah that overlooked the river.[12] Every Saturday night from 1957 to 1962, Aboriginal community leader Charlie King and the Boathouse committee would organise dances for local and regional Aboriginal people. These dances raised funds for the first Aboriginal football team in Brisbane and for an Aboriginal women's vigoro team.[13]

Queensland was a conservative state, and I was shocked to learn that curfews were imposed on Aboriginal people to restrict their movement. In the lead up to the 1967 referendum, the enforcement of draconian laws started to relax, but Native Affairs [the Queensland equivalent of the New South Wales Aborigines Protection Board] still held sway in many Aboriginal lives and they had the power to implement drastic restrictions upon Aboriginal people.

The Brisbane River and a road called 'Boundary Street' marked out the boundary for the imposed curfew on

Aboriginal people. During the curfew, Aboriginal people were not allowed on the north side of the river unless specific permission was given. By the 1950s, the north side of the river was generally considered by Aboriginal people to be the domain of white society.[14]

Faye Gundy recalled being stopped by a man on a red scooter (one of a number of suspected 'Native Affairs spies') from crossing the Victoria Street bridge. She told the person, 'Get out of my road or I'll knock you off!'[15] Aunty Faye found out that the man had informed on her:

> We used to have to report to the Native Affairs Department every Thursday. On our day off we had to go there and report to them . . . I remember there was this one time . . . and they said 'You were seen walking across that bridge.' Big Brother was watching you. You know because the boundary they used to have at 'Boundary Street', we weren't allowed to cross that.

Uncle Charlie King had to use 'deft intelligence and political manoeuvring' to obtain access to the Boathouse for Aboriginal people. To organise an All Blacks football club and gain official approval to do so, Uncle Charlie had to meet with Ron McAuliffe, the secretary of both the Queensland Rugby League and the Brisbane Rugby League. McAuliffe was discouraging, advising Uncle Charlie to form a team under the name of 'Souths' or 'Wests', but Uncle Charlie was adamant that he wanted a team named the 'Brisbane All Blacks':

> We're not ashamed to call ourselves Blacks we'll stay with the name, Brisbane All Blacks. Brisbane All Blacks, ay. We're not ashamed if they call us 'abo', because 'abo' is Aboriginal.

We are the originals! Let them call us that, we will love it! We love it because when I say 'abo' I say, you, we are the originals. We are the original one . . . First here, where'd you come from, ay? Boat people, you the original boat people, you're still coming out in boats. Huh, yeah! They come from other countries.[16]

Uncle Charlie also had to meet with other officials. The commissioner of Native Affairs, Frank O'Leary, summoned Uncle Charlie to the Brisbane offices to investigate what he was trying to do. The authorities both at Native Affairs and the Police Department did not like the idea of a large gathering of Aboriginal people and imposed the presence of two policemen, ordering the dance committee to pay their wages.[17]

The Boathouse dances were built around the notion of respect. The evenings were multi-generational, with Elders and children watching the dancing. The music was a combination of a three-piece band playing old time music for the Elders and a record player hooked up to a sound system for rock'n'roll. The tempo would start off slow and would increase during the night, building up the excitement of the dance, and then it would slow down in preparation for the close of the dance so everyone could make the last tram or bus home. Strict social codes were in place, including no broken glass or drinking, and (a courteous rule that my father remembers) no woman was to be left seated during a dance. It was an ideal opportunity to meet other Aboriginal people and 'check out the opposite sex'.[18] Dad said that the young people were absolutely expected to follow the rules, so you would see young strong All Blacks football team members getting the old Aunties and little kids up to dance.

The Boathouse dances were respectable, wholesome community events with well-behaved young people getting together, 'establishing new relationships and falling in love'. But at other places around town, young adults like George Bostock used to get into all kinds of mischief with 'the lads', including 'punch-ups' with other suburban Brisbane groups. Dad was unusual in that he socialised with two communities. He had his Aboriginal mates on the Southside, but he also 'knocked about' with his white mates known as 'The Albion Boys'. Some of these mates began knocking about with petty criminals and he realised that he would probably end up in gaol one day if he didn't step away from that life.

So, Dad went to Sydney, and he and my mother, Rita Anderson, began dating, then living together after Henry died in 1960. Mum became pregnant in March 1961 and Dad joined the army in May of that year, leaving her in Sydney while he underwent his basic training at Kapooka. When he arrived at basic training, he was very surprised to see that his brother Gerry was also there doing basic training.

Military service

The brothers were both posted to the 1st Royal Australian Regiment (1RAR), which was based in Sydney. Rita Anderson and George Bostock were married at Ingleburn Army Camp and their first child, a daughter, was born in December 1961, followed by another daughter in 1963, and then twin girls in 1964. I am one of the twins. When we were babies, both Dad and Uncle Gerry volunteered to join the 4th Royal Australian Regiment (4RAR), which was based in Woodside, not far from Adelaide. They made the move because the word was out that 4RAR would be the next battalion to be posted overseas. My father knew that, in those days, soldiers could not get war service home loans unless they had completed war service on an overseas posting.

The 4RAR tour during the Indonesian Confrontation was its first tour overseas. The soldiers arrived at Terendak Garrison, on the west coast of Malaya, in September 1965, where they carried out military exercises before being deployed to Borneo in 1966. Whole 4RAR families were posted, too, so we lived at the garrison while the soldiers were deployed.

It was a small-scale operation[19] and the signing of a peace treaty between Malaysia and Indonesia ended the conflict. 4RAR returned to Terendak, and members began returning to Australia from August 1967.[20]

Upon returning to Australia, Dad was posted to Brisbane. Later, he and his brothers served in the Vietnam War. As a historian, I noted that his decision to leave his extended family and city life to join the army, for the betterment of the lives of his children, echoed the decision that his parents' generation made to leave the country and move to the city. Norman and Edith Bostock had three of their four sons in the Australian Defence Force at this time, and at one time all three were on active service overseas. (Their oldest son, Uncle Lester, had his leg amputated as a young man and therefore was never in the military.) Dad decided that he and his brothers should have a portrait photograph done of them, all in uniform, and gift it to their mother before they departed, just in case one of them did not come back.

It must have been a very difficult time for my grandmother Edith during her sons' tours of Vietnam. Thankfully, all her soldier sons returned home physically unharmed.

Sydney in the early days

In the early 1960s, the Bostock family, minus the married army sons George and Lindsay, moved to live in the inner-city Sydney suburb of Glebe. Aunty Phemie (pronounced 'Fee-mee', and short for Euphemia) Bostock said she moved from Brisbane to Sydney in 1962 because:

> In Brisbane in the 1960s the credit squeeze was on and it was hard to find work. I was living on a deserted wife's pension, which was nothing. I read in the paper that there was a lot of work in Sydney so I came down, landed here in the morning and walked into a handbag factory by eleven o'clock.[21]

When Uncle Lester Bostock moved to Sydney in 1962, he attended Tranby College. Tranby College was founded in 1952 as Tranby Aboriginal College, and later, in 1962, became known as The Co-Op for Aborigines Ltd. The college's fundamental principles of communal ownership and self-management and the philosophy of shared working and learning environments remain with the organisation today.[22]

Political organisations such as the Aboriginal Australian Fellowship and the Federal Council for the Advancement of Aboriginal and Torres Strait Islanders (FCAATSI) were the only organisations in the inner city for Aboriginal people at the time. After the 1967 referendum, there was a surge in political activism by people who wanted to make a difference for Aboriginal people.[23]

In George Street, near Central Station, was the Foundation of Aboriginal Affairs (FAA), which operated from 1963 to 1975. It was set up as an organisation to assist rural Aboriginal people who were migrating to the city.[24] The FAA played a recognised role in Sydney's Aboriginal community during the 1960s and early 1970s, and Charlie Perkins said that apart from meeting Aboriginal people coming in from the country and looking after their obvious needs of education, employment and housing, it also looked after the social needs of Aboriginal people:

> We used to run concerts there, and oh, they used to come in their hundreds from all over the place, every Friday, Saturday and Sunday night. Concerts and dances. And they were legendary, you know. And a lot of the blacks around Sydney and around NSW and around Australia have all been to the concerts. And they've met each other, got married there, and had kids and you know. They've set them up for life in that sense, and they all remember that. And so it was brand new in everything we did.[25]

Former Aboriginal activist Professor Gary Foley remembered that when he first arrived in Redfern in 1966–67, the White Australia Policy was still in force, and you could walk all over the city and never see a non-white face. He made an interesting comment that 'from a couple of thousand people, within three years you had an Aboriginal community that was in excess of 20,000 people. It was the biggest Aboriginal community that ever existed in over 60,000 years of the history of Australia'. Foley aptly described Redfern as 'an impoverished community of landless refugees'. Many Aboriginal people often met for the first time at the FAA. According to Foley:

> Charlie sought to try and prevent young Aboriginal people from getting caught up in police brutality, so he tried to create opportunities for them to get employment. A place where they could meet socially on Friday, Saturday and Sunday

nights, and be relatively free of police harassment. So many of us at about the age of sixteen would go to the foundation. It was a place to meet beautiful young Aboriginal women on a Friday and Saturday night. On Sunday night they had the talent quest where anybody who thought they could sing or dance or do anything could get up on stage, and it was a great community social organisation.[26]

A number of active committees were set up as the FAA became more established, including education, social welfare, health, fund raising, a women's auxiliary and a dancing group. After the landslide 1967 referendum, it was the dancing committee who held a large-scale debutante ball in the centre of town.[27] My cousin Pearl Anderson (Aunty Ruby's daughter) famously danced with Prime Minister John Gorton at the FAA Debutante Ball in July 1968. Pearlie wanted to go to the ball, but Aunty Ruby could not afford it, so she went to the Smith Family (charity) in Crown Street, Darlinghurst, and asked a welfare worker for a white ball gown. The size 18 dress was way too large for Pearl, so Ruby got her sewing machine out, took the dress apart and remade it to fit Pearl's petite size. Unfortunately, halfway through, Ruby was broke and had to pawn the sewing machine to feed her children. Typical of Aunty Ruby, she just rolled up her sleeves and continued making the dress, hand-sewing it until it was done, just in time for the ball. Aunty Ruby said, 'I did up Pearl's hair' and 'Charlie Perkins bought her a pair of white shoes and gave me a free ticket to the Ball'.[28]

This is a great example of the outstanding work that Charlie Perkins did for Aboriginal people at the FAA, but it wasn't all about granting Aboriginal people's wishes, like a black fairy-godfather. It was continuous, exhausting work fighting against structural racism, and there were a number of people who worked alongside him in supporting Aboriginal people. Prior to the ball, the foundation had been fighting a Sydney council ban on the use of halls for Aboriginal dances at Darling-hurst and Redfern. At the Parliamentary inquiry into the Aborigines Welfare Board in 1966, Perkins gave evidence cata-loguing the mundane and demoralising racial discrimination directed at urban Aboriginal people, and later reiterated that there certainly was 'racial discrimination' because the Sydney council had never spoken to (or banned) the Greek community or any other cultural group that used council halls.

The documentary *Dancing with the Prime Minister* was made for ABC Television and aired on 22 August 2010 on an Indig-enous television program called *Message Stick*. Charlie Perkins was interviewed and told the reporter that the idea was to 'stimulate a sense of pride and dignity' and help Aboriginal people 'become part of the community in a way that, you know, we think is acceptable and I think that they would think would be acceptable too'. Aunty Ruby said that:

> there were a lot of questions asked about whether Aboriginal girls should be making their deb balls which was, you know, coming out of the white man's culture. It was something to show everybody that we were as good as anybody else and that we could dress up and be nice and pretty too.[29]

John Gorton became prime minister seven months after the 1967 referendum; he and his American wife were consid-ered to be modern thinkers who embraced the civil rights era. A debutante by the name of Sue Bryant recalled that she thought Charlie Perkins said to the prime minister that he should 'put his money where his mouth is' and if he really wanted to support Aboriginal people then he should come to the ball because 'we want our young Debutantes to be presented to you'. Prime Minister Gorton explained that he did two or three debutante balls every year and when asked to attend this one, said he was delighted to come. He said nonchalantly, 'Is there a significance in it? Perhaps there's this—that I think it might be the first time that a Prime Minister has been to an Aborigine Debutante Ball. I don't know, but I think it might be.'[30]

Historian Anna Cole said that while it was publicised in government media and national papers as 'proof' of the 'success of assimilation', the memories of the women involved have disturbed this myth. The presence of the prime minister had little impact on them. The Aboriginal women simply saw it as a big night out:

The Debutantes' real freedom from the historical processes all around them was not to be resisting assimilation or fighting it that night, but just to be themselves—young, stylish, 'groovy' women having fun. The taxis would not stop for them at the end of the night because they were 'Aboriginal', which some of the Debutantes remembered 40 years on, or the police presence outside because of a large gathering of 'Aboriginals' in central Sydney, are part of the same story. But having a Ball, neither fighting nor 'resisting' but being proud of whom you are, dancing and enjoying a night out, was the greatest freedom of all in that moment. As the former Debutantes told me it was about being with a big group of people, dressing up, looking great, feeling proud, knowing about the taxis and the police presence but knowing that we are more than the sum of our oppressions.[31]

Aunty Ruby and my mother Rita 'Pearl' Anderson were named after their grandmother Mabel's identical twin sisters, Ruby and Pearl Yuke, and when Aunty Ruby had her first daughter, she named her Pearl, bringing the name down to my generation. A year after the debutante ball, in 1969, my cousin Pearl died tragically after being hit by a car. She was buried with our grandfather Henry Anderson. Pearl's older brother Bill also died tragically in a drowning accident in 1970, a year after Pearl's death. He was buried near the graves of his sister and our grandfather.[32]

Aunty Ruby had her name down for a Housing Commission home for nine years when, in 1972, she was finally allocated a house in Green Valley, in the western suburbs of Sydney.[33] The Housing Commission was established in 1941 to answer the growing need for housing in Sydney and throughout New South Wales, especially for ex-servicemen. On top of building new homes, a program of slum clearance and rehousing people from some of the older, more densely crowded parts of the city of Sydney was undertaken. New blocks of medium-density and high-density high-rise flats on old sites like Redfern housed some inner-city residents, while others were moved to new housing estates like Green Valley. The population of Green Valley grew from about 1000 in 1960 to over 20,000 by 1965. Poor, fatherless and young families were given priority, and later, Aboriginal families were added.[34]

The house Aunty Ruby moved into was the first Aboriginal house in the valley, and the people who lived there before her were the first Aboriginal family to arrive in Green Valley. When Aunty Ruby and my cousins came to Green Valley, there were still only three or four Aboriginal families in the whole of the valley. She said that putting Aboriginal families together with whites was part of the government's policy of integration, but because there were very few Aboriginal people there in 1972, she felt very isolated from her friends and our culture:

> All my neighbours were white, and there weren't many black kids in the school. I found out that you were not supposed to create a nuisance or disturb any of the neighbours. You also weren't allowed to have anyone come and stay without permission from the commission. It reminded me of the missions. The rule was useless in our culture, where survival depended on being able to stay with friends and relatives. Here I thought I'd got away from this, finally.[35]

It was the same old 'carrot and stick' plan that the Australian Government had implemented in country New South Wales. It seemed as though there was a deliberate intention to isolate and separate Aboriginal people from their extended families, communities and culture—but instead of the housing being in country towns, it was housing way out in the western suburbs of the city. In contrast, the FAA tried to unite the Aboriginal community and bring them together. Its focus was on achieving equality, and the social activities it conducted were a means to achieve social inclusion and acceptance. It saw the need to assist Aboriginal people in their transition from dependence to independence. As Aunty Ruby said, our survival often depended on Aboriginal people looking after each other.

But Charlie's good intentions and the effort made by the FAA could not distract young Aboriginal people from the reality of their lives on the streets of Redfern. The young Aboriginal adults who previously enjoyed the social get-togethers organised by the FAA became dissatisfied with what they saw as the foundation's conformity to the white Australian Government's assimilation agenda and seemingly ineffectual attempts to achieve equality for Aboriginal people. They began to organise themselves politically and became vocal Aboriginal rights activists. The *Tribune* newspaper, also known as *Tribune: The People's Paper*, was published by the Communist Party of Australia (CPA) and it supported the young radicals.[36]

In March 1972, the young Aboriginal activists advertised their demonstration in support of Aboriginal rights and asked workers, students and others to stop work to attend a rally and a march. A *Tribune* newspaper article provides insight into how radical the politics of the young Aboriginal activists had become. Far from being like other mainstream newspapers of the time, the *Tribune* published articles explicitly detailing the voice of the Aboriginal activists and the wording of this article has me thinking that it was written by the activists themselves:

> National Aborigines Day has been marked in the past by such events as the former Prime Minister Gorton receiving Aboriginal debutantes at a National Aborigines Day Ball in Sydney. Militant young Aborigines in Sydney have decided that the farcical and paternalistic way National Aborigines Day has been celebrated in the past should not occur this year.[37]

The way that the young activists regarded the 1968 debutante ball shines a spotlight on their separation from the FAA and the Aboriginal establishment. Naturally, as a historian reading these words, I wanted to know why they were so angry. Hadn't the FAA proved itself to be a reputable organisation with the best interests of Aboriginal people at heart? From what I learned about Charlie Perkins, and the FAA, I felt its members deserved to be placed on a pedestal. It was Charlie Perkins who gave my cousin shoes to attend the ball, and it was Charlie Perkins and the foundation who made sure my aunty had a ticket to the ball to witness her beautiful daughter's *Cinderella* moment. Why was our wonderful Aboriginal solidarity becoming divided at this time? Why were the young radicals so angry and what was happening that caused them to feel this way?

Coming up to this timeframe in the chronology of my research, and knowing that my uncles, Gerry and Lester Bostock, were fully immersed in Aboriginal activism in Redfern in the 1970s, I often wished that they were still alive so that I could ask them questions about that dynamic time in Aboriginal history. Several times during my research journey, a pivotal document or source has come to me in a miraculous way, or with incredible timing. When I came across a documentary film by Darlene Johnson and Sue Milliken called *The Redfern Story*, it arrived just at the time I needed it most. I believe my uncles heard my wish and sent me the perfect gift.

The film was so important to me that I bought the DVD and painstaking transcribed the entire dialogue to capture the *exact* quotes straight from the mouths of my beloved Uncle Gerry and Uncle Lester, as well as other people who were active participants in the 'revolution' at Redfern. They were an amazingly creative, artistic and politically motivated group who brought about incredible historic change for all Aboriginal people. The film answered my pressing questions: 'Why were the young radicals so angry, and what was happening that caused them to feel this way?'[38]

The extent of police violence and racism Aboriginal people experienced in Redfern in the 1970s was shocking, and the film began with a number of short comments from former Aboriginal activists. Aboriginal actor (and former activist) Bindi Williams explained that back in the 1970s there was no Aboriginal liaison or modern 'go-betweens' to turn to, and so if there was a crime down the street, and you happened to be a blackfella who was nearby, then you would immediately be blamed for it.[39] Professor Marcia Langton (a former Aboriginal activist) described 'the war between the police and Aboriginal people' as constant, adding, 'It was a crime to be black. It didn't matter what the charge was, the real charge was walking while black.'[40] My uncle Lester Bostock said bluntly, 'If you were black, you were a thief'.[41] Former activist Gary Foley made one of the most insightful comments: 'Police harassment had a significant role in politicising all of us. I've always said that the beginning of my political education was when I got a good kicking from a bunch of thug coppers at the Regent Street Police Station.'[42]

Police brutality against Aboriginal people was not just confined to Sydney. Dad told me the same thing happened in Brisbane:

> Aboriginal people in Brisbane had their own special pubs, the places that only blackfellas went to drink. Ordinary black-fellas drinking at the blackfella pubs got arrested. They weren't *goomies* either, they were just your regular blackfellas. Back in those days they had the black mariahs . . . they were like a police prison transport vehicle, but bigger than a paddy-wagon, and you could get about eight to ten people in the one truck. You know, six of them black mariahs would be lined up, waiting outside the blackfella pubs at closing time.[43]

'Goomies' was an Aboriginal nickname for chronic Aboriginal alcoholics. The point being made here is that it was not just the goomies who you would expect to be arrested—it was also the regular Aboriginal pub patrons who were not drunk, but just out socialising, who were locked up for no reason.

The young Aboriginal activists in Redfern realised that they needed to educate themselves and learn how other coloured communities around the world were responding to police brutality and racism. They looked at ways in which they might adopt and adapt some of the strategies used by the Black Panther Party for Self-Defense, an African American political group formed in Oakland, California, in 1966.[44] The police at that time were a law unto themselves, so one of the strategies that the Redfern group decided to use was to monitor the police, and record exactly what they were doing in the community. Then they started a local legal service, staffed with volunteer lawyers on a rostered basis, to help the victims of the rampant arrests and assist Aboriginal people to mount at least some kind of defence within the court system. Foley proudly stated that 'Redfern Aboriginal Legal Service was the first ever free shop-front Legal Aid Centre in Australia for anyone, and once we started creating our own organisations, the Legal Service was just the beginning'.[45]

The idea of Black Power in Australia, and also the Black Theatre in Redfern, came directly from the Black Power movement in the United States. In 1970, Aboriginal activist Bob Maza travelled with other Aboriginal people to a Black Power conference in Atlanta, Georgia, and from there went on to New York, where he visited the National Black Theatre in Harlem. Maza immediately saw the possibilities of a political black theatre in Sydney and came back from his trip all fired up. He and Aboriginal actor Jack Charles had already produced a Nindethana Theatre production called *Jack Charles is Up and Fighting*. Nindethana Theatre was Australia's first

Aboriginal theatre, founded in Melbourne in 1971. Foley said that seeing this play really opened his eyes to the possibilities of a black theatre: 'I was a young crazy political activist and never thought about theatre in my entire life.' Maza moved his family to Sydney and set up the National Black Theatre at Regent Street, which became a kind of hub for Aboriginal people. My uncles were founding members and Uncle Gerry said that:

> The Black Theatre was used as a gathering place for a talk-fest every week, people from other organisations like the Aboriginal Legal Service, the Aboriginal Medical Service, and the Aboriginal Housing Centre would meet at the Black Theatre to discuss ourselves. In the community it was known as 'The Black Caucus' and so we were able to unite with one another and support all the other organisations . . . So people who were on the Board of the Black Theatre were also on the Board of the Legal Service and the Medical Service and other services around.[46]

In *The Redfern Story*, Rachael Maza, daughter of Black Theatre founder Bob Maza, said, 'Mind you, theatre was basically a political tool, it was a way to get our stories on the street. It actually started with street theatre. It was very . . . kind of almost pantomime-esque . . . the masks, very heavy metaphors and representations.' Former Aboriginal activist Bronwyn Penrith explained that they wanted to use street theatre to raise awareness of the land rights struggle, but it was also about the incursion of the mining companies onto Aboriginal land and the disturbance of sacred sites.[47] Aboriginal people gravitated to the new Black Theatre because it was like a one-stop shop for information and services from all the Aboriginal organisations.

In 1972, the Australian Government, under Prime Minister William McMahon, saw mining as a 'national interest' and allowed unimpeded access to Aboriginal reserve lands. W.E.H. Stanner and Nugget Coombs (from the Council for Aboriginal Affairs) were supportive of the Yirrkala people's right to claim royalties from the bauxite mining occurring on their lands. They favoured leasehold ownership of land in all states and advocated for the provision of funds to buy land outside the reserves. They conducted an interdepartmental study and advised the federal government that there were political opportunities for change.

Prime Minister McMahon's Coalition rejected the report and, on 25 January 1972, the McMahon government announced that the Yirrkala people would receive only paltry royalties. A weak form of Aboriginal leasehold was available in the Northern Territory only, and traditional ownership was not to be regarded as a reason for renewed tenure. There was no reference to land acquisition outside 'traditional' areas, nor any compensation for dispossession.[48] Prime Minister McMahon was basically saying that his government would never grant Aboriginal land rights. Infuriated, the young radicals decided to set up a 'Land Rights' protest on the lawns of Parliament House in Canberra, with the initial intent of getting a photograph in the *Canberra Times* so that the world would know they rejected McMahon's statement.[49]

Less than two days after McMahon's announcement, four young men were sent to Canberra. Tony Coorey, Bertie Williams, Billy Craigie and Michael Anderson arrived at Parliament House and, in the early hours of 27 January 1972, they set up a beach umbrella and declared it the site of the Aboriginal Embassy. They boldly explained that McMahon's statement had relegated them to the status of aliens in their own country and they needed their own representation. This stunt captured the national imagination. A few weeks later, Opposition Leader Gough Whitlam visited the protesters and told them that if he was elected he would reverse McMahon's decision.[50]

In another newspaper article published in the *Tribune* on 30 May 1972, Aboriginal activist John Newfong responded to those who thought of the Tent Embassy as an eyesore by saying, 'They ought to go and see some of their own government settlements.' Newfong is described by the *Tribune* as an 'Aboriginal Embassy spokesman', and it was not until I read his comments that I fully appreciated the full extent of the New South Wales Government's embarrassment internationally. The dramatic embassy gesture received worldwide coverage in the media.

Regardless of the scrutiny of the international press, a decision was made on 20 July that saw 100 Canberra police officers forcibly remove the tents. This became a violent clash that was televised and resulted in eight Aboriginal people being arrested. Three days later, another violent clash was televised. Fanned by opponents, fear grew that the overall black–white relations would become more violent. However, with the benefit of hindsight, historian Jane Lydon explained why it was so effective:

> The 1972 Tent Embassy was a stroke of genius for several reasons. As a statement of alienation it was deeply embarrassing to the government in its failure to represent its Indigenous citizens. Second, as an 'eyesore' it effectively disrupted the smooth lawns and symmetrical vistas of Canberra's monumental landscape, peopling its empty spaces with a scruffy makeshift straggle of campers that precisely illustrated the

relationship between comfortable white Australia and the living conditions of most Aboriginal people.[51]

By creating a fringe camp at a site considered to be the symbolic heart of the nation, the embassy 'exploded at a blow all those familiar images of assimilation showing neatly marshalled houses filled with docile black families as proof of successful assimilation and management of the Indigenous population'.[52] 'Demands for freedom were no longer marginalised or quietly intellectualised; rather, they became the stuff of public theatre.'[53] Uncle Gerry, Uncle Lester and Aunty Phemie Bostock were present at the Tent Embassy demonstrations, and in *The Redfern Story* there is footage of my Aunty Phemie dancing in a street performance with other Aboriginal dancers from the Black Theatre. In Foley's opinion, these acts were all relatively harmless but effective, because it was a tremendous embarrassment for the McMahon government to be asked by foreign journalists: 'An embassy? An internal embassy? Is there an internal nation of people?'[54]

Another tremendous embarrassment to the Australian Government was the controversial journeys that Aboriginal activists embarked on in 1972 and 1974 to visit the People's Republic of China (PRC). The first visit in 1972 was led by Charles 'Chicka' Dixon and included Uncle Gerry Bostock, Ruby Hammond, Lynette Thompson, Lilla Watson, Cheryl Buchanan, Terry Widders, Peter Long and Ken Winder.[55] At the invitation of the Chinese government, the 1972 delegation went on an all-expenses-paid trip, with the intention of seeking 'China's support in forming an international lobby directed at shaming Australia to alter its policy toward Aborigines'.[56] The second delegation went to China in 1974 and included Gary

Foley as leader of a ten-member group who were guests of the Chinese Association of Friendship with Foreign People. The Australian Government was ignoring them, so their next move was 'to take the entire case of Aboriginal Land Rights into the international sphere and embarrass Australia that way'.[57]

In 1961, the Communist Party in the Soviet Union declared its support for 'all peoples who are fighting for the complete abolition of the colonial system' and, as a result, the CPA started to refer to Aboriginal Australians as a 'national minority' and began to attack the government's policy of assimilation. The director of the Australian Security Intelligence Organisation (ASIO) concluded that the 'CPA now regards the aborigines and their problems as an issue to be developed and used by the Party for political purposes, and for the furtherance of its own programme for the political power in Australia'. ASIO viewed Aboriginal dissent as associated with the international communist movement, which Foley described as 'a convenient way to ignore the legitimate claims of the Aborigines themselves'.[58]

Foley did not find out until 2002 that ASIO maintained extensive files on the Aboriginal Embassy and kept files on numerous Aboriginal organisations and people, himself included. ASIO's interest in the surveillance of the Aboriginal political movement provides a better understanding of what Foley calls 'ASIO's specific, obsessive preoccupation with possible communist infiltration, or manipulation of the Aboriginal rights movement from 1951 until the end of the cold war'.[59]

On the night of 21 January 2014, a documentary series called *Persons of Interest: ASIO's dirty war on dissent*, written and directed by Haydn Keenan, was screened on SBS. The documentary told the story of four different men who were targeted by ASIO between the 1950s and 1970s, and Foley was one of them. I made sure I watched the documentary because I wanted to know more about Aboriginal activism in Sydney in the years my uncles were there. In the documentary, Foley expressed gratitude to ASIO, saying, 'I'm able to piece together vast tracts of my life that had disappeared from my memory . . . some of the files are very good historical records . . . in certain ways ASIO has done us a bit of a service.'[60] This documentary series alerted me to the possibility of there being files on my family members as well.

While watching the documentary, I was absolutely stunned to see footage of my grandmother Edith Bostock. Knowing that these kinds of documentaries are often re-run the following day, I made sure I watched it again, with my notepad and pencil. I took down notes and recorded that the footage was of a 'March Against Racism' rally in 1971, and while the television camera scanned those present, Nan popped her head up, so the camera zoomed in on her for a close-up. In a later photograph, she is seen standing beside other marchers, and the photo showed that she and two other people were identified by red numbers handwritten onto the surveillance photograph. The narrator explained that the numbers indicated that there were ASIO surveillance files on these 'persons of interest'.[61]

I was shocked, but also intrigued, so I made inquiries at the National Archives of Australia. They informed me that they could not locate a file on my grandmother Edith Bostock; however, my two uncles, Lester and Gerry Bostock, like Gary Foley and other Aboriginal activists, had ASIO files.[62] Buzzing with excitement, I immediately ordered copies of their files. ASIO surveillance of my family members included the bugging of my grandmother's telephone, and also the bugging of both my uncles' telephones when they lived together in a house in an inner-city house in Sydney. The ASIO files diligently record the movements of my uncles, the people they associated with, and the political meetings and social events they attended. From the transcriptions of conversations in the ASIO files, it was clear the Aboriginal activists sometimes knew they were being recorded and they often joked about it.

I couldn't help but smile with pride as I read that Uncle Gerry and his friends were like cats tormenting mice. They played games with ASIO, joking about being bugged and deliberately not using names when speaking about others. One transcript details Uncle Gerry saying, 'And which one was that on the phone? Was that the one with the Italian husband?'[63] After one conversation, a frustrated ASIO agent wrote, 'It's impossible to work out whether the above conversation was serious or not, as their conversation was conducted in a very light-hearted manner.'[64]

I knew my uncles were activists in the 1970s, but it was not until I read their ASIO files that I fully understood how deeply they were immersed in working for organisations involved in the advancement of Aboriginal people. Uncle Gerry articulated his political convictions predominately through the arts, while Uncle Lester chose the more hands-on path of working tirelessly for a large number of organisations that supported Aboriginal advancement.

The ASIO file on Uncle Gerry had a group photograph taken from a Western Australian newspaper. There was also another surveillance photograph taken at Mascot (Sydney's International Airport), and these photographs were of the first Aboriginal delegation's departure for China on 22 October 1972. Seeing Uncle Gerry's ASIO file for the first time, I was blown away by the photographs that were taken by an undercover agent using a concealed camera in a briefcase. It felt so surreal, like something out of a James Bond film.

These files enable me to piece together important aspects of my uncles' lives. The files are also a record of the government's fear of Aboriginal people being influenced by communism. These records show the surveillance of Aboriginal activists was like a version of post-war American McCarthyism, fortunately without the witch hunts and testimonies before a House Committee on Un-Australian Activities.[65] For the Aboriginal activists, the China visits were more about learning how China treated its minorities, than communism. The activists certainly wanted to highlight the plight of Aboriginal people to the world, but they mainly wanted to increase awareness in Australia.

Uncle Lester's ASIO file begins in 1964 with a secret ASIO list of people on the boards of the Aborigines Progressive Association (APA) in Sydney and the Aboriginal Advancement Leagues in Newcastle, Nowra, the South Coast and Blacktown. Interestingly, the APA Board list included the names of three of my family members. The document states that the APA was 'formed on initiative of: Ruby Langford, Charles Perkins and Raymond Peckham'. The president was Herbert Groves, the secretary was Isabelle McCallum, and the treasurer was Lester Bostock. There was also four vice presidents: Ray Peckham, Joyce Mercy, Clive Williams and my grandmother Edith Bostock.[66]

In her book, Aunty Ruby mentioned that Isabelle McCallum was the daughter of the founder of the original APA, Bill Ferguson. The APA elected Charles Perkins as a spokesman and Aunty Ruby became the editor of their newspaper, *Churringa*, which means 'message stick'. Although she attended meetings, including an important meeting of the APA at Martin Place on National Aborigines Day (in the presence of the governor-general and other dignitaries), her time with the APA was short-lived. She said her de facto husband was unhappy about looking after her children, 'so I had to give up my political work before I'd edited the first issue of *Churringa*'.[67] Uncle Lester, however, continued his political work as treasurer of the APA in Sydney, and his ASIO file reveals more about his political interests.

In August 1964, Uncle Lester Bostock's name was on an ASIO list of 'National Sponsors' of the Australian Congress for International Co-operation and Disarmament.[68] The file also contained a translation of a *Pravda* newspaper article titled 'The Fifth Continent says "No!" to War'. *Pravda* was the official newspaper of the Communist Party of the Soviet Union at the time. Lester Bostock was named as 'the aboriginal representative' and cited as stressing that 'the ideas of peace, race equality and social justice are penetrating more and more deeply into the ranks of the aboriginals. We are marching side by side with all progressive Australians'.[69] On the next page of his ASIO file was the photocopy of an article from the *Bulletin* magazine (26 December 1964) which mentioned Uncle Lester's trip to attend a Christian Youth Council in Manila. On the same page there was a trade unions section with an article called, 'New Men and New Ideas'. This article states that 'probably the most significant feature in Australian Trade Union affairs for 1964 was also the least reported, a growing social consciousness. The major efforts in this direction centred on Australian Aborigines.'[70]

In Brisbane, the Australian Workers' Union (AWU) applied for equal wages for Aboriginal workers in Queensland who were working under awards, which would affect Aboriginal workers in other states working under AWU awards. The general secretary of the AWU, Mr T. Dougherty, applied for a new federal pastoral award that would give Aboriginal workers the same wages, rights and privileges as white workers covered by the same award. Dougherty told the court:

> We are deliberately setting out to prove the rights of the people, irrespective of who they are, to receive the award rates and conditions . . . It is the right of Aborigines to be employed under the same wages as their fellow Australians, whatever their colour and nationality.[71]

The CPA is frequently mentioned in Uncle Lester's ASIO file, but I cannot see any evidence to support the possibility that he was a card-carrying member. Both the CPA and the trade unions supported Aboriginal activists not just politically but also in practical ways. A document in his ASIO file reveals that Uncle Lester's phone call to Noel Hazard, the photographer at the *Tribune*, was recorded and transcribed. Uncle Lester asked Hazard to take photographs for an upcoming 'State Aboriginal Conference'. Hazard also agreed to develop photographic film that had already been taken by conference organisers.[72] Interestingly, on the night of 26 January 1972, it was Noel Hazard who drove the four Aboriginal activists to Canberra to establish the legendary Tent Embassy. Foley described Hazard as 'a close friend of many activists at the time'.[73]

Foley also added that Aboriginal people 'didn't judge their white friends on whether they were Communists or not, but rather on the quality of their personal character'. Their relationships with them were based on mutual respect, and there was never any question of them (communist or otherwise) trying to manipulate the Aboriginal activists. Tabloids inspired the idea that the people involved in the Black Power movement were racists who hated white people, and ASIO bought into this nonsense. Foley concluded that 'the lunacy of their logic was that, despite thinking we were black racists, they still believed that we were taking orders from white communists'.[74]

The most interesting document that I found in Uncle Lester's ASIO file is a letter dated 19 January 1965. The letter is written on the letterhead of the Australian Embassy Moscow by Australian attaché D. Wallace to the secretary of the Department of External Affairs, Canberra, and is a translation of a lengthy article by Canberra *Pravda* correspondent Yuri Yasnev, published in *Za Rubezhom* (a weekly review of foreign press published by the Union of Journalists of the USSR).

In a general discussion of everyday Australian economics and politics, Yasnev also wrote about the peace forum, surmising that the reason for its success was that the trade unions in Australia played an active role in the struggle for peace. He stated, 'here the slogan, "Peace is the affair of the Trade Unions" is not just an empty slogan but meets with material support'. Yasnev added that the movement of peace workers was coming more and more to include Aboriginal people, describing them as 'the original inhabitants of the Fifth Continent who are given unequal rights both politically and socially, who live as outcasts: these people instinctively find themselves drawn to the peace forum, the most progressive section of the Australian people'.

Yasnev wrote that when he caught sight of an Aboriginal man called Lester Bostock on crutches, he immediately thought that he must have been injured in the Second World War. What Yasnev wrote next had me staring at the page for several moments in a state of open-mouthed shock . . . before I burst out laughing. He wrote:

It turned out that Bostock had lost his leg in another war—the war for a dry crust of bread. For a long time his only weapon for the struggle for existence was pearl hunting. Together in the Torres Strait with other aborigine youths he had to dive to a great depth to seek out the valuable shellfish. The manager of the boat paid comparatively good wages, but it was dangerous work and many were frightened away from it. The divers sought out the pearl but sharks hunted them. More than one of them perished in the jaws of these monsters. Bostock did not escape unscathed.[75]

Dad shared with me how Uncle Lester took great delight in telling him funny stories about his encounters with people who believed his made-up stories about how he lost his leg. He had never been a pearl diver, or anywhere near the Torres Strait. Uncle Lester had an injury (Dad said he thought it was from playing football) that did not heal properly and a terrible infection set in. That is why he lost his leg. But it was this intrepid story, of the courageous survival of an oppressed Aboriginal man, who dived in shark-infested waters for a 'dry crust of bread', that was published by journalists in the USSR's communist newspaper during the Cold War!

My family members and their peers were not communists, they were just Aboriginal people who experienced prejudice, oppression and racism, and decided to come together in solidarity to fight for equality. In Redfern, various groups of Aboriginal people used different strategies for the same goal. Whether it was through showing non-Indigenous Australians that Aboriginal people were 'just as good as they were', or through angry public protests to demand land rights and equality, or through creative expression and satire, there was one common denominator—and that was that non-Indigenous Australians could no longer ignore Aboriginal people or pretend they didn't exist. Aboriginal people had come out of the shadows and into the public arena to make their presence known.

9

Embracing the arts

'We believed that we could change the world . . . and we did.'

GARY FOLEY, *THE REDFERN STORY*

Although untrained, the young Aboriginal activists in Redfern passionately embraced the arts and creative expression, and their theatre productions were well received by the wider Australian community. The Black Theatre in Redfern was more about presenting to the audience all kinds of things that were happening to Aboriginal people. Bob Maza wanted to attack preconceived ideas that non-Indigenous people had about Aboriginal people. He saw regular theatre as exclusive and elitist and wanted to bring theatre to the grass roots. He enlisted Gary Foley as a member of the cast of *Basically Black*, a revue with a series of skits and parodies. The Aboriginal activists realised that public speeches were received with hostility by the wider white Australian community, but through satire and ridicule on stage, they were able to get their message to white Australians. *Basically Black* played to packed houses and good reviews.[1]

It was an exciting time for the theatrical activists, because *Basically Black* was picked up by ABC TV and was given a pilot series. It was a great forum for humour, but it only had a short run. Bob Maza's daughter Lisa Maza thought 'people weren't ready for that kind of in your face, satirical, hard-core kind of stuff from blackfellas'.[2]

A wonderful example of this humour was an endearing character that Gary Foley wrote exclusively for Zac Martin called 'Super Boong'. Imitating early Superman comics and television shows, the 'Super Boong' segment was preceded by an excited narrator reporting:

Look up in the sky, is it a bat, is it a crow, is it the flying doctor??? No . . . it's SUPER BOONG! Strange visitor from a northern tribe, who came to the city possessing powers far beyond those of mortal Kooris. Faster than a killer boomerang . . . and able to leap over tall gum trees in a single bound! SUPER BOONG uses his secret identity as a mild mannered Aboriginal ex-boxing champion, Lionel Mouse, to fight a never-ending battle against racism wherever it may be found!!!

[*Lionel Mouse in a suit approaches two Aborigines outside a pub*] 'Hi guys, seen any racism around?'

[*They answer*] 'Not today, Bud.'

[*A short distance away a fight breaks out*]

[Lionel Mouse] 'Looks like someone's in need of help from an artful Abbo! I think I'll race into the toilet of this hotel and change.'

[Super Boong] 'What's up, Bud?'

[Aboriginal Man] 'They don't allow Blacks in that Pub!'

[*Super Boong rushes in to save the day*][3]

Aboriginal actor Ernie Dingo, like me, remembers Super Boong as an endearing character:

> Yeah, Super Boong was just a deadly character, man. Somebody calls you a name and as soon as you go to think about it, Super Boong appears on the scene, 'Step aside, son, I'll fix this for you!' and then you'd watch Super Boong tell these people that their racist actions, well there's no place for it . . . and have a good laugh about it, and teach whitefellas that you don't mess with blackfellas, because we've got Super Boong on our side.[4]

The Black Theatre moved to a new residence at Cope Street, Redfern, just around the corner from the original Black Theatre at Regent Street. Uncle Gerry said that the building was originally owned by the Uniting Church and was handed over to the Aboriginal people of Redfern, making it 'the first land settlement that Aborigines had'.[5] I remember going there as a child of nine or ten years old with my sister to do karate classes and attend the dance classes organised by Carole Johnson, an African-American woman who came to Australia in 1972. Johnson worked with Indigenous Australians for 35 years and taught Australians how to 'discover the richness of Indigenous dance'. She was a founding director of the National Aboriginal and Islander Skills Development Association and established the Bangarra Dance Theatre Australia Company.[6]

When Uncle Lester Bostock went to the Australian Arts Council to try to get funding for the theatre, the Arts Council agreed on the condition that they have white directors come in and do the directing and the producing. Uncle Lester refused. He was adamantly against that and said, 'We needed to do everything from top to bottom, otherwise it could not be called a Black Theatre.'[7] Around that time, and after sixteen months of lobbying, the Black Theatre received minimal government funding (of $9200) from the Department of Aboriginal Affairs. In June 1975, the theatre received a grant of $86,000. Indigenous former blues singer Bettie Fisher became the administrator of the newly established Black Theatre Arts and Cultural Centre, and used the money to renovate the old warehouse and develop a theatre and studio area.[8]

The first full-length Aboriginal play to be performed at the Black Theatre in Redfern was *The Cake Man* by Aboriginal writer Robert Merritt in 1975, and it received positive reviews. The story is about a family—Ruby, Sweet William and their child Pumpkin Head—as they struggle to survive.[9] It was a milestone for Aboriginal people because it was written, directed, produced and initiated by Aboriginal people. Bob Merritt wrote the play from his prison cell as part of his prison workshop, and Bob Maza rushed back and forth from the prison to collect script pages.

In 1976, a season of 'Black Plays by Black Artists' was planned, with works by Uncle Gerry Bostock and others. However, after the manager of the Black Theatre, Bettie Fisher, died in May 1976, the theatre lost its funding. Tension grew between the Aboriginal Arts Board and the management of the Black Theatre. The board accused the theatre of 'being irresponsible and/or perhaps acting illegally within the terms of their own article'. The board was critical of Uncle Lester Bostock's appointment as Fisher's replacement, and the Black Theatre's application for funding of $76,000 for the 1976/77 financial year was unsuccessful.

In an interview with Maryrose Casey, the author of *Creating Frames: Contemporary Indigenous theatre 1967–1990*, Marcia Langton said that there was a clash of agendas between some Indigenous arts bureaucrats and the Black Theatre's management. Langton believed the difficulties faced by the Black Theatre were in many ways a 'last gasp of assimilation' because its work challenged the accepted expectations of Aboriginal people:

> We were a serious theatre and we weren't taken seriously, certainly not by Aboriginal bureaucrats ... there was never a misappropriation of funds but the bureaucrats were terrified of expressions of Aboriginal life. Their job, whether they recognised it or not, was to convince their 'white masters' that Aborigines were assimilating and living useful lives, in three bedroom brick veneer homes ... [This was compounded by] the Anglo hang-up about theatre. It infected them as much as it did anyone else ... [an underlying message was] that a 'good Aborigine' was one who played soccer or football. It was a psychological war-zone.[10]

In a newspaper article, Uncle Gerry Bostock was quoted as saying, 'If white Australia has ignored the fact that urban blacks have a culture, the more respectable Aboriginal cultural organisations don't seem too interested or excited about the idea either.'[11] The Black Theatre was completely dependent on government grants and the loss of funding was a crisis. Uncle Lester Bostock and members of the company met with church groups and arts organisations and established a committee to raise funds for the theatre. They focused their limited resources on producing his brother Gerry's play *Here Comes the Nigger*.[12]

Here Comes the Nigger

Uncle Gerry's play deals with racism and sexism in Australia. He said, 'If you scratch a sexist you'll find a racist and vice versa.' The play was about a blind Aboriginal man named Sam who was tutored by a white Australian woman called Odette. It explores the racist attitudes of both the white Australian and the Aboriginal sides when other characters wrongly assume there is a sexual relationship between the two young people. In the play, Sam's brother, Billy, and his partner, Verna, are militant Aboriginal activists, and they accuse Sam of selling out his people. Odette's brother, Neil, a Vietnam veteran, is a self-proclaimed racist and horrified that she is having a relationship with an Aboriginal man. Neil and his army mates set out to teach Sam a lesson, and the play ends tragically when Sam is beaten to death.

Uncle Gerry's play was quite different to the early 1970s work of early Aboriginal playwrights like Kevin Gilbert, Jack Davis and Harry Williams, in that their works were about Aboriginal fringe dwellers, and did not impinge upon the mainstream themes of plays by the broader theatre community. Kevin Gilbert's iconic play *The Cherry Pickers* focused on the experiences of itinerant Aboriginal rural workers, and Robert Merritt's *The Cake Man* focused on Aboriginal mission life— but Gerry Bostock's play was the first to offer a place for urban Aboriginal voices in the heart of the city.[13]

Marcia Langton played the role of Verna in *Here Comes the Nigger* and in 2014, she spoke about her memories of the play:

So what the play *Here Comes the Nigger* by Gerry Bostock did was take the heart of racism and serve it up to the audience in a way that they had never seen it or thought about it before.

269

And even the title . . . *Here Comes the Nigger!* Shocking! The play was shocking! That's why it was so exciting.[14]

In mid-1975, non-Indigenous Australian actor Bryan Brown was performing in a play at Sydney's Nimrod theatre when he was approached by Bob Maza, who offered him a part in a new play at the Black Theatre.[15] Brown described *Here Comes the Nigger* as 'a raw, gutsy drama, and I played the role of a Vietnam vet [Neil] who doesn't like the idea of his sister being involved with a black man'.[16] The play generated a lot of excitement in the Redfern community. Uncle Gerry noted that the support of the Aboriginal community even extended to the goomies, who immediately recognised what these young people were trying to achieve:

> When we started putting on the performances, the goomies, the Aboriginal local alcoholics, would bypass the theatre, they would skirt right around it, because they didn't want to give the white audience any bad vibes about the theatre—because they wanted them [he pauses] . . . there was a pride in the community about people giving their bit to the Black Theatre performance.[17]

Marcia Langton worked during the day at the Aboriginal Medical Service and would go from there to rehearsals at the Black Theatre:

> I was a nurse or a receptionist or something, you know, so I was like the barrel girl, I would walk on and say, 'Frank's here', you know, or 'There's somebody to see you', . . . so I had a very small role, but it was so tremendously exciting.

Bryan Brown laughed as he explained how his role in the play made him nervous about being a whitefella in Redfern at that time:

> Of course, doing *Here Comes the Nigger*, where, you know, in that play I get to kick the shit out of Kevin Smith, you know the terrific Aboriginal actor, who's since passed away . . . but you know, I beat the shit out of him, and it was a bit scary me wandering around Redfern after that . . . a lot of the time people can't get the difference between what goes on stage and what doesn't, you know.[18]

An Aboriginal audience member, an elderly lady who had never seen a play before, got out of her seat during his performance (when he was acting as a white racist) and started hitting him with her umbrella. Marcia Langton said that they had to stop the performance, calm everyone down, and explain that they were just acting.

As the CEO of the Black Theatre, Lester Bostock's role was to find funding for the theatre. So, he went to the local bank manager at Redfern and the bank gave them an overdraft.[19] Bryan Brown said:

> At that time in Redfern, police arrests of Aboriginal people were so frequent that the theatre staff and actors were forced to be prepared for the more than likely event that someone would be locked up by the police. There had to be someone available to run up to the police station and bail them out, otherwise the show could not go on.[20]

Bryan Brown explained how tight the money was and how the play ran on a week-by-week basis:

come Friday we would never know if we were going to get paid, and we knew that Lester was down there, late afternoon Friday, talking to the local bank manager to convince him to give the money to pay the cheques, because next week there was crowds coming to the play! Each Friday we'd go, 'Well, are we on next week or not?' and he'd pay out the money and he'd say, 'Yep! We're on for another week!'[21]

At a certain point, Marcia Langton realised that the work they were doing was ground-breaking—when they saw the impact the play had on the white audience and how very powerful that impact was.[22] Bryan Brown added:

It had no hype, it had no money for marketing, it wasn't in the mainstream theatre there of Sydney . . . the only way it could get recognised or known was to have its door open and to have a play on—and people to discover it.[23]

By 1977, there had been no grants for a year and the Black Theatre was in serious financial difficulty. It continued to operate for the community even after the phones and electricity were disconnected, but it could not continue without money for rent. People became burnt out from having to try and find money for the theatre while also trying to make their own living.

According to the late Aboriginal actor Kevin Smith, the Black Theatre in Redfern 'inspired confidence among the community'.[24] Another Aboriginal actor, Bindi Williams, added that 'Just seeing someone like yourself can change you, and you begin to think, Yes, I can do that! If they can do it, I can do it! If she can do it, we can do it!'[25]

At the end of *The Redfern Story*, Gary Foley makes a comment that at first I perceived to be somewhat vain, but later, upon reflection, I recognised was true. 'We believed that we could change the world . . . and we did, we changed the world around us, we changed the way in which the world around us related to us, we changed the shape of Australian society.'[26]

Lousy Little Sixpence

Progress for Aboriginal people in Sydney did not end with the demise of the Black Theatre in 1977. Uncle Lester continued to be passionate about the arts. He helped form Radio Redfern (now Koori Radio) in the early 1980s and was the first Aboriginal presenter on SBS radio. Later, he joined SBS Television and was part of the first Aboriginal program, teaming up with Rhoda Roberts, another Bundjalung woman.[27] He then took some time off from SBS to help make the ground-breaking documentary film *Lousy Little Sixpence* with Uncle Gerry and Alec Morgan, who was the film's director. Uncle Lester said:

> I was one of the producers on that. Because we had a bit of knowledge, we'd be working on those programs. So, those types of things came about not because one had a desire to pursue some sort of career, but one reacted to what the situation was at the time.[28]

Lousy Little Sixpence is based on interviews with five elderly Aboriginal people, some of whom I've mentioned: Margaret Tucker, Bill Reid, Geraldine Briggs, Flo Caldwell and Violet Shaw, who were part of what we now call the Stolen Generations. They were my grandmother's generation, and, as discussed earlier, they talk about how the Aborigines

273

Protection Board created a servant class on Aborigines reserves, with little regard for human rights. Uncle Gerry and Alec Morgan wisely decided that the stories that the old people were telling had to be backed up with archival evidence, and so they found photographs, newspaper articles and newsreel footage, most of which had never been seen by the general public.[29]

They travelled through Victoria and New South Wales, with the film taking three years to research and produce. Their research was not funded, so they lived off unemployment benefits and slept in a caravan. They had some small investors from a variety of sources, such as the Australian Film Commission and the Nurses Union, but they needed $10,000 to finish the film. At that time, Bob Hawke was the newly elected prime minister, so Uncle Gerry Bostock, Alec Morgan and Chicka Dixon set up a meeting with the new Minister for Aboriginal Affairs, Clive Holding. Uncle Lester Bostock remembered, 'The Labor Party needed to show they were on side with Aboriginal people. We were euphoric when we got the money and Clive Holding took us out to dinner.'[30] With this support, they were able to finalise the film.

Alec Morgan described the film as 'a phenomenon' when it opened in 1983, but after six weeks at the Dendy Theatre in Martin Place, there was trouble. 'It was the same time as Henry Reynolds' book *The Other Side of the Frontier* was released, and there was a hunger in the wider community to learn more about Aboriginal people, as nothing was out there.' Mainstream white Australian society was ready to accept this raw kind of Australian history, but Uncle Gerry said that even though they backed up the Elders' stories with archives, 'we were accused of fabricating the evidence'.

The ABC was not interested in screening the film, so, like our earlier freedom fighters, they got a petition together. Aboriginal politician Linda Burney was then the head of the Aboriginal Education Consultative Group. She supported the film and it was used in schools. Morgan explained that back then there was no terminology or words used to describe what we now know as the Stolen Generations, so the film was very significant in bringing this whole issue to public attention. *Lousy Little Sixpence* was a forerunner for 'an explosion of Aboriginal life-writing, fiction, poetry, film, drama and music'. But it took another 25 years for the Prime Minister of Australia to apologise to the Stolen Generations.

While Uncle Gerry and Uncle Lester had been successful in the film industry, they noticed, however, that there were very few Indigenous people working in film. Uncle Lester said:

> I was producing. My brother Gerry was directing. You could count them all on one hand, the number of [Indigenous] film and television makers around at that time in 1990. And that's not too long ago. And the only way we're gonna get Aboriginal crew is train them ourselves. So I went and saw some film-maker friends of mine, and I ran into Tom Jefferies, who was then head of the film school. About 30 Aboriginal people came out of those two courses.[31]

Uncle Lester wrote policies and protocols on filming in Aboriginal communities and for Indigenous employment in the industry. In the 1990s, Uncle Lester ran accelerated workshops in television at the Australian Film Television and Radio School (AFTRS). His work paved the way for the formation of the AFTRS Indigenous Unit. Uncle Lester has received numerous awards for community service over the years, including a Centenary Medal, the NSW Law and Justice Foundation Award for Aboriginal Justice and, in 2010, he was NAIDOC's Male Elder of the Year. AFTRS Chair Julianne Schultz said Uncle Lester's training programs were instrumental in increasing production of Indigenous drama among emerging filmmakers, and he has contributed greatly to the talented pool of Indigenous filmmakers we have today.[32] AFTRS graduates trained by Uncle Lester and Uncle Gerry include Aboriginal actor and director Wayne Blair, who directed the drama series *Redfern Now*, and Nakkiah Lui, actor, director and producer of the *Black Comedy* series.

Aboriginal literature

The literature of the 1970s was inspired by the drive for more political and territorial self-determination, which demonstrated 'a fusion of political and creative energies'. Aboriginal social and political life delivered new forms of agency, and new types of authorship were explored and invented. The *Macquarie PEN Anthology of Aboriginal Literature* described Aboriginal writers like Kath Walker, Jack Davis, Kevin Gilbert, Gerry Bostock, Monica Clare and Lionel Fogarty (who were all politically active while simultaneously writing their own creative literature) as 'catalysing a nascent Aboriginal publishing industry' and writing their own vanguard pieces of creative literature.[33] Just as Bindi Williams explained when he said, 'If they can do it, I can do it', it was these creative and literary Aboriginal activists who truly inspired other Aboriginal people to tell their own stories, because they gave their people the confidence to do what they had done.

Pioneering Aboriginal dramatists, filmmakers, musicians and writers like my Uncle Gerry gave aspiring Aboriginal people permission to show their lives to the world; after two centuries of oppression, racism, subordination and white control, Aboriginal people were just beginning to believe in themselves and their own capabilities again.

Aunty Ruby Langford Ginibi started writing her first book, *Don't Take Your Love to Town*, in 1984. She described it as 'a true story of an Aboriginal woman's struggle to raise a family of nine children in a society divided between black and white cultures in Australia'.[34] *Don't Take Your Love to Town* was published in 1988 and Aunty Ruby went on to write another four books: *Real Deadly* (1992), *My Bundjalung People* (1994), *Haunted by the Past* (1999) and *All My Mob* (2007).

In a 1999 interview with ABC Radio National, Aunty Ruby said that she was always going to write a book because (at that time) 'there was nothing taught in this country about Aboriginal history'. She thought that if she could tell people what it was like from the Aboriginal perspective, 'then maybe they'd understand us a little better'.[35] Ruby Langford Ginibi was one of a large number of Indigenous female writers who published in the late 1980s and 1990s. American academic Belinda Wheeler claims that the first time the wider Australian public showed genuine interest in Australian Aboriginal people, their culture and their literature was, arguably, in the lead up to the bicentennial celebrations in 1988.[36]

Dad's story

My father, George Bostock, always laughed and joked (in front of his chuckling brothers and family) that he was 'sick and bloody tired' of how every time he introduced himself to blackfellas, they always asked him, 'Are you related to Lester and Gerry Bostock?' Well, he may have been a 'late bloomer', but eventually, and unintentionally, he began to make his mark creatively. In fact, he always said that his life began at 60, because the strange and wonderful direction his life took was rejuvenating.

Dad's play *Seems Like Yesterday* was staged by Kooemba Jdarra Indigenous Performing Arts Company in 2001. It was about a young Indigenous soldier who goes on active service to fight in the Vietnam War. The poster tagline read, 'In Vietnam there were no blackfellas or whitefellas, we were all tarred with the same brush, our colour was green'. When Dad met Kooemba Jdarra's Indigenous artistic director, Nadine MacDonald, he gave her a copy of his play, and she suggested to him that he should audition for a role in Aboriginal director Wesley Enoch's upcoming play for the Queensland Theatre Company (QTC). The character called Henry was an Aboriginal Elder, and Dad said:

> At 60 years of age with a nice grey beard she [Nadine] said I was ideal for the part, but I had my doubts. I knew I had the good looks, but I had no acting experience. Now the QTC is the biggest company in the state so you can imagine my surprise when I got the part. I was now a Playwright/Actor and it sounded good.[37]

Aboriginal playwright George Landen's *Fountains Beyond* was about a group of Aboriginal people living as fringe dwellers next to a country town. When the play was first performed in 1942, there were no Aboriginal actors, and so the white Australian cast members blackened their faces to play the Aboriginal roles. The QTC's production had an all-Aboriginal cast, so they put on white face paint to play the role of the

Europeans. Dad loved that as the performance neared the end, the white paint was wearing off and only the black faces were left to be seen on stage.

Dad thought he must have impressed someone in the business because it was not long after that production that he got a phone call from the Sydney Theatre Company, asking if he would like to play the role of Chucka in their production of *The Cherry Pickers* by Kevin Gilbert. Like Henry in *Fountains Beyond*, the character Chucka was an Aboriginal Elder. The story revolves around itinerant Aboriginal workers wandering around their own Country looking for work wherever they can find it. It was brutally honest about family, spirituality and dispossession. My father was quite surprised that he didn't have to audition for the role and I remember teasing him: 'Geez, Dad, there must be a shortage of short, fat blackfellas!'

On 17 August 2001, *Seems Like Yesterday* opened in Brisbane, and my father decided to be bold, so he rang Government House and asked if the governor would like to come to the opening night. The Queensland governor, Major General Peter Arniston, was also a Vietnam veteran. A day or so later, the Government House office staff rang and told him that the governor would be very pleased to attend. Once word got out that the Governor of Queensland was coming to opening night, executives in the performing arts industry, who had previously refused Dad's invitations, suddenly became available.[38]

A year or so later, Wesley Enoch asked Dad if he would like to reprise his role in *The Cherry Pickers* and go on tour with the original cast. After a split second his immediate reaction was 'What the fuck!' and he agreed to go, but nearly fell over when Wesley told him they were touring England. *The Cherry Pickers* opened in Manchester in May 2002 and continued to Brighton,

Exeter, Salisbury and Nottingham. The following is an extract from an interview given by cast member Tessa Rose:

> *The Cherry Pickers* tour was an exciting and anxious prospect because we were not sure how it was going to be received. The historical content of the play and the way it was directed and delivered was humorous, bold and sexy . . . The theatres that we were in did not have back exits so you had to depart after the show through the foyer, giving us an opportunity to talk to the audience, which really proved to us the success of the play. They, like Australians, are not taught the true history of our countries. All the ugliness is covered up so the English audiences were astounded at what actually happened. They were totally dumbstruck, and the people were openly express-ing how emotionally moved they were . . . The play was a huge success in that it educated the audiences, made them laugh, made them sing songs, tell jokes and made them cry.

A few years later, in 2013, Dad was asked if he would like to be a part of an all-Aboriginal cast for the QTC and the Queensland Performing Arts co-production of *Mother Courage and Her Children*. My father responded, 'Look, as an actor, I'm no Bob Maza or Jack Charles. I think that it helped that I was an *elder-looking* bloke who just happened to live locally.' He laughed at himself as he remembered, 'They had to make sure they didn't give me too many lines to remember!'

Mother Courage reunited him with his mate from the cast of *The Cherry Pickers*, Luke Carroll. Luke was (and still is) a very successful Aboriginal stage, television and film actor. He was about 21 years old when he and Dad met, and despite their 42-year age difference, they became great friends. Both Luke and Dad were cast for the 2014 play *Black Diggers*, by Tom Wright, which had another all-Aboriginal cast; this time it was nine men. The QTC and Sydney Festival Production play opened at the Sydney Opera House and toured around Australia. A week before rehearsals began, Dad got a call from Wesley Enoch. Wesley was then the artistic director at QTC and he asked Dad if he would meet him in his office:

> When I got there it turned out to be a job interview. He asked if I would work with the team as the Creative Consultant. My job was to talk to the actors about military culture, and to show them basic drill movements and weapons handling. Then he asked if I'd be interested in taking a part in the play, and of course I said yes. My role was like being at the Recruit Training Battalion. I had to turn these young men into soldiers within a couple of weeks. What made my task easier was that they were professional actors, and they were keen to learn. By the end of rehearsals, they not only knew their lines, but they were walking the walk and talking the talk, and most importantly they had bonded like soldiers. The characters I played were given very few lines, and for that I was thankful.[39]

Wesley Enoch told a newspaper journalist, 'There were no formal records kept of Indigenous servicemen, so we've had to rely on oral tradition as well as formal records.' He hoped by highlighting the role played by Indigenous servicemen, the play would encourage more families to come forward with their stories.

Another actor in the play, Trevor Jamieson, told the journalist that both his grandfathers served in the First World War, and one of the reasons that Aboriginal people enlisted to fight was to create equality in Australia—an equality that was not achieved when they returned, and still had a long way to go. 'They wanted the war to change Australia. When they served with each other, there was a huge bond of camaraderie. They looked after each other and never saw the blackness or whiteness of each other's skin.'[40]

Both political activism like the Tent Embassy and the growing number of public performances in the arts scene in Redfern fed and sustained Aboriginal pride. They seeded, then nurtured, then spread the Aboriginal belief that Aboriginal people did not have to forsake or renounce their Indigeneity to be a part of Australian society. Storytelling has always been an intrinsic part of Aboriginal culture, and I do not think we have ever lost that need to tell our stories. I think it is in our Aboriginal DNA. In saying that, I have known for a long time that it's certainly in *my* DNA.

10

The Truth is a Healer

'I always assumed it was as a direct consequence of my drawing attention to the dynamite they contained.'

PETER READ, ON THE CLOSURE OF THE ABORIGINES
PROTECTION/WELFARE BOARD ARCHIVES

This book is filled with stories about my family members' experiences from colonisation right up to my father's *thespian* adventures, but I just have two more stories to squeeze in. The first is a postscript to my stories about the Aborigines Protection Board Manager, J.P. Howard—and the second, undoubtedly the most important in this whole book, is about my experience with accessing the New South Wales State Records archive.

The sins of our ancestors

Towards the end of my research journey, I was telling my husband Allan that I had so many copies of archival letters and documents written by the Kyogle Reserve Manager Mr J.P. Howard that I was really curious to know what he looked like; I couldn't find any photographs of him. Allan was a family history researcher long before I was ever interested, and he asked me if I had tried Ancestry.com. I mumbled something about not being a subscriber then I washed, dried and put away the dishes that were in the sink; wiped down the kitchen benchtops; grabbed the rubbish bag and took it outside to the wheelie bin—and by the time I walked back inside the house, he was standing at the top of the stairs with a smug smile on his face.

On Ancestry.com, J.P. Howard's grandson's wife, Carolyn, had uploaded the Howard family tree, and attached to it was a portrait photograph of the man himself. I had read some-where that he was an Englishman, and as I examined his perfect Windsor knot tie, tucked into the buttoned-up waistcoat of his three-piece suit, I thought, *Of course he looks like that*. It made perfect sense that such a fastidious man would dress accord-ingly. As I looked at him it felt like I knew him. I had read so many of his letters and seen his handwriting so many times that even if he hadn't signed a letter, I could immediately recognise that he had written it.

I was stunned when Allan asked me if I would like to contact Carolyn. He told me that through Ancestry.com, you can send an email to any person who uploads their family tree. The website acts as a go-between for potential family members who might like to share their family history research. I instantly thought, *Wouldn't it be great if she had some photographs of my ancestors?* I had learned long ago that if something is put in front of you, then maybe there's a reason for it, so I said, 'Let's do it.'

Allan sent an email to Carolyn briefly explaining that I was an Aboriginal descendant of people who lived on Kyogle reserve, doing doctoral research on Aborigines reserves and that I was particularly interested in any photos from the period. We got an immediate email response. She said Joseph Percival

Harris Howard was her husband Alan's grandfather. Carolyn knew he worked on Aborigines reserves, and she said they had some photos which they could scan and send. She also said that one of Joseph's daughters was still living and we could find out if she had any photos.

Later, Carolyn and I made phone contact and she said straight up, 'Call me Lucky! It's my nickname; no one ever calls me Carolyn.' Lucky then said that I was more than welcome to visit anytime to see their photographs. In my experience, if you rely on other people to send you scans of photographs via email, they often don't do as good a job of it as you would do. The most terrible mistake people often make is not scanning the back of the photograph when it has a handwritten caption. These captions can sometimes have dates and names, so I packed my portable scanner and laptop in my car and headed down to Lismore again—this time to see Lucky and Alan Howard.

I was nervous about how our meeting would go because, like the Aboriginal people in history who had lived on reserves, I certainly disliked J.P. Howard. On the drive there my thoughts were scattered. *How do I tell someone that their ancestor played a role in taking Aboriginal children from their families? What if I upset them or cause them distress?* Then I thought, *I wonder what they have photographs of?* and lastly I thought, *This is about history, just calmly discuss the history.* The empath, the photo-collector and the historian, however, had vanished by the time I pulled into the Howard's driveway. Lucky came out to greet me. She looked as though she was a bit younger than my parents, and had a big smile on her face as she came towards me. I put my hand out to shake her hand, but she pulled me into her arms, gave me a hug and a kiss on the cheek. Alan's brother Geoff was there as well, so I was able to speak to two of J.P Howard's grandsons. Geoff had brought some original photographs for me to scan.

The Howard family were keen to know what I knew about J.P Howard. I told them that at home, I had many archival documents and letters that he had written that painted a very clear picture of his role as the manager of the reserve. When I said he was a prolific writer, they smiled in agreement, and happily remembered how he would send long-winded, typed letters to all his children. Lucky's husband Alan is a retired bank manager, and he talked about Aboriginal people not being able to handle money. He said that his father, Deric, was a policeman who lived in country New South Wales, and he had taken over the running of Cabbage Tree Island while J.P. Howard was away for a year. Then Alan said something about blackfellas blowing all their money, spending it as soon as they got it and not saving it. I had a little laugh at that and said, 'Your grand-father said exactly the same thing.'

I told them about the letter J.P Howard had written about the bunch of blackfellas who got some good contract work and, as soon as they got paid, went back to the reserve and took the whole mob on an excursion. J.P. Howard was baffled by their choice to spend the money on hiring a truck to visit family and friends, rather than save the money for their future. Then I said to his descendants, this is where J.P. Howard had great diffi-culty understanding Aboriginal people. This was a cultural thing. From J.P. Howard's perspective he saw it as a terribly frivolous thing to do, but I urged them to think about it from the people's perspective.

I asked them to think about how miserable life was for the people living on the reserve, surviving with only the incompe-tent Aborigines Protection Board to assist them, contained on reserves, segregated from nearby towns and controlled by a racist bureaucracy. I said 'Imagine how freeing it would be to have the money to hire a truck to take the whole tribe to see distant family, or to take the whole mob to the beach for the day. Imagine how great it would be as a parent to see your kids squealing with excitement and delight at having a great big day out!' I laughed as I said, 'They piled the whole mob onto that truck, young kids and the old people too, so that *everyone* could enjoy a great big family day out, and just for that one day they could all escape from the reserve.'

I explained that it if we place Aboriginal history on a timeline we can see that it has taken Aboriginal people a much longer time to achieve things that white Australians take for granted, like saving and owning your own home. There are so many 'firsts' for Aborigines that are recorded decades, or even over a century, later than the non-Indigenous experience of the same milestone. For example, our first university students graduated as recently as 1959 (Margaret Weir née Williams), and 1965 (Charlie Perkins). Then, out of the blue, Alan spoke about his father Deric (the country policeman) and said, 'My father hated Charlie Perkins for all that trouble he caused.' I immediately knew what he was talking about, and asked him if he had heard of the Freedom Rides in 1965, and what they were all about. He said he hadn't.

I gave Alan an outline of the Freedom Rides and told him the details about how Charlie Perkins led a civil rights movement that was inspired by Martin Luther King in the United States. White Australians thought that racism was an issue that only ever happened overseas (like apartheid in South Africa), but in country towns in New South Wales there was shocking and blatant racism. We didn't have 'whites only' signs out in the open in Australia, but behind the scenes there definitely was a colour bar. Aboriginal people were barred from swimming in the public pool or going to theatres and cafes. Charlie Perkins took a bus load of students from Sydney University to see for themselves the shocking racism, and when they protested the townspeople were enraged. When Charlie Perkins tried to take six Aboriginal children to the public swimming pool, hundreds of angry townspeople fought with the Freedom Riders. That was what the 'trouble' was all about. Lucky agreed, saying, 'Yes, there were places that Aborigines couldn't go, like the movie theatres, and drink in the pubs.' Alan listened to what I said and accepted it. I remember thinking to myself that this was exactly why these stories need to be told, and I am thankful for the Howards' willingness to listen.

We organised another time for me to visit because the family wanted to have copies of all the archives pertaining to their grandfather. I said I would bring my husband Allan with me for a drive.

For my second visit, Alan Howard insisted on doing a barbeque. His brother Geoff was again present, and I gave the Howards copies of all the archives I had relating to J.P. Howard. What happened next was so peculiar, I was completely engrossed in every moment. We, the granddaughter of incarcerated Aboriginal people, and the grandsons of an Aborigines Protection Board Manager, sat down together and over coffee and tea and biscuits, talked about our family histories. That included me telling them frankly that their grandfather was hugely disliked by Aboriginal people, because he played a role in the Aborigines Protection Board's removal of Aboriginal children. I gave them my DVD copy of *Lousy Little Sixpence* and explained that, as a historian, I was genuinely interested in knowing their thoughts on it. They said they'd watch it later and let me know.

When the history discussion was over, they brought out some photo albums. They mostly contained Howard family photographs. There were some taken on the reserve, but these were mostly farming and scenery shots. There were only a few photographs with Aboriginal people taken on the reserve. The first photograph I saw was of the reserves people nicely dressed in their 'Sunday best' for the outdoor church service on a grassy hill. J.P. Howard's handwritten caption said '126 natives attended Sunday Service'. I wondered if they were coerced to be there. I have read about instances on other reserves where rations were withheld by managers to ensure Aboriginal compliance. Religious indoctrination was approved and nurtured on Aborigines reserves and I suspect it was part of a broader government agenda. When you enlarge the photograph, you can see that they all look absolutely miserable.

The second photograph I saw was of Aboriginal children planting potatoes and corn. I kept my thoughts to myself and didn't make any comments, and while I was pleased to see that our people had crops of fresh vegetables to supplement the lousy, unhealthy rations of the Aborigines Protection Board, I was also angered to see that our children were working in the field. Did white Australian children have to plant crops in the field? Without knowing what I was thinking, the Howards told me that J.P. Howard's requests for financial support from the Aborigines Protection Board were not always approved, and there were times when he had to pay for things out of his own pocket.

On the back of a photograph labelled by J.P. Howard as 'Boys and girls pulling corn', he also wrote 'Efforts made to train children. No assistance from Board. Used my son's horses and plants.' The Howards were very proud that he tried to provide food for Aboriginal people, and that he set up bank accounts for the people to help them save money.

The last surviving child of J.P. Howard and his wife Irene's eight children is Alan and Geoff's Aunty Pat, a knowledgeable 86-year-old. After our first meeting, Lucky and Alan had told her about our intention to meet again and they asked if there was any information she wanted to pass on to me. Patricia Howard wrote an email, which the Howards forwarded to me:

Managed various Aboriginal Stations for over 30 years. Began his first assignment in Yass in 1916. Went from Yass to Maclean in 1918, then to Moree in 1921 and onto Inverell in 1922. From there he went to Kyogle in 1936 and then onto Cabbage Tree Island around 1940 (can't be sure if that is the right year) and retired in 1945. He taught the Aboriginal children at Primary School level and had one of the first Aboriginal children (a boy) to attend High School. He was able to get the men jobs in the cane fields and helping on farms. His wife, Irene, taught the Aboriginal ladies how to cook, wash clothes, do housework and plant vegetable gardens. She also helped the ladies and young girls to sew and knit—they began to knit socks and scarves for the soldiers—also showed them how to make butter and soap. She also taught the Aboriginal men to milk cows, look after poultry, and how to look after bees and collect the honey. Dad would never allow any alcohol onto the Stations as it made things uncomfortable due to the way it had an effect on the Aboriginal people. He taught them how to handle money that they were paid for doing work. Years after Dad retired, my parents took a return trip to Cabbage Tree Island. The new Manager had allowed alcohol onto the Island and the place was in ruins. No gardens, no cattle, poultry or bees and children were not being taught. It reduced them both to tears and they never returned.

From the perspective of my Aboriginal family members and other Aboriginal people, J.P. Howard was a sycophantic minion who carried out the cold, heartless orders of the 'Destruction Board'. This included, among other things, cutting off rations to a large group of Aboriginal people to force them to move from one reserve to another, and actively removing Aboriginal children from their families. But to be frank, I'm seeing a lot of survival skills being taught here. Knowing what I know about Protection Board managers on other reserves, I doubt many of them would have even bothered to teach Aboriginal people survival skills. From the Howard family's non-Indigenous perspective, he paid for crops out of his own pocket to feed Aboriginal people, found employment for the men, and he and his wife taught banking and a number of survival skills to Aboriginal people.

Each side brought different pieces of information about J.P. Howard to the table, and we came together to exchange that information. Each side learned something that they didn't know about this man. There was something extraordinary about this meeting with the Howard family. Upon reflection, I realised that the beauty of that meeting with the Howards was that descendants of the Protection Board's Aborigines Reserve Manager, and a descendant of Aboriginal people who lived on the reserve, came together in a mutually respectful way.

Lucky and I recently had a conversation on the phone about what the Howards had learned from watching *Lousy Little Sixpence*. She told me that she and Alan didn't know anything at all about J.P. Howard's role in the removal of Aboriginal children, and she said they were 'very, very sad when they heard about what happened'. She imagined that he probably thought he was just doing his job, and did what they told him to do. 'But it's still so sad, isn't it . . . I just don't know what to say.' This took me way back to the beginning of my research journey when I found out that my ancestors were slave traders. I could clearly see that the Howards are no more responsible for their ancestor's actions than I am for the actions of mine. Neither of us should carry the burden of the sins of our ancestors.

The archives

Without a doubt, the most important pieces of evidence that I have collected and presented in this book are the Aborigines Protection Board files about my family members. There is an interesting, even shocking story behind the New South Wales Government's Aborigines Protection Board and Aborigines Welfare Board files: how they were taken from public access—and how I was able to access them.

At the very beginning of my PhD research, Peter Read told me that he was 'the last person to see all the archives', and, at the time, I didn't know the whole story. It's important to reiterate here that Peter was the historian who in 1981 revealed the history of what is now known as 'The Stolen Generations'. He explained that:

> The Stolen Generations was a pamphlet that I wrote in 1981 following a request from a small New South Wales (NSW) Government agency. Fresh from reading the painful archives relating to removed [Aboriginal] children in the NSW State Archives (now closed), and listening to dozens of interviews

with Wiradjuri people when conducting doctoral research—and full of fury that such things could have happened in our country—I wrote it in a day. Though the agency's director was significantly unimpressed, some members of the then Wran government were, and soon more than 10,000 copies were distributed free throughout the state.[1]

Coincidentally, the same year that Peter Read's work on the Stolen Generations was published, the New South Wales Government created the Ministry of Aboriginal Affairs (now known as Aboriginal Affairs NSW), and after this government department was created in 1981, all the personal files of the Aborigines Protection and Aborigines Welfare Boards were removed from the public domain of the New South Wales State Records archive and locked away in the Ministry of Aboriginal Affairs. Access to these records through Aboriginal Affairs New South Wales is strictly conditional. The declaration 'Due to the personal and sensitive nature of the information contained in these records, many of the records are closed to public access' appears on all material related to their Aboriginal Family Records Service.

Over time, the reasons for these kinds of restrictions have been reduced to a catchphrase: 'cultural sensitivity'. Every time I hear this phrase, I have a vision of a white government official's hand gently patting my brown hand and saying consolingly, 'It's cultural sensitivity, dear'. In my opinion, the term 'cultural sensitivity' has been over-used for decades as an excuse to restrict public access to government-held material about Aborigines. When reflecting on the New South Wales Government's closeting away of the Aborigines Protection/Welfare Board's files, Peter Read said, 'I always assumed it was as a direct consequence of my drawing attention to the dynamite they contained.'

The Aboriginal Affairs NSW policy is that researchers can only access the records with the permission of the individuals recorded in the files, or their descendants. Peter added that, 'It may sound reasonable, but in effect it prevents historians from ever seeing the big-picture workings of a government department. It's a real disgrace.'[2] Not surprisingly, I agree with him. Peter's comment, which was made in 2016, was like a foreboding prophecy, because that is exactly what happened.

A team of Aboriginal PhD historians, led by Aboriginal Professor John Maynard and his (non-Indigenous) wife, Professor Victoria Haskins, came together to collaborate on a research project called 'The NSW Aborigines Protection/Welfare Board 1883–1969: A History'. John Maynard said the history of Aboriginal people in New South Wales when they were under the control of the Aborigines Protection/Welfare Board is remarkably under-researched. The time between the Aborigines Protection Board's legislated empowerment in 1909 and its reinvention as the Aborigines Welfare Board in 1940 was when state control was at its most extreme. It was a time when Aboriginal people, confined to and restrained on Aborigines reserves, were subject to extremely discriminatory restrictions on their basic civil rights, and this timeframe can be considered 'a period of erasure and silencing that is perpetuated in historiographical inattention'.[3]

But Maynard, Haskins and their team of Aboriginal academics were denied access to the archives. Maynard and Haskins believe that 'the decision of Aboriginal Affairs NSW to refuse permission stems from their fears of criticism and litigation from Aboriginal community members, rather than hiding anything in particular' and Maynard and Haskins believe that 'they are genuine in their concern'. That said, they add that 'ongoing secrecy not only makes it impossible to write a full history of the Board, but it also reinforces the impressions that the authorities' actions and policies are being hidden from public exposure'.[4] The historians said the archive staff were kind, and tried to be helpful, but unfortunately their efforts were to no avail.

The Aboriginal academic research group were refused permission to look at significant sections of the materials, including 'Ward Registers 1916–28', 'Correspondence files of the Welfare Board 1949–69', and 'Chief Secretary Letters Received—Files Relating to Aboriginal Affairs, 1938–49'. Haskins has warned that 'there are certainly real and powerful issues to be confronted when researchers work with records containing information on Indigenous peoples' and communities'.[5] I find it bewildering, however, that as late as the second decade of this millennium, two renowned professors of Aboriginal history and their esteemed all-Aboriginal team of PhD research scholars were refused access to NSW state government archives.

Maynard and Haskins' efforts to gain access, while unsuccessful, did manage to reveal that what Peter Read accessed over 40 years ago did not include the more recently discovered 'Chief Secretary, Letters Received—Files Relating to Aboriginal Affairs, 1938–49', which showed up around 2008. I was curious about how a large collection of archives could just magically 'show up' after such a long absence. It turned out that 166 boxes of the Aborigines Welfare Board records were discovered to be contained within the 'Chief Secretary's Correspondence'. After the State Records Authority completed an indexing project, the records were made open to the public, but with very limited access.[6] It is not known how many researchers have been denied access to the Aboriginal Affairs NSW files relating to the Aborigines Protection/Welfare Boards' records; however, a large number of the archives that I have sourced for this book have come directly from the abovementioned 'Chief Secretary, Letters Received—Files Relating to Aboriginal Affairs, 1938–49'. I was allowed access because I am 'directly related' to several people who are named in the files.

To access records held by Aboriginal Affairs NSW, I had to submit multiple personal documents to prove my direct genealogical lineage to every person whose file I applied for. Aboriginal Affairs NSW's insistence on 'direct' lineage meant that I could only access my biological grandparents', great-grandparents' and great-great-grandparents' records. The application I compiled for access to the records was approximately 27 pages long. These pages were a compilation of numerous proofs of identity papers, including my driver's licence, and multiple birth, death and marriage certificates (BDMs) from my parents', grandparents' and great-grandparents' generations, as well as family tree charts to map out my genealogical relationship to family members.

Some time after my initial access request was approved, I found an Aborigines Protection Board minutes book record that implied that my great-grandaunt might have actually been my great-grandmother. I suspect that as the great-grandaunt was a single mother, she gave her baby to a married sibling to raise. After finding this record, I wrote a letter explaining the circumstances, and sent the letter and a second application to Aboriginal Affairs NSW for access to my great-grandaunt's file. Yet even armed with this 'government record' as a reference, they still denied me access to her file—because she was not on my 'direct line'. It felt like they had shut the door in my face.

I wondered if non-Indigenous researchers experience the same kind of restrictions on accessing non-Indigenous archival material. Do non-Indigenous Australians have to go through such rigmarole to gain access to historical government documents? Are non-Indigenous government documents sequestered away with strict access conditions too? Do non-Indigenous people have to lay down multigenerational proof of identity papers on all their non-Indigenous ancestors before they can gain access to their files? Do everyday researchers, seeking a file on an unrelated non-Indigenous person in history, first have to gain permission from that person's descendants?

In December 2022, I asked John Maynard if anything had changed. He told me that the access conditions were still in place. Surely, in this day and age, a team of qualified historians (regardless of race) should be given access to *all* of the archives, to investigate the history of the Aborigines Protection/Welfare Boards, and the 'big picture workings' of this government department once and for all?

In the introduction to this book I explained what the Great Australian Silence was. W.E.H Stanner's observation basically brought an end to 'the cult of forgetfulness practised on a national scale'.

Archival access restrictions in the present could rightly be considered a contemporary version, 'The Great Australian Silence 2.0', if you will. This is another way for the state governments to perpetuate the silence and maintain the erasure of Indigenous people from the nation's history. Over 40 years ago it was white historians who smashed open the window so that all Australians could have a view of the *whole* landscape (and not just a quadrant). I am so grateful to these pioneering white historians, because as a result of their work, Aboriginal people are no longer relegated to being thought of as a 'melancholy footnote' in Australian history. But there still exists, as W.E.H. Stanner observed, 'a structural matter': the government's decision to separate Aboriginal archives from other Australian archives and restrict access to them has, over time, become a continuing practice that remains unchallenged.

Their cache of historical, archival documents needs to be brought out of the darkness and into the light, so that all Australians can learn the *whole* truth about Aboriginal history. When speaking about the (at that time) upcoming apology to the Stolen Generations in 2008, Peter Read warned Prime Minister Kevin Rudd, 'It's best to say sorry not for what "we" have done, but for what the Australian Government has done. Our nation is going to have to confront the enormity of the managed reserve system which degraded, abused and humiliated Aboriginal people for 90 years after 1870. That's as big and as hurtful as the Stolen Generations themselves.' My research, combined with the access I had to the Aborigines Protection/Welfare Board's files of my ancestors, has been able to shed *some* light on the managed reserve system—but I'm sure that the stories that I have been able to tell merely scratch the surface of the *whole* truth of Aboriginal history in New South Wales.

Duality exists everywhere and throughout my research journey I have always acknowledged that there were both 'good' and 'bad' non-Indigenous people involved in the history of Aboriginal people in this country. As much as there were shocking stories about the mistreatment of Aboriginal people in history, there were also contrasting stories with shining examples of non-Indigenous kindness and support. Throughout my research journey I have found evidence that has completely upended my previously held ideas and assumptions about Aboriginal and Australian history. But how can we learn from history when it is hidden from public view?

The aim of my family history research has always been to trace my four Aboriginal grandparents' family lines as far back as I could go in the historical record, and because both sides of my family are Aboriginal, I descend from a large number of Aboriginal people. I don't believe that I am simply lucky to have had access to a large number of the Aborigines Protection/ Welfare Board's files. I believe it was my calling. Spiritually, I believe that it was all part of God's plan that I was born into this family as the daughter of two Aboriginal people with so many Aboriginal ancestors—because it was my biological relationship to my ancestors that was the key that has unlocked the padlock on my access to archives held by Aboriginal Affairs NSW. If I was not directly related to these people—my ancestors—then these records would never have seen the light of day.

Epilogue

On the cover of this book is the John William Lindt photograph of Mary Ann of Ulmarra, my great-great-grandfather's sister. That she is indeed related to me was recently confirmed by Uncle Lewis, a Wahlubal-Bundjalung man who is a Language and Lore-keeper, and recognised by the Bundjalung Council of Elders as a Knowledge Holder. Meeting Uncle Lewis was such an extraordinary experience it felt like my ancestors had orchestrated it, rather than my friend Sharon, who introduced us.

Uncle Lewis lives in a remote location on Country beside one of the tributaries of the Clarence River. Sharon had met him several times as a supporter of a community nearby. When she told him all about me and my research, Uncle Lewis said he'd like to meet me, and she organised a visit. I showed him my doctoral thesis, flipping through the pages. As I got to the photograph of 'Mary Ann of Ulmarra', Uncle Lewis tapped on the photograph with his index finger. I said, 'Yes Uncle, I know. That dingo tail headband, and that snake bone necklace are for males only, not females.' He said, 'They're all wrong, all them photographs. They shouldn't have done that. They shouldn't have dressed her up like that.'

I commented that Lindt must have given them food or money as an incentive to pose for those photographs because they all look incredibly sad and it's obvious they don't want to be there. Uncle raised his eyebrows:

In some of these photos, when you look at the original ones, and you zoom right in on the eyes, you can see the reflection of them, you see this [then he held up his arms as though he was aiming an imaginary rifle] . . . and then on the side you will see the camera man in their pupils, in their reflections. *Oolamurra* that's my great-great-grandmother. That's Mumma's Country, yeah. *Oolamurra* is a bandicoot, the land of the sleeping giant bandicoot, that's their Dreaming. She was born and bred there; big tribe used to be there too. Yoway. Big story there!

As he looked at more Lindt photographs in my thesis he said, 'Should be one of my grandfather here, grandfather Pluddroon in one of them photos.'

I was gobsmacked. 'Do you mean the boy they called Pundoon, that was taken by Edward Ogilvie? The boy who taught Ogilvie to speak the local language?'

A smile spread over Uncle Lewis's face and he was very pleased that I knew the story. 'His name was Pluddroon, that's my grandfather.' (Except for his parents, sometimes he used the word 'grandfather' for male ancestors, and 'grandmother' for female ancestors. He didn't bother much with the 'greats'.) Uncle Lewis pointed to the landscape nearby saying:

See that big mountain there, you right in the heart of the story that was created from right here over them mountains, Yoway . . . Pluddroon was great-grandfather . . . he was a mythological little forest wallaby that lived beneath the canopy, he was sacred. He had all the secrets, and all the tracks, and all the fruit and vegetables and herbs and he was a medicine man. They found Pluddroon that's when they stole him, and they took him . . . and they brought him back to Solferino mines, so that's my grandfather, big story there, Yoway. Edward Ogilvie started speaking language and all of them old people started looking at each other, 'that white man he speaking our language'. Pluddroon must have taught him language, that's why he was still alive . . . so he [Toolbillibam] waved him over. Ogilvie was on his white horse, and early in the morning, this happened in the fog, they come up there. The day before they seen the smoke in the mountains, that's where they spotted it. They went up then. That's when grandfather said 'Begone white man, go! We gave you enough country to graze, you and your cattle and everything else. Leave me and my people to the mountains. Begone!' . . . Yoway. Then there's another story. When he took his wife home . . . his wife died and he fell in love with a *goorie* woman. [an Aboriginal woman] . . . that's another story, yeah. That's not written down.

I noticed how Uncle often said 'Yoway' and I asked him what it meant. He told me it means 'Yes, okay'. He said, 'It also means "I'm telling you the truth" and it can be an acknowledgement that you are speaking the truth, like when you say something and I agree. Sometimes it can mean "Our Goddess" as in Mother Earth.' When Uncle Lewis talks about Mother Earth his voice has a gentle lilt when he says 'Yoway'.

I also noticed how detailed Uncle Lewis's oral history was. He said Ogilvie had a 'white horse'; that it was 'early in the morning'; and 'this happened in the fog': and it was 'the day before' that they had seen the smoke. Those details are not found in Ogilvie's letter to *The Sydney Morning Herald*, nor in George Farwell's book, *Squatters' Castle*. Uncle Lewis also mentioned Ogilvie's *goorie* mistress, unaware that the story had been recorded in a book. At home I found the reference. Farwell wrote that when Ogilvie was 75, long after his first wife Theodosia had died, he married 45-year-old Alice Tottenham. When Alice arrived at Yulgilbar Castle, each time she went to the side entrance she found a stout grey-haired *goorie* woman sitting outside the door. Nothing was said. The woman merely stared. Alice found this unnerving, and finally, with impatience, she asked, 'Do you want something? If not, please go away.' The woman looked at her impassively and said, 'I see you'm little bit flash, missus. I bin Mrs Ogilvie longa time afore you.'[1]

In Chapter 2, I reproduced the original letter that Edward Ogilvie sent to *The Sydney Morning Herald* in 1842, which told the story of the encounter he and his brother Fred had with Toolbillibam and his tribe on the mountains near Ogilvie's Yulgilbar station. Ogilvie had kidnapped Uncle Lewis's 'grandfather', Pundoon, after a terrible massacre, with the intention of learning the local language (which we now know as Wahlubal). Ogilvie wrote, 'Since the hostile encounters with the blacks, which took place upon this river about a year ago, in consequence of the murders committed by them, they have rarely shown themselves'—but this was a fabrication no doubt meant to portray himself as a humanitarian, when in fact he was quite the opposite. The look on Uncle Lewis's face, and the tone of his voice gave emphasis to his comment, 'Big story there!'

Ogilvie failed to mention that while a fellow squatter, Peter Pagan, and his men were working, an Aboriginal person stole two blankets from his hut. Pagan ordered his men to chase down Aboriginal people and when they found an innocent Aboriginal group some distance away, they started shooting. Pagan was killed by a warrior, and eight of his workers fled to the shepherd's hut. One got away and took two days to travel 80 miles for help. Major Oakes then led a posse of eight men north and camped a night at Yulgilbar. The next morning, they found Pagan's men still barricaded in the hut long after the Aboriginal 'attackers' had vanished. For the next three days Oakes and his posse followed tracks through the bush. Ogilvie was sent to Swanlea for reinforcements, and when Oakes heard of a tribal party building gunyahs miles away from Yulgilbar, they assumed they were Pagan's killers. So, they camped out overnight and at dawn they attacked. Several Aboriginal people were shot, and a New Zealander, the police flogger, tomahawked all he could get—young or old.

One of Pagan's men and two policemen followed another set of tracks. They found two camps of Aborigines and dashed through the middle 'firing left and right'. The Aborigines retaliated by killing 150 sheep over three nights on Dobie's station. Major Oakes then led a posse to Orara River, where they rushed an Aboriginal encampment, and men, women and children were shot down indiscriminately. According to Farwell, 'Their dead bodies subsequently floated down past the settlement.'[2] Uncle Lewis quietly told me:

Ogilvie's brother [Fred] was very racist, and he teamed up with Peter Pagan and Thomas Coutts. They were impersonating [Christian] Reverends, stealing our people and raping them. True! I found Peter Pagan over here, in the fields over here, back in 1986, yeah. Horse dead and bones of horse and cart. He had all his stuff in there [the hut]. One thousand two hundred bones I got from that massacre site right on the river down there, the Clarence River.

After a long silent pause, Uncle Lewis looked me in the eye and started speaking to me in Wahlabal language, and although I couldn't understand a word he was saying, the intensity of his dark eyes staring into mine carried such emotional weight that I felt as though my heart had suddenly become cold and heavy.

Mala yogimbah mooginah abrubra
(There were no thunderclouds above)
Ngna mala jugan ngar juganah
(As the earth was shaking)
Nga mala jarjums nar bowgie nar jangbah
(As the children were swimming and laughing)
Mala nugung nar booglemah malah wagalare gngi
(And the Elders were sharing their stories)
Nga berla yuddaman yarh mala berla yuddaman
(Two horses, and then another two horses)
Bana nublenar jarjums
(Coming towards the children)
Mala goombinj
(But it was too late)
Mala balin nar banah nar wahl goomah
(The river has already turned into blood)

We sat in silence for some time. It was very important to him that people know about the large number of massacres of innocent people on Bundjalung Country. When he spoke again, I wasn't sure if Uncle Lewis was re-telling the previous story, or whether this was a story about another massacre:

306

We laughed, our old people laughed a long time ago . . . as they sat maybe there . . . or over there, or here . . . as the children played and splashed in the river, and laughing and carrying on. Then all of a sudden, thunder rumbles . . . the old people look up to the sky, no cloud? Ground vibrating . . . no wind, no thunder? As the children laughed and carried on being happy . . . the white men came on their horses and came galloping through. It happened there at a place called Myrtle Creek, not far from our Country here, and that's where that happened, as they laughed and played. But that memory, and the bloodstains will remain on that country until we all heal together.

As we talked, I explained that I have lived in big cities all my life, and I have always had a burning desire to learn more about my cultural heritage. I told him I am especially interested in what tribal life was like before colonisation. I asked him, 'What is a songline, Uncle? Can you explain it in a way that you can tell a person who doesn't know?'

A songline is always there. Over there is a songline, there at that songline, it will tell you where to sleep if you're a visitor for the first night. The next day it will tell you where to go over there, the other side of the track, and then it will tell you there is food over there, near the river, the food is in there at the river, at the songline from the river, on the carving on the rock an arrow will tell you where to go, keep follow-ing, it will tell you where to sleep on the side of the river. Which side? That side could be woman. Men's side if you're a man. You sleep there. It will tell you not to go that side. You keep walking an hour or so next day when you wake up, and an arrow will tell you where to go. It'll tell you to go up the hill and over, because there's a big cliff face there. You're not allowed to cross to the women's area, so you got to go around so you climb up the mountain, and come right around and join your men's place. And on the other side of the mountain it will tell you where to go, come to a big giant tree. The carving is there right in front of you. It'll tell you where to sleep and set up camp, and what to eat and what's around there. There are only vegetables, no meat, you're not allowed to kill meat here. Not allowed to cook after dark. So, no killing. So, they draw little vines and vegetables and fruit, so they know what to eat and where to go. At the end of the songline, after the food, it'll tell you where you're coming to your destination. You're coming to a mountain. It'll tell you where to go and set up. On the flat walking path, a big flat rock will appear. On that flat rock, it'll tell you where to go and look at it. 'Oh yeah, that line there go around that mountain . . . that must be the, oh yeah, that's that mountain there, that line must be the track that comes around, so I've got to go this way then come around . . . right.' So it would tell you what to do, with these kind of markings and lines. Why you got to go all the way around is because you're crossing a birthing site. You're crossing a woman's site, so you got to go right around, and pay the respect, and show the respect. And the songline ends and finishes there for you. And that's your journey. And you know how to come back. And share all that journey back from where you start. Share it from the home, where you started. That's a songline!

I asked Uncle, 'So, past that place, is your songline connected to other songlines on someone else's Country, and they join up?'

Uncle said yes. I asked, 'If you join up with a songline that is outside your Country, what happens?'

Before you even cross another man's Country, where the songline ends, like if the songline has got to go to the other side of the river, then you make the fire. But, back in them days, the old people already know someone was coming, three days ahead of you. 'Someone is coming to the river' because they can feel the songline. So, the other mob on the other side of the river, they'd already know that Lore went through it. They hold the Lore on the other side of the river. So, if you was on this other side of the river [wanting to come into another mob's Country] you'd hold a boondi up, a nulla nulla, and he'd hold it straight up first, and he'd tell the other fella to 'stand up straight'. 'Who are you?' He'll turn that nulla nulla sideways, so he'll turn around and show his back, and hold his hand up . . . so he'll turn his nulla nulla sideways and then he'll hold his weapon up and turn it sideways, put down all his weapons, and then he'll turn his nulla nulla upside down, and then the fella on this side go to put all his weapons down, everything to the ground and then he'll wave. 'You are welcome, come'. And when he comes to the other side old mate will give sign language. [Uncle gestures with all fingertips of one hand touching lips] Means, 'I only come to hunt food to eat, not to take, to eat!' [then gestures fingers walking in a line] Means, 'I'm passing through on your Country'. It was all sign language back in them days also, because language wasn't spoken. Old mate would say, 'You can come'. [Uncle gives the universal 'Come' gesture with his hand]. Then the visitor would say 'I'm going to make a fire' by rubbing his hands together, 'I'm going to sleep' [Uncle put his palms together with hands on cheek, head to the side, eyes closed] and telling them with index finger up, 'One night'. Then does this [Uncle gestures with one arm, a pointed index finger doing a large arching semi-circle, which points to a far destination]. Means he's going on to other Country. Old mate then walk away. Old mate go back over there, grab his stuff and set up camp to hunt. Next day he's gone away through Country, on his journey through the songlines.

To summarise I said, 'So, Uncle, it's a courtesy thing because he told him in sign language, "I'm going to hunt for something to eat, I'm going to make a fire, I'm going to sleep for one night, and then I'm going to move on" to other Country, right?'

'Without taking anything! Not disturbing anything!'

'Only taking what he's going to eat, and then he's going to go.'

'Yes, and that was that protocol. Protocol is very important for us many rivers. So, these are part of that songline also. When going to another tribe, there was no expectations because that tribe doesn't know you. He'll feel if you're a good fella or a bad fella straight away. But the old womans feel it before the mens. They feel it four days before the mens does. And then say, "Nah someone coming, don't let him come." [But] no one know nothing in the tribe then, about that stranger.'

'Nobody knows anything about that stranger who's coming?' I asked.

'That's how well hidden they keep that kind of knowledge. They only share it to certain people to protect the people, for the future.'

'Oh, so the tribe didn't know when a stranger was coming, or when they sent them away. So, what happened if he came to Country, and he did the sign language, and he was refused, what happened then?'

'He goes back to where he came from. He's not allowed. He break Lore anywhere else he'll get punished. But not by our mob. He was told to go. And our old womans always knew the Country. They had the Spirits roam our land to protect our people . . . and keep them kind of people away.'

I loved the way Uncle Lewis explained things so well. He also told me there were seven seasons on Bundjalung Country and there's 'all these medicines in between, the vegies and the herbs'. Uncle stressed that it's not just a calendar, and elaborated that:

A calendar to us is a flower. The flowers let us know when the fish is fat, and the goannas are fat, Yoway. Let us know when the turtles are fat, the catfish, all that. If there's a catfish nest in there, we wait for a big storm. We've already had a couple of big storms, so finished now. When the catfish lays their eggs in the nest, it's the male that look after the nest, and when big lightning and thunder comes along, opens the nest up. Then the mother comes out, the father goes out hunting again and try and protect them. So, we go by that little cycle of lightning/thunder, then the third big storm, then we are allowed to go turtle diving. We wait for them to lay their eggs over there on the beaches [of the river] over there, yeah, on the sandy beaches, Yoway. Then, after they lay their eggs, big thunder let us know, then we see a lot of flowers come of the bloodwood tree, so that means that everything's all fat and ready to eat.

That's the last tree here to show us flowers yeah. So, we go by that and we know that when the bark is peeling off the trees, and it strips back to just white ghost gum, when it goes back to nothing, that's when we know in the salt-water on the coast the sharks are ready, look for sharks. He out there now, and the mullets coming upstream to freshwater to spawn again. So, we watch the trees and we don't go mullet hunting because he's going to come back up and spawn. We wait until they're finished and then we go hunting them. Take the middle pack. Never take the one in front. The one in the middle, not the one in the back, the one in the middle, take about six or seven, maybe 30 or 40 in the middle. Yoway.

So, there's plenty of food, but also on the ocean there's flowers that let you know. You can eat some, and you know there's a lot of trevally out there and there's a lot of flathead and whiting. [So there is] all that knowledge, you know. And you know what's up on the rocks, the ocean meat, periwinkles. We used to get the ocean meat and when you squeeze it water squirts out it and when you cut it open there's meat in there, red meat there. We used to go and get seaweed, roll it up, flatten it out, and get the periwinkles out and put six or seven in and roll it up and eat it. It was all bush tucker, it was all food . . . but knowing when it was ripe, knowing when it was ready, yeah. Yoway.

This is the kind of connection that we need to teach our young ones, how to connect back to country again, how to connect back with our animals again. The trees let you know, and the birds will talk to you, let you know if there's any animals, danger ahead of you. They come and talk in mysterious ways. The land is so sacred when you're out on Country, especially when you're out here. That's how we know about the seasons, yeah, it changes, and it's all about the flowers, Yoway, and the leaves, and all the bark. Some bark hangs, some bark it stays straight up and down on the tree. That's another message. You know that means the possums are having their babies, and the koala they're having their babies. It's time for breeding season now for winter. So, it's all a cycle now, yeah.

Some of the big trees get their barks all straight see. There's nothing hanging off. Some of the other ones you see them hanging off, peeling off is a different sign. That means the platypus going into breeding, and the ones that have already had the babies, bringing them out, and teach them how to hunt. Especially a full moon they teach them how to hunt, too dangerous in the daytime, too open for them. The white river eagles come down and have a go, try and get him . . . You see a lot here. It's a good documentary!

We talked for hours on my first visit, and on my second visit, a few days later, I stayed for the full moon. I am so grateful to Uncle Lewis for his priceless gift of knowledge, and the precious gift of his time. He believes that the time has come for us all to stand together as one. He said, 'Bygal nar jugun', which means 'we are people of this land', adding, 'That goes for all people on this land. It's important to belogaman yubra, to "come together as one". Mala boogle ma: "we shall do it right".'

I listened to Uncle Lewis as he explained to me our traditional ways of *knowing* and *being* and *doing*. I could clearly see the stunning beauty of Aboriginal culture, and its symbiotic and loving relationship with Mother Earth. The word 'esoteric' means something that is understood by few, or 'only for the initiated'. The structure of our culture is esoteric because it is based on progression through levels of initiation. Each level of knowledge requires the initiate to take on certain responsibilities and

practices. An example of having to start at the bottom is practised on tourists today at Uluru. Travellers on guided tours who
are taken to waterholes and caves and shown rock art are told
the stories behind each place, but these are children's stories.
Like any education it begins with simple stories, and the stories
grow more complex, with more meaning, over time.

My Uncle Gerry was a Bundjalung kurradji, who was
taught traditional healing from a young age. He told me
that new age people tend to look to the heavens for spiritual
connection, following the principle 'as above, so below', but
he believed that the traditional way embraced both this and
the parallel principle, 'as below, so above'. I imagine people
as human trees, reaching up into the heavens, and those same
trees secured by an underground root system that taps into the
songlines of Mother Earth.

Scientists have discovered a whole underground network
of communication and connection. In *The Hidden Life of Trees*,
Peter Wohlleben explains how 'mother trees recognise and
talk with their kin, shaping future generations . . . and these
discoveries have transformed our understanding of trees from
competitive crusaders of the self to members of a connected,
relating, communicating system'.[3] Dr Stephan Harding is
an ecologist who has explored 'how Earth science can help
us to develop a sense of connectedness with the "more-than-
human" world'.[4] He tells us that we have overlooked 'a whole
kingdom of life that exists hidden from our gaze in the soil,
and in rotting trunks and fallen trees'.[5] US mycologist and
fungi expert Paul Stamets has described mycelia as 'a complex
network of fungal pipelines' that allow fungi to 'create networks
of phenomenal communicative power that strongly resemble
our blood system or the neuronal connections in our brains.'

They are the 'neurological network of nature'. He writes that they actually 'sense the movements of organisms upon the land and the impact of fallen trees on the ground (potential food for decomposing fungi) thanks to complex molecules that course through the communal spaces of intercommunicating pipelines'.[6]

I can't help but think that our ancestors were like human trees, that our people were also connected to that vast 'neurological network of nature'. We had an invisible energetic and psychic connection to Earth's own network. That would explain a lot of the mystical elements of Aboriginal culture, and the uncanny, extraordinarily symbiotic and harmonious relationship with Mother Earth. Ours was a supremely civilised culture that the Western world simply could not see, let alone try to understand. But our connection to Earth was violently severed.

Uncle Lewis said, 'Bygal nar jugun', which means 'we are people of this land', and he added, 'that goes for *all* people on this land'. He said it's important to 'belogaman yubra', to 'come together as one'—but how do we come together as one after such incredible injustice? For Aboriginal people, colonisation was a cataclysmic, violent upheaval that continues to impact us. We are survivors of invasion, massacres, violence, land theft, segregation, stolen children and inequality. European colonists brought with them a foreign concept called *government* that robbed us of our financial equity, our land (which was our independence and livelihood), and stripped us of our soul equity (the wealth of our cultural way of life, the use of our language, and even our children). We were kicked off our sacred Country and forced to become propertyless paupers in a nation overflowing with natural abundance. There was absolutely nothing *civilised* about the way European society, then Australian society, treated Aboriginal people.

We were bound by rules of the dominant (at times racist) government, and the more I thought about the stacks of documents that I have seen in the archives, tied up with cotton tape bindings, the more the files felt like a metaphorical representation of our unknown, forgotten Aboriginal ancestors. We can't see them when they are locked away in the darkness of the archives of the Aborigines Protection/Welfare Board. We don't know their names, and no one knows who they were, where they were from, or what they experienced in their lifetimes. They are still bound.

I have been able to free my family's ancestors from their bindings. I know their names, I know who they were, and I know something about what they experienced in their lives. I have been able to construct a bridge between my ancestors— who witnessed colonisation—and my life today as an urban Aboriginal woman. The New South Wales Government's archives contained the information that I needed to reconstruct their lives, see their experience and restore their humanity.

We need individual and collective remembrance and mourning. Aboriginal people must be able to tell their ancestors' stories so that their experience is validated and honoured by the wider community. When this doesn't happen it is very difficult for descendants to process what has happened to their families.[7] Especially Indigenous people, who have experienced generations of racism, dispossession, displacement, oppression and continuing uncertainty.

Uncle Lewis urges us to embrace belogaman yubra, 'to come together as one':

Black, white, doesn't matter what colour. We live in this country together. We got over the fear, but we never got over the trauma. We will never forget the past, but we should never live in the past. The past is a spiritual journey that leads us to the truth right until this day, and as I speak, we are living proof, me, you, my nieces, nephews, cousins, aunties, uncles. We are living proof of what happened back then. [A] page for every person . . . they've been stolen, they've been taken away, they've been gaoled, they've been forced into something that we didn't know nothing about.

Getting over that fear will make a better place for our community, and setting the foundation down for community is a big responsibility. That's what my big brother's trying to do, and my older sister's trying to do in the community. Holding the woman together, holding woman's Lore together, trying to keep it strong again, keep the bond.

Keep sticking together, you womans, keep talking about old days. Our children need to see that now, yeah. It's all about reconnecting Songlines for the future of our children and our grandchildren, and their future children's childrens. Let's not lose our identity. Our identity is truth.

Historian Henry Reynolds said:

I understood those many people who took the view that a troubled history was best forgotten, that it was preferable to look to the future and not dwell on the past. But it was always hard to equate those sentiments with that most revered phrase in Australian history, 'Lest We Forget'. Australians are sensitive about the past and most people have strong views about First Nations people. It is a subject about which almost everyone is willing to express an opinion, no matter how poorly informed . . . there is now a better chance than at any time in the recent past to initiate a process of truth-telling.'[8]

This book is my contribution to truth-telling. Our history was beginning to be revealed 40 years ago, yet I still hear the same old response, 'We were never taught about that when I was in school', and I still sigh and feel a twinge of pain from that old wound that hasn't healed properly. Telling our ancestors' stories is a way to address this unfinished business.

When I was researching the slave trade, I came across a quote from Professor Kofi Anyidoho, a celebrated national poet of Ghana. He told Thomas DeWolf, the descendant of three generations of American slave traders, 'Slavery is the living wound under a patchwork of scars. The only hope of healing is to be willing to break through the scars to finally clean the wound properly and begin the healing.'[9]

The history of Aboriginal people in this country is also 'a living wound under a patchwork of scars' but the process of truth-telling creates healing. By reaching through time and pulling our ancestors' files out of the archives we restore their humanity. They are not just 'Aborigines': they are One My, a traditional Aboriginal woman from Wollumbin/Mount Warning; and Sam Anderson, an Aboriginal county cricketer who caught Don Bradman out for a duck; and Nellie Solomon, a gutsy girl who pushed back against the Aborigines Protection Board; and the long-suffering Henry Anderson, who finally found peace and happiness in Redfern—just to name a few.

I have often wondered if there was some kind of existential significance to my non-Indigenous ancestors being slave traders, the Bostock family becoming blackfellas and my attention being frequently drawn to slavery themes in my research.

There are similarities between slaves and Aboriginal people's experience of racism—being treated as lesser human beings, indenture, exploitation and oppressive control. Ruminating on the slavery theme, I wondered if family history research was the key to emancipation, because researching my ancestors' lives has spiritually unshackled them.

I too am unshackled. I am freed from the emotional sadness that I carried for their pain and suffering because I now know their stories of bravery and courage, and their valiant determination to extract themselves from the bindings of colonialism, to push forward on the road to equality. I truly believe that they would not want their descendants to carry the burden of our history. Uncle Lewis said that family history research is 'a protocol for overcoming these experiences and releasing trauma and allowing us to heal together. When they see these pictures, and the memory of their great-grandfather and great-grandmother, and the story and the names—that's healing!'

And I say, 'Yoway'.

Acknowledgements

The moment that this book became a potential reality for me was when the late author (and convict history historian) Babette Smith marched up to me after a conference where I presented my research and said, 'I loved your presentation and I'm going to help you! I'm going to introduce you to my publisher!' Sending gratitude to you in heaven, Babette, because, true to your word, you did introduce me to Elizabeth Weiss, Publisher at Allen & Unwin.

Elizabeth, you are blessed with the patience of a saint! I feel like a moogal jarjum for testing your steadfast, long-suffering perseverance. Thank you for staying in touch while I completed my PhD, and thank you for your encyclopaedic knowledge, your sage advice, and especially your kindness and grace when I was stressing out with writer's block.

So chuffed to have the rockstars of Aboriginal history agree to writing my endorsement quotes, thank you Peter Read, Ann McGrath and Jackie Huggins. Double thanks for Peter Read and Ann McGrath, who along with Maria Nugent, were the supervisors of my PhD.

I am especially grateful to Thelma (Bostock) Birrell, and Associate Professor Emma Christopher for their incredible genealogical and historical research on 'the two Roberts'. Emma, you were so encouraging to me in the early days when I was nowhere near as confident as I am now. Mr Ian Fox, thank you for generously sharing your extraordinary knowledge (and library!), and heartfelt thanks to you and Teena for your enduring friendship and hospitality.

My gratitude goes to Andrew Pike (Ronin Films), Sue Milliken (Samson Productions) and film-maker Darlene Johnson for allowing me to use the transcript of their documentary film *The Redfern Story*. Thank you, Gary Foley, for permission to use your scripts for *Basically Black*, and for gifting Aboriginal people with our very own superhero. God bless Super Boong!

Thanks so much to the Howard family for your willingness to hear my stories and share your stories.

To my dear friend Pam Lane, thank you (and Claire and Julia and Phil) for my happy times in Canberra. Pam, you were a guardian angel who always intuitively knew when I needed you. Thank you Nancy Valentine-Smith, Belinda Pate-Macdonald and Jacinta Louise Sinclair (three Spiritual Goddesses who have helped me many times in my life). Uncle Lewis, I am so grateful to you for the gift of your time, and your knowledge of our Bundjalung sacred Lore, our Dreaming, and our stories.

My dear family, Luana, David and Abbey Gallagher—and Tania, Danny and Allira Schafer—I'm so excited that you will finally get to read what your history nerd Sister/Sister-in-Law/ Aunty has been working on all these years. Thanks to my father, George Bostock, for sharing your captivating memories. My husband, Allan, and my beautiful daughter Brenna, you were with me on every single step of my epic journey past to present.

ACKNOWLEDGEMENTS

Especially the heart-warming praise, and high fives from you beautiful Brenna. I love you both so much!

Lastly, my eternal love to my mother Rita, my twin sister Janna, and all our ancestors who are no longer with us. I have heard your whispers and felt your presence every step of the way.

Notes

INTRODUCTION

1 H. Reynolds, *Why Weren't We Told? A personal search for the truth about our history*, Camberwell, Vic: Penguin Books, 1999: Reynolds quote, p. 4; journalist quote, back cover.

2 Stanner, in Reynolds, *Why Weren't We Told?*, pp. 91–2.

3 H. Reynolds, *The Other Side of the Frontier: Aboriginal resistance to the European invasion of Australia*, Townsville, Qld: James Cook University, 1981.

4 T. Griffiths, *The Art of Time Travel: Historians and their craft*, Carlton, Vic: Black Inc., 2016, p. 140.

5 J. Maynard & V. Haskins, '"For the Record": A history of the New South Wales Aborigines Protection Board', in J. Damousi & J. Smart (eds), *Contesting Australian History: Essays in honour of Marilyn Lake*, Clayton, Vic: Monash University Press, 2019, p. 134.

6 Maynard & Haskins, '"For the Record"', p. 134.

7 H. Reynolds, *Truth-Telling: History, sovereignty, and the Uluru Statement*, NewSouth Publishing: Sydney, p. 239.

CHAPTER 1: SINS OF THE ANCESTORS

1 T. Birrell, *Mariners, Merchants . . . then Pioneers*, Kawana, Qld: Campbell Printing, 1993, self-published.

2 Birrell, *Mariners, Merchants . . . then Pioneers*, p. 32.

3 F. Watson & P. Chapman, Parliament, Library Committee (eds), *Historical Records of Australia*, series 1, vol. 8, *July 1813 to December 1815, Despatches*, Sydney: Library Committee of the Commonwealth Parliament, 1914, pp. 602–3.

4 E. Christopher, *Freedom in Black and White: A lost story of the illegal slave trade and its global legacy*, Madison, Wisconsin: University of Wisconsin Press, 2018.

5 Christopher, *Freedom in Black and White*, pp. 23–4.

NOTES

6 Birrell, *Mariners, Merchants . . . then Pioneers*, p. 10.

7 Christopher, *Freedom in Black and White*, p. 24.

8 Christopher, *Freedom in Black and White*, p. 23.

9 Christopher, *Freedom in Black and White*, p. 10.

10 Christopher, *Freedom in Black and White*, p. 27.

11 Christopher, *Freedom in Black and White*, p. 29.

12 Christopher, *Freedom in Black and White*, pp. 50–5.

13 Christopher, *Freedom in Black and White*, pp. 91–3.

14 Christopher, *Freedom in Black and White*, p. 111.

15 Christopher, *Freedom in Black and White*, pp. 139–40.

16 Christopher, *Freedom in Black and White*, p. 149.

17 Christopher, *Freedom in Black and White*, p. 159.

18 Christopher, *Freedom in Black and White*, p. 160.

19 Christopher, *Freedom in Black and White*, p. 181.

20 Christopher, *Freedom in Black and White*, pp. 188–9.

21 Christopher, *Freedom in Black and White*, p. 206.

22 'The Black Natives', *The Hobart Town Gazette*, 11 November 1826, <https://trove.nla.gov.au/newspaper/article/8791038>, accessed 4 January 2022.

23 Christopher, *Freedom in Black and White*, p. 218.

24 Christopher, *Freedom in Black and White*, p. 219.

CHAPTER 2: WOLLUMBIN ONSLAUGHT

1 R. Harrison, *Shared Landscapes: Archaeologies of attachment in the pastoral industry in New South Wales*, Sydney, NSW: University of NSW Press, 2004, pp. 2 & 29.

2 Museums of History New South Wales, 'Crown Lands Occupation Guide', <https://mhnsw.au/guides/crown-lands-occupation-guide/#outside_the_settled_districts>.

3 H.W. Denning, *Historical Manuscript of the Tweed*, Murwillumbah, NSW: Tweed Shire Council Civic & Cultural Centre, 1988, p. 20.

4 Denning, *Historical Manuscript of the Tweed*, pp. 20–2.

5 Denning, *Historical Manuscript of the Tweed*, pp. 20–2.

6 G. Farwell, *Squatters' Castle: The saga of a pastoral dynasty*, Sydney: Lansdowne Press Pty Ltd, 1973, pp. 106–7.

7 N.C. Keats, *Wollumbin: The creation and early habitation of the Tweed, Brunswick and Richmond Rivers of New South Wales*, Tweed Heads, NSW: Tweed Heads Historical Society Inc., 1988, pp. 317–18.

8 Farwell, *Squatters' Castle*, p. 136.

9 Farwell, *Squatters' Castle*, p. 136.

10 M. Ryan, unpublished, 'Original Correspondence: Edward Ogilvie's Letter to The Sydney Morning Herald', 8 July 1842 (Shauna Bostock Private Collection). See also Farwell's version in *Squatters' Castle*, pp. 145–50.

325

11   H. Goodall, *Invasion to Embassy: Land in Aboriginal politics in New South Wales, 1770–1972*, chapter 4, St Leonards, NSW: Allen & Unwin, 1996, pp. 45–57.

12   Goodall, *Invasion to Embassy*, pp. 45–7.

13   Goodall, *Invasion to Embassy*, pp. 47–8.

14   NSW Government, Crown Lands Alienation Register 1887 & 1891, Colonial Secretary, Conditional Land Purchases, CP 82-201[10/35310 & 87/321] & CP 88.75 [10/17759 & 91/50], Sydney: State Records NSW.

15   F.J. Lever, 'Letter to Mr R. Whittle about the original Aboriginal camps on the Tweed River Basin', Tweed Heads, NSW: Tweed Heads & District Historical Society, 1964.

16   M. Kinsman, *Joshua Bray: A Tweed Valley pioneer*. Chatswood, NSW: Bannermann Bros. Chatswood, 2007, p. 13.

17   Kinsman, *Joshua Bray*, p. 15.

18   Kinsman, *Joshua Bray*, pp. 19–20.

19   Kinsman, *Joshua Bray*, p. 25.

20   J.J. Byrne, 'Hundreds of Blacks Lived on the Tweed', *Tweed Daily*, 18 December 1945, p. 2, <http://trove.nla.gov.au/newspaper/article/192801988>.

21   'Settlement on the Tweed', *Sydney Mail and New South Wales Advertiser*, 21 November 1885, <https://trove.nla.gov.au/newspaper/article/162818771>.

22   A. Curthoys & A. McGrath, *How to Write History that People Want to Read*, Sydney: University of NSW Press, 2009, pp. 38–9.

23   'Cleverfella' or 'Kurradji' are Aboriginal terms used to describe what other Indigenous peoples, such as First Nations Americans, would call a 'Shaman' or 'Medicine Man'. They were intuitive, shamanic healers, keepers of spiritual knowledge, and communicators with the metaphysical ancestral realm.

24   NSW Government, 'Conditional Purchases, Augustus John Bostock', CP82.201 [10/35310, 87/321] & CP88.75 [10/17759, 91/50], Crown Lands & Alienation Branch of Lands Department, Sydney: State Records NSW, 1882 and 1888.

25   Denning, *Historical Manuscript of the Tweed*, pp. 56–7.

26   Denning, *Historical Manuscript of the Tweed*, pp. 56–7.

27   M. Bundock, 'Notes on the Richmond River Blacks', in Papers of the Bundock family of Wyangarie Station, Richmond River, ca. 1835–1898, Microfilm CY2227, A6939 Original Call Number (Sydney: Mitchell Library, State Library of New South Wales, 1835–1898).

CHAPTER 3: MY FATHER'S SIDE OF THE FAMILY

1   C. Henderson, 'Main Camp Reminiscences, 1864–1950, with Miscellaneous Writings, Manuscript Number 910761, M.L.M.S.S. 1863', in Manuscript Collection (Sydney: Mitchell Library, State Library of NSW, 1864–1950). See also C. Henderson, 'Australian Aborigines, by Cunningham Henderson "Mynumi", Coraki, New South Wales, 1864–1950', in J. Hart (ed.), Tweed

Heads, NSW: Tweed Heads Historical Society Inc., 1864–1950, p. 17. I have referenced both the Mitchell Library's and Tweed Heads Historical Society's copies of Henderson's reminiscences because both are missing chunks of writing, but when combined they fill in each other's missing sections.

2   A. McGrath, *Illicit Love: Interracial sex and marriage in the United States and Australia*, Lincoln, Nebraska: University of Nebraska Press, 2015, pp. 5–6.

3   C.A. Mann, 'A Dying Race: Authentic Stories of Australian Aboriginals: Mr W.M. Flick's Experiences: Peace and War', *Northern Star*, 25 April 1925, <http://nla.gov.au/nla.news-article93484947>.

4   Anglican Church of Australia, 'Baptism Register Entry for Augustus Bostock, 1st Nov. 1894', in *Baptism Administered in the Parish of Tweed River, County of Rous in the Year 1894*, Grafton, NSW: Grafton Diocese of the Anglican Church, 1894, p. 13; Anglican Church of Australia, 'Baptism Register Entry for Meta Bostock, 1st Nov., 1894', in *Baptism Administered in the Parish of Tweed River, County of Rous in the Year 1894*, Grafton, NSW: Grafton Diocese of the Anglican Church, 1894), p. 14.

5   Chief Protector of Aborigines, Exemption Correspondence (1909–1914) [A/58730 QSA]—Folio 14/823, Letter dated 25 March 1914; Chief Protector of Aborigines, Exemption Correspondence (1909–1914) [A/58730 QSA]—Folio 14/1585, Letter dated 14 June 1914.

6   'Blacks Want "Relic" Back', *Sunday Mail*, 11 May 1975, p. 6.

7   J. Macdonald, 'Descendants of Kitty Family Tree Chart', Group 2, Tweed Heads, Qld: J. Macdonald.

8   Queensland Government, 'Marriage Certificate of Edward Williams & Ina Bostock, 8th August 1906, No. 1906/1655', Brisbane: Queensland Registry of Births, Deaths and Marriages, 1906. Ina's descendants remember her as being an Aboriginal woman. I thought 'Walumba' and 'Wollumbin' were two different ways to spell the same word. Transcriptions of the spoken word can vary. According to Keats in his book *Wollumbin* (1988, p. 228), Samuel Gray and Joshua Bray were the original graziers at 'The Walumban Run', which later became known as 'Wollumbin' and finally as 'Kynnumboon'. Other history researchers concur that 'Walumba' and 'Wollumbin' are the same word with different spellings. Ina married Ted Williams, who was an Aboriginal man.

9   McGrath, *Illicit Love*, p. 343.

10 Queensland Death Certificate No. 1929/B008763 for Matilda Sandy Fogarty.

11 'Beaudesert', <https://queenslandplaces.com.au/beaudesert>.

12 Australian Government, 'McDermott, Claude: Series No. B883, Control Symbol: Q.X. 22571, Personnel Dossiers 1940–1947', Second Australian Imperial Force, Canberra: National Archives of Australia, 1941–1946. The photocopies of the telegrams were given to me by Aunty Joyce Frater (née Byerley), oldest surviving grandchild of Gus and Lena Bostock. The direct quotation of Uncle Claude is from a letter he wrote to the war gratuity officer,

Victoria Barracks Brisbane, undated but between 27 October 1949 and 5 December 1949, p. 31 of the file.

13   Australian Government, 'McDermott, Claude, Personnel Dossiers 1939–1947'. An 'allotment' was a regular payment of a portion of a soldier's wage to send to dependants back home.

14   J. Feller, 'The Light of Day', *Australian Story*, season 18, episode 1, screened 4 February 2013, Sydney: ABC, 2013, television broadcast, <www.abc.net.au/austory/the-light-of-day/9170148>.

15   J. McBean (ed.), *Dreaming the Past: The Lindt story*, Grafton, NSW: Grafton Regional Art Gallery, 2012, p. 58.

16   S. Bostock-Smith, 'Connecting with the Cowans', in J. Lydon (ed.), *Calling the Shots: Aboriginal photographies*, Canberra: Aboriginal Studies Press, 2014, pp. 61–5.

17   F. Gale, 'Roles revisited: the women of Southern South Australia', in P. Brock (ed.), *Women Rites & Sites: Aboriginal women's cultural knowledge*, St Leonards, NSW: Allen & Unwin, 1989, p. 123.

18   J. Hoff, *Bundjalung Jugun: Bundjalung Country*, Lismore, NSW: Richmond River Historical Society Inc., 2006, p. 236.

19   M. Bundock, 'Notes on the Richmond River Blacks', p. 2. There are also photographs of Bundjalung men wearing the dingo tails in this way, see Hoff, *Bundjalung Jugun*, pp. 106, 150, 234, 258.

20   K. McLeish, 'Postcards of 19th century Brisbane Aboriginal people on display at "Captured" exhibition in Brisbane', Australian Broadcasting Commission, 31 March 2014, <www.abc.net.au/news/2014-03-28/early-photos-of-brisbane-aboriginal-people-in-captured-exhibit/5336752>.

21   Lydon, *Calling the Shots*, pp. 61–5.

22   V. Haskins & J. Maynard, 'Sex, race and power', *Historical Studies*, 2005, vol. 36, no. 126.

23   K. Ellinghaus, 'Margins of acceptability: class, education, and interracial marriage in Australia and North America', *Frontiers: A journal of Women Studies*, 2002, vol. 23, no. 3, pp. 55–75.

24   McBean, *Dreaming the Past*, p. 58. What the Elders told me correlates with what is recorded in McBean's book.

25   McBean, *Dreaming the Past*, p. 58.

26   Goodall, *Invasion to Embassy*, p. 111.

27   Goodall, *Invasion to Embassy*, p. 119.

28   Goodall, *Invasion to Embassy*, pp. 121–2.

29   Goodall, *Invasion to Embassy*, p. 123.

CHAPTER 4: MY MOTHER'S SIDE OF THE FAMILY

1   State Library of Queensland, 'Deebing Creek Aborigines Reserve Station, Group Photograph of Inmates, Negative Number 18939 & 48639', Brisbane:

John Oxley Library, State Library of Queensland, 1895. This image was sent to Aunty Ruby by Maurice Ryan with a letter, dated 30 March 1998.

2 M. Ryan, *Dusky Legend: Biography of Sam Anderson, Aboriginal cricketer*, Lismore, NSW: Northern Rivers Press, 2001, p. 14.

3 Queensland State Archives, Cherbourg Social History card for Kathleen Black (née Anderson, Sam's sister), CHHC/B169—according to this card, Kathleen was born at Mt Esk on 18 September 1897 to a 'White man' and an Aboriginal woman called Mary Jane; Tindale noted Mary Jane was a Wakka Wakka woman, Tindale Genealogy, Cherbourg sheet 105; an Aboriginal woman named Mary Jane was listed as living at Eskdale in 1882, COL/A337 82/2918 Return of blankets issued to Aborigines at Esk on May 1,1882. Mary Jane, Sam Anderson's mother, and Sam Anderson were identified by the daughter of Mr Ivins, manager of Deebing Creek Mission, Queensland, in a photograph of mission residents, taken c. 1895. See Ryan, *Dusky Legend*, p. 13.

4 D. Smith, 'Letter from Mrs Doris Smith to Mrs Margaret Keller identifying Sam Anderson in Deebing Creek photograph, written 4th August 1977', Byron Bay, NSW, 1977 (Shauna Bostock Private Collection).

5 Ryan, *Dusky Legend*, p. 65.

6 'Narrow Win: Kippax Team's Visit: District Men Shape Well', *Northern Star*, 17 September 1928. <https://trove.nla.gov.au/newspaper/article/94046801>.

7 Ryan, *Dusky Legend*, p. 36.

8 H. Reynolds, *Frontier: Reports from the edge of white settlement*, St Leonards, NSW: Allen & Unwin, 1987, pp. 49–50.

9 Henderson, 'Australian Aborigines', p. 17.

10 Henderson, 'Australian Aborigines', p. 17.

11 R. Langford Ginibi, *My Bundjalung People*, St Lucia, Qld: University of Queensland Press, 1994, p. 98.

12 Langford Ginibi, *My Bundjalung People*, p. 90.

13 Ryan, *Dusky Legend*, pp. 71–2.

14 Henderson, 'Main Camp Reminiscences, pp. 17, 18.

15 G. Phillips, 'An introduction to the study of the iso-haem-agglutination reactions of the blood of Australian Aboriginals', *Medical Journal of Australia*, 7 April 1928, vol. 1.

16 Phillips, 'An introduction to the study of the iso-haem-agglutination reactions', p. 431.

17 Dr Steven Lane, email correspondence, 14 January 2019; Dr Steven Lane is a leukaemia researcher and clinical haematologist. He is a professor and, in April 2018, was appointed as the head of the Cancer Program at QIMR Berghofer Medical Research Institute. He is currently working from the Icon Cancer Centre, Chermside, Brisbane, and his bio is available on their website <https://iconcancercentre.com.au/doctor/steven-lane/>.

18   D. Habermann & Ipswich (Qld) Council, *Deebing Creek & Purga Missions, 1892–1948*, Ipswich, Qld: Ipswich City Council, 2003, p. 31.

19   Phillips, 'An introduction to the study of the iso-haem-agglutination reactions', p. 432.

20   A. Haebich, *Broken Circles: Fragmenting Indigenous families 1800–2000*, Fremantle, WA: Fremantle Arts Centre Press, 2000, p. 183.

21   Full text copies of these Acts, policies and amendments, as well as summary notes, are available online at NSW Government, 'Aborigines Protection Acts in New South Wales: Legislation/Key Provisions', <https://aiatsis.gov. au/collections/collections-online/digitised-collections/remove-and-protect/ new-south-wales>.

22   NSW Government, 'Aborigines Protection Acts'.

23   NSW Government, 'A.P.B. Minute Book References to Nellie Solomon, 9 Nov. 1911 to 26 Sep. 1912', Original Location 4/7117, Aborigines Protection Board (APB), Sydney: State Records NSW, 1911–1912.

24   NSW Government, 'Aborigines Protection Amending Act, No. 2 1915', APB, Canberra: AIATSIS, 1915, <https://aiatsis.gov.au/sites/default/files/docs/ digitised_collections/remove/52290.pdf>.

25   Goodall, *Invasion to Embassy*, p. 123.

26   P. Read, 'Reflecting on the Stolen Generations', *Indigenous Law Bulletin*, July/ August, vol. 8, issue 13, p. 6.

27   Goodall, *Invasion to Embassy*, p. 45.

28   Goodall, *Invasion to Embassy*, p. 47.

29   Goodall, *Invasion to Embassy*, p. 49.

30   Goodall, *Invasion to Embassy*, pp. 52–3.

31   Goodall, *Invasion to Embassy*, p. 57.

32   Goodall, *Invasion to Embassy*, p. 62. 'Tucker' is an Australian slang word for food.

33   Goodall, *Invasion to Embassy*, pp. 88–9.

34   NSW Government, 'Aborigines' Protection: Report of the Public Service Board, 16th August 1938', Reel 1649, Public Service Board, Sydney: State Records NSW, 1938, p. 7.

35   NSW Government, 'Protection of the Aborigines (Report of the Board)', Legislative Assembly, Sydney: APB, 1883–1884, p. 4; NSW Government, 'Aborigines. (Report of the Board for the Protection of, for Year 1910)', Legislative Assembly, Sydney: APB, 1911, p. 1.

36   NSW Government, 'Aborigines. (Report of Board for the Protection of, for Year 1910)', p. 1.

37   Goodall, *Invasion to Embassy*, p. 119.

38   Goodall, *Invasion to Embassy*, p. 119.

39   Goodall, *Invasion to Embassy*, pp. 119–23.

40   Goodall, *Invasion to Embassy*, pp. 122–3.

CHAPTER 5: RESERVES AND WHITEFELLAS

1   'Aborigines' Reserve', *Northern Star*, 26 August 1922, <http://nla.gov.au/nla. news-article93403237>.

2   T. Connor, 'Closer Settlement Schemes', *The Australian Quarterly*, March 1970, vol. 42, no. 1, pp. 72–3.

3   Goodall, *Invasion to Embassy*, pp. 122–4.

4   A. McGuigan, 'Occasional Paper Number (No. 4): Aboriginal Reserves in New South Wales: A Land Rights Research Aid', Sydney: NSW Ministry of Aboriginal Affairs, undated, p. 25.

5   NSW Government, 'Letter from Mr Homersham to A.P.B. Secretary, 3 June 1916, Coraki Aboriginal School Files 1886–1939, Item Number 5/15528.1', Sydney: State Records NSW, p. 23.

6   Goodall, *Invasion to Embassy*, p. 143. I choose to call them 'Aborigines Only schools' to highlight the racist segregation of Aboriginal children from white Australian children at 'public' schools. These schools may have been called 'public schools', but the 'public' did not include Aboriginal children.

7   C. Brown, 'Cabbage Tree Island Reserve', *Northern Star*, 9 August 1922, <http://nla.gov.au/nla.news-article93390682>.

8   Brown, 'Cabbage Tree Island Reserve'.

9   Goodall, *Invasion to Embassy*, p. 144.

10 Brown, 'Cabbage Tree Island Reserve'.

11 'Primary Producers' Union: Lismore Branch', *Northern Star*, 21 January 1918, <http://nla.gov.au/nla.news-article92928082>.

12 'Blacks at North Lismore', *Northern Star*, 27 November 1918, <http://nla.gov. au/nla.news-article92910513>.

13 'Lismore District: A Suitable Home', *Northern Star*, 3 December 1918, <http:// nla.gov.au/nla.news-article92911179>.

14 'The Lismore Contacts', *Northern Star*, 24 February 1919, <http://nla.gov.au/ nla.news-article92979382>.

15 'Influenza Pandemic: 1919: Influenza reaches Australia', National Museum of Australia, <www.nma.gov.au/defining-moments/resources/influenza-pandemic>.

16 L. Ogilvie, 'Australian Aborigines', *Northern Star*, 25 May 1919, <http://nla. gov.au/nla.news-article92989771>.

17 'Aborigines' Reserve', *Northern Star*, 28 July 1921, <http://nla.gov.au/nla. news-article93101951>.

18 'Aborigines' Houses: Insanitary and Dilapidated: On Dunoon Aborigines Reserve', *Northern Star*, 10 May 1922, <http://nla.gov.au/nla.news-article 223949134>.

19 'Lismore: Aborigines' Reserve', *Northern Star*, 24 June 1922, <http://nla.gov. au/nla.news-article20533608>. Stoney Gully was also known as Runnymede or Kyogle reserve.

20 'Refuse to Leave: Aborigines Standing for Rights', *Northern Star*, 12 June 1922, <http://nla.gov.au/nla.news-article179016251>.

21 'Dunoon Aboriginal Reserve', *Northern Star*, 19 July 1922, <http://nla.gov.au/nla.news-article93387327>.

22 'Won't Disturb Those Aborigines', *Evening News*, 7 October 1903, <http://nla.gov.au/nla.news-article113798254>; 'Aborigines Protection', *Evening News*, 21 June 1895, <http://nla.gov.au/nla.news-article108095474>, accessed 17 February 2017; 'Land Business', *Clarence and Richmond Examiner*, 31 March 1903, <http://nla.gov.au/nla.news-article61393256>; 'The Clarence Electorate', *Clarence and Richmond Examiner*, 10 May 1910, <https://trove.nla.gov.au/newspaper/article/61519109>.

23 'Official Information', *Clarence and Richmond Examiner*, 29 August 1914, <http://nla.gov.au/nla.news-article61634700>.

24 NSW Government, 'Letter from Mr Ellis to Inspector Henderson, Dept. of P.I., 16 Sep. 1907, Nymboida School Files, Item Number 5/17197.1', Department of Public Instruction, Sydney: State Records of NSW, 1907, p. 12.

25 NSW Government, 'Letter from Inspector Henderson to DPI Chief Inspector, 16 Sep. 1907', Nymboida School Files, Item No. 5/17197.1, Department of Public Instruction, Sydney: State Records of NSW, 1907, p. 13.

26 NSW Government, 'Completion of Contract Form, 8 August 1908, Nymboida School Files, Item Number 5/17197.1', Department of Public Instruction, Sydney: State Records of NSW, 1907, p. 6.

27 NSW Government, 'Inspector Henderson's Summary Report for the Application of the Establishment of an Aborigines Provisional School, 1 April 1908, Nymboida School Files, Item Number 5/17197.1', Department of Public Instruction, Sydney: State Records NSW, p. 7.

28 'Nymboida', *Daily Examiner*, 30 March 1916, <http://trove.nla.gov.au/newspaper/article/194988176>.

29 'Darkies and Officialdom: Trouble on the Clarence', *Richmond River Herald and Northern Districts Advertiser*, 2 February 1915, <http://nla.gov.au/nla.news-article125928005>.

30 'The Nymboida Aborigines Case', *The Grafton Argus and Clarence River General Advertiser*, 1 February 1915 <https://trove.nla.gov.au/newspaper/article/235455929>.

31 NSW Government, 'Aborigines (Report of the Board for the Protection of, for Year 1912)', Legislative Assembly, Sydney: APB, 1913, p. 4.

32 When I attended an international science and documentary filmmakers conference, one of the conference organisers repeatedly introduced me as 'Gerry Bostock's niece', and several well-known Australian documentary filmmakers told me what a landmark film *Lousy Little Sixpence* was. The conference was the World Congress of Science and Factual Film Producers Conference, Brisbane Convention Centre, Brisbane, 27–30 November 2018. I was invited as a member of a panel for a discussion on the topic of history.

33 A. Morgan & G. Bostock, *Lousy Little Sixpence*, directed by A. Morgan, Sydney: Ronin Films, 1983, YouTube, Part 2 of 4, 3:04–4:27, <www.youtube.com/watch?v=J7z2Ad5K27s&t=20s>. The whole documentary can be seen in four parts on YouTube.

34 Aunty Violet is not my biological aunt, nor is Aunty Margaret. It is customary in Aboriginal culture to show respect for our Elders by addressing them as 'Aunty' or 'Uncle'. For non-biological Aboriginal Elders, I initially state their full name and later in references call them 'Aunty' or 'Uncle' followed by their first name.

35 Morgan & Bostock, *Lousy Little Sixpence*, Part 2 of 4, 0:20–2:01, <www.youtube.com/watch?v=J7z2Ad5K27s&t=20s>.

36 Morgan & Bostock, *Lousy Little Sixpence*, Part 2 of 4, 2:39–3:04, <www.youtube.com/watch?v=J7z2Ad5K27s&t=20s>.

37 I. Walden, '"That Was Slavery Days": Aboriginal domestic servants in New South Wales in the twentieth century', *Labour History*, 1995, no. 69, pp. 196–209.

38 NSW Government, 'Aborigines. (Report of the Board for the Protection of, for Year 1913)', Legislative Assembly NSW, p. 4.

39 For more on Miss Lowe, see V. Haskins, *One Bright Spot*, New York: Palgrave MacMillan, 2005.

40 M. Goulding, 'Ukerebagh Island Aboriginal Place Nomination Background Investigation', Hurstville, NSW: NSW National Parks & Wildlife Service Cultural Heritage Division, Department of Environment & Conservation NSW, 2004.

41 NSW Government, 'Aborigines Welfare Board (Annual Report for the Year Ended 30th June 1940)'; 'Aborigines Welfare Board (Annual Report for the Year Ended, 30th June 1941)'; and 'Aborigines Welfare Board (Annual Report for Year Ended, 30th June 1944)', Legislative Assembly NSW.

42 Goulding, 'Ukerebagh Island Aboriginal Place', p. 31.

43 Goulding, 'Ukerebagh Island Aboriginal Place', p. 51.

44 Goulding, 'Ukerebagh Island Aboriginal Place', p. 34.

45 Goulding, 'Ukerebagh Island Aboriginal Place', p. 53.

46 A. Burger, *Neville Bonner: A biography*, South Melbourne, Vic: Macmillan, 1979, p. 2.

47 (Senator) N. Bonner, 'The Senate Adjournment: Ukerebagh Island New South Wales Commonwealth Scientific and Industrial Research Organisation – Candidate: Bass Electoral Division Speech Wednesday 11th June 1975', ed. The Senate: Parliamentary Debates, Canberra: Commonwealth of Australia, 1975, p. 2568.

48 NSW Government, 'Letter from Inspector Henderson to Dept. Head Office, 3 March 1907, Item Number 5/15528.1, Coraki Aboriginals School Files 1876–1939', Sydney: State Records NSW, 1907.

49 NSW Government, 'Letter from Mr Homersham', p. 23.

50 Although the grandaunt was Dad's grandfather's brother's wife, the huge age difference between the brothers and her youth at marriage made her seem more like an aunt than a grandaunt to my father and his siblings. (Name of grandaunt intentionally withheld.)

51 NSW Government, 'Letter from Mr Homersham', pp. 39–40.

52 NSW Government, 'Letter from Mr Homersham', pp. 39–40.

53 Goodall, *Invasion to Embassy*, pp. 121–2.

54 Goodall, *Invasion to Embassy*, p. 142.

55 J. Jacobs, C. Laurence & F. Thomas, 'Pearls from the deep: re-evaluating the history of the Colebrook Home for Aboriginal Children', in D.B. Rose & T. Swain (eds), *Aboriginal Australians and Christian Missions*, Bedford Park, SA: The Australian Association for the Study of Religions at the Australian College of Advanced Education, Sturt Campus, 1988, pp. 140–55.

56 'Alma Smith and Alva Atkins Papers and Photographs Relating to Missionary Work', Australian Aborigines Mission, 1908–1929, Mitchell Library.

57 'Farewell Party at Coraki – Gratitude of Aborigines', *Richmond River Herald and Northern Districts Advertiser*, 25 August 1936, <http://nla.gov.au/nla.news-article126094853>.

58 A. Cole, 'Unwitting soldiers: the working life of Matron Hiscocks at the Cootamundra Girls Home', *Aboriginal History*, 2003, vol. 7, p. 147.

59 'Wedding on Coraki Abo Reserve, Anderson–Walker', *Richmond River Herald and Northern Districts Advertiser*, 4 September 1934, <http://trove.nla.gov.au/newspaper/article/127178675>.

60 'Aboriginal Wedding – Interesting Function at Coraki – Bostock–Cowan', *Richmond River Herald and Northern Districts Advertiser*, 24 November 1933, <http://nla.gov.au/nla.news-article127169918>.

61 *The Australian Aborigines Advocate*, 31 August 1925, in 'Alma Smith and Alva Atkins Papers and Photographs Relating to Missionary Work'.

62 'Alma Smith and Alva Atkins Papers and Photographs Relating to Missionary Work'.

63 *The Australian Aborigines Advocate*, 28 December 1920, in 'Alma Smith and Alva Atkins Papers and Photographs Relating to Missionary Work'.

64 *The Australian Aborigines Advocate*, 28 December 1920, in 'Alma Smith and Alva Atkins Papers and Photographs Relating to Missionary Work'; Morgan and Bostock, *Lousy Little Sixpence*.

65 J. Maynard, *Fight for Liberty and Freedom: The origins of Australian activism*, Canberra: Aboriginal Studies Press, 2007, p. 1.

66 Goodall, *Invasion to Embassy*, p. 120.

67 V. Haskins, 'A better chance? – Sexual abuse and the apprenticeship of Aboriginal girls under the NSW Aborigines Protection Board', *Aboriginal History*, 2004, vol. 28, p. 53. See also Haskins, *One Bright Spot*.

68 Maynard, *Fight for Liberty and Freedom*, p. 141.

69 A. McGuigan, *Aboriginal Reserves in New South Wales: A Land Rights Research Occasional Paper, No. 4*, Sydney: NSW Ministry of Aboriginal Affairs.

70 Morgan & Bostock, *Lousy Little Sixpence*, Part 1 of 4, 5:15–6:15, <www.youtube.com/watch?v=2TfaXdI5Z8Q>. When Aunty Geraldine refers to 'so much' land, she means 'an undefined quantity' of land, and not 'a great amount' of land. This was common vernacular at the time and should not be taken literally. For example, if I asked my grandmother for some flour to bake a cake, she would narrate that to her friend by saying, 'Well, I gave her so much flour, put the tin away, and then asked her what else she needed.'

CHAPTER 6: THE DESTRUCTION BOARD

1 Goodall, *Invasion to Embassy*, p. 220.

2 Goodall, *Invasion to Embassy*, p. 220.

3 Goodall, *Invasion to Embassy*, p. 220.

4 Morgan & Bostock, *Lousy Little Sixpence*, Part 1 of 4, 10:42–11:22, <www.youtube.com/watch?v=2TfaXdI5Z8Q>.

5 NSW Government, 'Letter from Mr Howard to A.P.B. Head Office, 6 March 1939, NRS 905, A48/228 [12/7773.1]', Files Relating to Aboriginal Affairs, 1938–1949, Chief Secretary Letters Received (CSLR), Sydney: APB, 1939, p. 13.

6 Morgan & Bostock, *Lousy Little Sixpence*, Part 1 of 4, 11:26–12:22, <www.youtube.com/watch?v=2TfaXdI5Z8Q>.

7 NSW Government, 'Death Certificate of Mabel Anderson, 19 Sep. 1937, No. 1937/016975', Sydney: NSW Registry of Births, Deaths and Marriages, 1937.

8 NSW Government, 'Minute of Order—Maintenance of Wife and Children: Deserted Wives and Children Act, 1909–1931, Complainant: Howard, J.P. Manager Aboriginal Station Kyogle, 17 August 1938, NRS 905, A48/228 [12/7773.1]', p. 1.

9 NSW Government, 'Letter from Mr Howard to A.P.B. Head Office, 6 March 1939'.

10 Morgan & Bostock, *Lousy Little Sixpence*, Part 1 of 4, 12:08–14:37, <https://youtu.be/2TfaXdI5Z8Q>.

11 NSW Government, 'Letter from Mr Howard to A.W.B. Secretary, 14 April 1942, NRS 905 A44/2309 [12/76881.1]', CSLR, p. 1.

12 NSW Government, 'Minute of Order—Complainant: Howard, J.P. Manager Aboriginal Station Kyogle', p. 1.

13 NSW Government, 'Letter from A.P.B. Inspector Mrs English to Mr Howard, 5 April 1939, NRS 905 A48/228 [12/7773.1]', CSLR, p. 14.

14 NSW Government, 'Memorandum from Mr Howard to A.P.B. Secretary, 29 August 1938, NRS 905 A4176 [12/7592.1]', CSLR, p. 1.

15 NSW Government, 'Memorandum from Mr Howard to A.P.B. Head Office, 1 March 1939, NRS 905 A4176 [12/7592.1]', CSLR, p. 8.

16 NSW Government, 'Accounts Ledger of Mr Howard, 2 March 1939 – 6 May 1939, NRS 905 A4176 [12/7592.1]', CSLR, p. 11.

17 NSW Government, 'Memorandum from Mr Howard to A.P.B. Head Office, 1 March 1939, NRS 905 A4176 [12/7592.1]', CSLR, p. 8.

18 NSW Government, 'Letter from Mr Howard to A.P.B. Head Office, 26 Nov. 1939, NRS 905 A4176 [12/7592.1]', CSLR, p. 17.

19 NSW Government, 'Memorandum from Mr Howard to A.P.B. Head Office, 29 August 1938, NRS 905 A4176 [12/7592.1]', CSLR, p. 1. Also shown in the accounts ledger pages.

20 NSW Government, 'Aborigines Protection Acts in New South Wales: Legislation/Key Provisions', <https://aiatsis.gov.au/collections/collections-online/digitised-collections/remove-and-protect/new-south-wales>.

21 Commonwealth of Australia, 'Initial Conference of Commonwealth and State Aboriginal Authorities: Held at Canberra, 21st to 23rd of April 1937', Canberra: APB, 1937.

22 A. Francisco, 'Creating space for exemption in New South Wales', in L. Aberdeen & J. Jones (eds), *Black, White and Exempt*, Canberra, ACT: Aboriginal Studies Press, 2021, pp. 52–3.

23 Goodall, *Invasion to Embassy*, p. 267.

24 Goodall, *Invasion to Embassy*, pp. 193–5.

25 Goodall, *Invasion to Embassy*, pp. 265–8.

26 Goodall, *Invasion to Embassy*, pp. 267–9.

27 Haebich, *Broken Circles*, 502–3.

28 NSW Government, 'Memorandum from Mr Howard to Secretary A.P.B. 8 April 1940', NRS 905 [12/7682.1], p. 1.

29 NSW Government, 'Letter from Mr Howard to A.P.B. Head Office, 6 March 1939'.

30 NSW Government, 'Letter from Mr Howard to A.P.B. Head Office, 26 Nov. 1939', CSLR, p. 17.

CHAPTER 7: CONTROL OF ABORIGINAL LIVES

1 NSW Government, 'Aborigines' Protection: Report of the Public Service Board, 16th August 1938', p. 15.

2 NSW Government, 'Department of Community Services, Endowees List as 31 July 1938, A.G.Y. 114, NRS 1063 [4/8565.2]', in 'Aborigines' Protection: Report of the Public Service Board 1938–1940', Sydney: Department of Community Services, 1938, p. 1.

3 NSW Government, 'Letter from Mr Howard to A.P.B. Head Office, 17 Sept. 1939, NRS 905 A47/483 [12/7746.1]', CSLR, p. 1.

4 NSW Government, 'Letter from Mr Rayner to the Commissioner of Family Endowment, 27 Sept. 1940, NRS 905 A47/483 [12/7746.1]', CSLR, pp. 128–9.

5 NSW Government, 'Application for Direct Payment of Family Endowment for Evelyn Anderson, 21 Nov. 1940', NRS 905 A47/483 [12/7746.1], p. 7.

6 NSW Government, 'Aborigines' Protection: Report of Public Service Board' (1938), pp. 9–11.

7 NSW Government, 'Letter from Mr Rayner to the Commissioner of Family Endowment, 27 Sept. 1940', CSLR, pp. 128–9. 'Letter from Acting Secretary A.P.B. to Taree Reserve Manager, 14 Feb. 1941', CSLR, p. 28.

8 NSW Government, 'Letter from Police Constable McKinnon to Sergeant Madelin to A.W.B. Secretary, 24 Feb. 1941, N.R.S 905 A47/483 [12/7746.1]', CSLR, p. 38.

9 NSW Government, 'Letter from Constable Ryan to A.W.B. Head Office, 12 May 1942, NRS 905 A47/483 [12/7746.1]', CSLR, p. 48.

10 All these letters are from the same AWB file on Evelyn Anderson.

11 NSW Government, 'Letter from Constable Ryan to A.W.B. Head Office, 12 May 1942, NRS 905 A47/483 [12/7746.1]', CSLR, p. 49.

12 NSW Government, 'Letter and Direct Payment Form from Constable Thomas to A.W.B., 15 June 1942, NRS 905, A47/483 [12/7746.1]', CSLR, pp. 50 & 52.

13 NSW Government, 'Letter from Henry Anderson to A.W.B. Head Office, 14 May 1943, NRS 905 A47/483 [12/7746.1]', CSLR, p. 87.

14 NSW Government, 'Letter to A.W.B. Head Office, 12 Sep. 1944, NRS 905 A47/483 [12/7746.1]', CSLR, p. 100.

15 NSW Government, 'Memorandum to A.W.B., re: Maintenance of Children of Henry Anderson, 28 Sep. 1944, NRS 905 A47/483 [12/7746.1]', CSLR, p. 103.

16 NSW Government, 'Letter from A.W.B. Head Office to Matron Hiscocks, 28 Sep. 1944, NRS 905 A47/483 [12/7746.1]', CSLR, p. 101.

17 NSW Government, 'Letter from Henry Anderson to the A.W.B., NRS 905 A47/483 [12/7746.1]', CSLR, p. 108.

18 NSW Government, 'A.W.B. Direct Payment of Endowment Form for Henry Anderson, 9 Nov. 1944, NRS 905 A47/483 [12/7746.1]', CSLR, p. 112.

19 R. Langford Ginibi, Don't Take Your Love to Town, Ringwood, Vic: Penguin Books, 1988, p. 9.

20 NSW Government, 'Letter from Constable Ryan to A.W.B. Head Office, 12 May 1942', p. 49. He noted Evelyn's desertion was two months earlier, so the approximate date was around 12 March 1942.

21 NSW Government, 'Letter from A.W.B. Superintendent Liscombe to Mr L. Austen, 16 Jan. 1947, File: C1058', CSLR, p. 8.

22 NSW Government, 'Telegram from Mr Austen to A.W.B., 16 Dec. 1946, File: C1058', CSLR, p. 2.

23 NSW Government, 'Telegram from Mr Austen to A.W.B., (Illegible Date) 1946, File: C1058', CSLR, p. 3.

24 NSW Government, 'Austen's Report for A.W.B., 16 Dec. 1946, File: C1058', CSLR, pp. 5–6.

25 NSW Government, 'Letter from Evelyn Anderson to Mr Howard, 23 August 1938, NRS 905 A393 [2/7582.1]', CSLR, pp. 1–2.

26 NSW Government, 'Diary Entry of Mrs I. English, A.W.B. Inspector, 12 Jan. 1945, NRS 905, A46/96 [12/7717.1]', CSLR, p. 1.

27 'Wedding on Coraki Abo Reserve, Anderson–Walker'.

28 'Aboriginal Wedding – Interesting Function at Coraki – Bostock–Cowan'.

29 Haskins, *One Bright Spot*, p. 187.

30 Haskins, *One Bright Spot*, p. 72.

31 NSW Government, 'Letter from Mr Austen to A.W.B. Head Office, 16 Jan. 1947, File: C1058', CSLR, p. 7.

32 NSW Government, 'Letter from A.W.B. Superintendent Mr Liscombe to Mr L. Austen, 16 Jan. 1947, CSLR, p. 8.

33 NSW Government, 'Letter from Henry Anderson to A.W.B., 23 Jan. 1947, File: C1058', CSLR, p. 9.

34 NSW Government, 'Letter from A.W.B. to Henry Anderson, 10 Feb. 1947, File: C1085', CSLR, p. 11.

35 NSW Government, 'Letter from A.W.B. to Bonalbo Police, Direct Payment Form, 5 Feb. 1947, NRS 905, A47/483 [12/7746.1]', CSLR, p. 128.

36 NSW Government, 'Letter from Police Bonalbo, Direct Payment Form to A.W.B., 13 Feb. 1947, NRS 905, A47/483 [12/7746.1]', CSLR, p. 130.

37 McGrath, *Illicit Love*, pp. 271–2.

38 Langford Ginibi, *Don't Take Your Love to Town*, p. 42.

39 Langford Ginibi, *Don't Take Your Love to Town*, p. 42.

40 Langford Ginibi, *Don't Take Your Love to Town*, p. 46.

41 Langford Ginibi, *Don't Take Your Love to Town*, p. 54.

42 Langford Ginibi, *Don't Take Your Love to Town*, p. 58.

43 Langford Ginibi, *Don't Take Your Love to Town*, p. 62.

44 Langford Ginibi, *Don't Take Your Love to Town*, pp. 68–71.

CHAPTER 8: REDFERN WAS A POWERHOUSE

1 NSW Government, *Report on City of Sydney Industrial & Warehouse Buildings Heritage Study*, Sydney: City Plan Heritage, 2014, p. 27.

2 Qld Government, 'Death Certificate of Nellie Anderson, 15 June 1954, No. 2521/1954', Brisbane: Qld Registry of Births, Deaths and Marriages, 1954. See also Langford Ginibi, *Don't Take Your Love to Town*, p. 71.

3 Langford Ginibi, *Don't Take Your Love to Town*, p. 71. My mother told me she had worked there, but I am not sure if it was her first ever job as a machinist.

4 Langford Ginibi, *Don't Take Your Love to Town*, pp. 48–9.

5 Langford Ginibi, *Don't Take Your Love to Town*, p. 47.

NOTES

6   Gary Foley, interview, in D. Johnson & S. Milliken, *The Redfern Story*, directed by D. Johnson, Australia: Samson Productions Pty Ltd/Ronin Films, 2014, 3:52–4:18. Permission to reproduce dialogue from the documentary film *The Redfern Story* was kindly granted by Andrew Pike of Ronin Films <www.roninfilms.com.au> and producers Sue Milliken and Darlene Johnson for Samson Productions Pty Ltd.

7   Lester Bostock, interview, in Johnson & Milliken, *The Redfern Story*, 4:18–4:25.

8   Langford Ginibi, *Don't Take Your Love to Town*, p. 71.

9   Cited as '*Northern Star* of May 25th 1959' by Maurice Ryan in *Dusky Legend*, p. 75.

10 Langford Ginibi, *Don't Take Your Love to Town*, pp. 100–4.

11 T. Whyte, C. Matthews, M. Balfour, L. Murphy & L. Hassall, 'Getting to know the story of the Boathouse dances: Football, freedom & rock 'n' roll', in J. McDonald & R. Mason (eds.), *Creative Communities: Regional inclusion & the arts*, Bristol, UK: Intellect, 2015, p. 81.

12 Whyte et al., 'Getting to know the story of the Boathouse dances', p. 84.

13 Whyte et al., 'Getting to know the story of the Boathouse dances', p. 82. Vigoro is an old-fashioned women's sport that is like a version of cricket. The bat has a long handle with a thick, teardrop-shaped base, where the ball is struck. There are two teams, one batting and one fielding, and they score runs between the wickets, just like cricket. But there are no overs and the rules are different to cricket in many ways.

14 Whyte et al., 'Getting to know the story of the Boathouse dances', p. 84.

15 Whyte et al., 'Getting to know the story of the Boathouse dances', p. 86.

16 Whyte et al., 'Getting to know the story of the Boathouse dances', pp. 86–7.

17 Whyte et al., 'Getting to know the story of the Boathouse dances', p. 87.

18 Whyte et al., 'Getting to know the story of the Boathouse dances', p. 86.

19 Australian War Memorial, '4th Battalion, Royal Australian Regiment, Claret Operations', <www.awm.gov.au/collection/U60457>, accessed 13 August 2018.

20 Australian War Memorial, '4th Battalion, Royal Australian Regiment, Claret Operations'.

21 E. Bostock, 'Euphemia Bostock: Artist', in L. Thompson (ed.), *Aboriginal Voices: Contemporary Aboriginal artists, writers & performers*, Marleston, SA: JB Books, 1999, pp. 123–7. My Aunty's family nickname is Phemie (pronounced 'Fee-mee'), and she only uses her full name, Euphemia, professionally as an artist.

22 Tranby College, 'Tranby: National Indigenous Adult Education & Training', Co-operative for Aborigines Ltd, <http://tranby.edu.au/about-us/history/>.

23 Lester Bostock, interview by Rachael Maza, 'Best Foot Forward', ABC TV, 5 September 2003.

24 D. Horten (ed.) and AIATSIS, *The Encyclopaedia of Aboriginal Australia, Volume 1 (A–L)*, Canberra: AIATSIS, 1994, p. 388.

25 Charlie Perkins, *Australian Biography Interview Transcript*, tape 5, <www.nfsa. gov.au/collection/curated/australian-biography-charles-perkins-0>

26 Gary Foley, interview, in Johnson & Milliken, *The Redfern Story*, 3:17–6:34.

27 A. Cole, 'Making a debut: Myths, memories and mimesis', in F. Peters-Little, A. Curthoys & J. Docker (eds), *Passionate Histories*, Canberra: ANU Press, 2010, pp. 205–16.

28 Langford Ginibi, *Don't Take Your Love to Town*, p. 140. Like the Salvation Army, the Smith Family is a charitable organisation (established in 1922) that works to support disadvantaged children and young people in Australia.

29 Cole, 'Making a debut', p. 209.

30 L. Cole, 'Dancing with the Prime Minister', in *Message Stick*, ABC TV, Neutral Bay, NSW: Enhance Videos, 2010, <www.abc.net.au/tv/messagestick/ stories/s2988499.htm>.

31 A. Cole, 'Making a debut', pp. 205–16.

32 Langford Ginibi, *Don't Take Your Love to Town*, p. 159.

33 Langford Ginibi, *Don't Take Your Love to Town*, p. 174. Aunty Ruby writes about having moved there in 1972, thus I deduced the nine years.

34 B. Kingston, *A History of New South Wales*, Port Melbourne, Vic: Cambridge University Press, 2006, pp. 172–3.

35 Langford Ginibi, *Don't Take Your Love to Town*, pp. 173–4.

36 'Tribune (Sydney, NSW: 1939–1991)', National Library of Australia, <http:// trove.nla.gov.au/newspaper/title/1002>, accessed 5 January 2017.

37 'Black Rights March July 17', *Tribune*, 27 March 1972, p. 12, <http://trove.nla. gov.au/newspaper/article/237868494>.

38 Johnson & Milliken, *The Redfern Story*.

39 Bindi Williams, interview, in Johnson & Milliken, *The Redfern Story*, 6:43–7:00.

40 Marcia Langton, interview, in Johnson & Milliken, *The Redfern Story*, 7:03–7:11.

41 Lester Bostock, interview, in Johnson & Milliken, *The Redfern Story*, 7:12–7:15.

42 Gary Foley, interview, in Johnson and Milliken, *The Redfern Story*, 6:34–8:59.

43 Interview with (my father) George Bostock.

44 Gary Foley, interview, in Johnson & Milliken, *The Redfern Story*, 10:31–14:59.

45 Gary Foley, interview, in Johnson & Milliken, *The Redfern Story*, 14:59–16:17.

46 Gary Foley, Rachael Maza, Lisa Maza and Gerry Bostock, interviews, in Johnson & Milliken, *The Redfern Story*, 17:43–21:28.

47 Gary Foley, Rachael Maza and Bronwyn Penrith, interviews, in Johnson & Milliken, *The Redfern Story*, 21:28–22:10.

48 Goodall, *Invasion to Embassy*, p. 338.

49 Gary Foley, interview, in Johnson & Milliken, *The Redfern Story*, 3:17–6:34.

50 Jane Lydon, *Flash of Recognition: Photography and the emergence of Indigenous rights*, Sydney: NewSouth Publishing, 2012, pp. 230–1.

51 Lydon, *Flash of Recognition*, pp. 230–1.

52 Lydon, *Flash of Recognition*, p. 231.

53 J. Clark, *Aborigines & Activism: Race, Aborigines & the coming of the sixties to Australia*, Crawley, WA: University of Western Australia Press, 2008, p. 242.

54 Gary Foley, in Johnson & Milliken, *The Redfern Story*, 23:59–25:11.

55 '9 Aborigines Go to China', *Tribune*, 24 October 1972, p. 12, < https://trove. nla.gov.au/newspaper/article/237867326>.

56 'Ten Aborigines Going to Peking', *Sydney Morning Herald*, 23 October 1972, <www.kooriweb.org/foley/images/history/news/china/med72b.html>.

57 'Blacks to Tell China', *The Melbourne Age*, 17 January 1974, <www.kooriweb. org/foley/news/1974dx.html>.

58 G. Foley, 'ASIO, the Aboriginal Movement, and me', in M. Burgmann (ed.), *Dirty Secrets: Our ASIO files*, Sydney: NewSouth Publishing, 2014, pp. 93–6.

59 Foley, 'ASIO, the Aboriginal Movement, and me', p. 94.

60 M. McKenna, 'ASIO Surveillance in Persons of Interest', *The Monthly*, February 2014, <www.themonthly.com.au/issue/2014/february/1391173200/ mark-mckenna/asio-surveillance-persons-interest>.

61 H. Keenan, 'Episode Three: Gary Foley – Native Title is not Land Rights. Reconciliation is not Justice', *Persons of Interest: ASIO's dirty war on dissent*, episode 3, directed by Haydn Keenan, Melbourne: Smart Street Films, 2013.

62 Australian Government, 'ASIO File: Bostock, Lester Fraser, Volume 1, Series No. A6119, Control Symbol 6060, Barcode 13161348' and 'ASIO File: Bostock, Gerald Leon, Volume 1, Series No. A6119, Control Symbol 6088, Barcode 13161339', ASIO, Canberra: National Library of Australia.

63 Australian Government, 'ASIO File: Bostock, Gerald Leon', p. 65.

64 Australian Government, 'ASIO File: Bostock, Gerald Leon', p. 64.

65 For a useful explanation on McCarthyism, see US History Online Textbook, 'McCarthyism', Independence Hall Association, Philadelphia, <www.ushistory. org/us/53a.asp>.

66 Australian Government, 'ASIO File, Bostock, Lester Fraser', p. 7.

67 Langford Ginibi, *Don't Take Your Love to Town*, pp. 115–18.

68 Australian Government, 'ASIO File, Bostock, Lester Fraser', p. 9.

69 Australian Government, 'ASIO File, Bostock, Lester Fraser', p. 9.

70 Australian Government, 'ASIO File, Bostock, Lester Fraser', p. 10.

71 *The Bulletin* magazine, 26 December 1964, p. 9.

72 Australian Government, 'ASIO File, Bostock, Lester Fraser', p. 58.

73 Foley, 'ASIO, the Aboriginal Movement, and Me', p. 104.

74 Foley, 'ASIO, the Aboriginal Movement, and Me', pp. 104–5.

75 Australian Government, 'ASIO File, Bostock, Lester Fraser', p. 10.

CHAPTER 9: EMBRACING THE ARTS

1 Gary Foley, interview, in Johnson & Milliken, *The Redfern Story*, 25:30–31:43.

2 Bob Maza, Lisa Maza and Gary Foley, interviews, in Johnson & Milliken, *The Redfern Story*, 32:55–33:54.

3 Gary Foley and Zac Martin as Lionel Mouse, in Johnson & Milliken, *The Redfern Story*, 35:21–36:38. Permission to reproduce the script dialogue from *Basically Blacks Super Boong Skit* was granted by Mr Gary Foley.

4 Ernie Dingo, interview, in Johnson & Milliken, *The Redfern Story*, 36:38–37:15.

5 Gerry Bostock, interview, in Johnson & Milliken, *The Redfern Story*, 38:01–38:30.

6 Australian Dance Council, Ausdance Inc. '1999 Hall of Fame: Carole Johnson', <www.australiandanceawards.net.au/award-winners/hall-of-fame/carole-johnson>.

7 Lester Bostock, interview, in Johnson & Milliken, *The Redfern Story*, 44:13–44:41.

8 A. Cole & W. Lewis, 'Fisher, Bettie (1939–1976)', *Australian Dictionary of Biography*, vol. 14, 1996 <http://adb.anu.edu/biography/fisher-bettie-10187>.

9 Mary Rose Casey, in B. Wheeler (ed.), *A Companion to Australian Aboriginal Literature*, Rochester, New York: Camden House, 2013, p. 157.

10 M. Casey, *Creating Frames: Contemporary Indigenous theatre 1967–1990*, Brisbane, Qld: University of Queensland Press, 2004, pp. 108–9.

11 Casey, *Creating Frames*, pp. 109.

12 Casey, *Creating Frames*, pp. 109–10.

13 Casey, *Creating Frames*, pp. 110–11.

14 Marcia Langton, interview, in Johnson & Milliken, *The Redfern Story*, 49:45–50:08.

15 Bryan Brown, interview, in Johnson & Milliken, *The Redfern Story*, 49:10–49:45.

16 Bryan Brown, interview, in Johnson & Milliken, *The Redfern Story*, 50:09–50:19.

17 Gerry Bostock, interview, in Johnson & Milliken, *The Redfern Story*, 50:24–50:51.

18 Bryan Brown, interview, in Johnson & Milliken, *The Redfern Story*, 51:21–51:48.

19 Lester Bostock, interview, in Johnson & Milliken, *The Redfern Story*, 52:39–52:50.

20 Marcia Langton, interview, in Johnson & Milliken, *The Redfern Story*, 53:17–53:36.

21 Bryan Brown, interview, in Johnson & Milliken, *The Redfern Story*, 53:37–54:01.

22 Marcia Langton, interview, in Johnson & Milliken, *The Redfern Story*, 54:08–54:26.

23 Bryan Brown, in Johnson & Milliken, *The Redfern Story*, 54:27–54:41.

24 Casey, *Creating Frames*, p. 117.

25 Bindi Williams, interview, in Johnson & Milliken, *The Redfern Story*, 55:31–55:44.

26 Gary Foley, interview, in Johnson & Milliken, *The Redfern Story*, 55:06–55:20.

27 S. Irvine, 'Uncle Lester Bostock Awarded an Honorary Doctorate by AFTRS', First Peoples Disability Network Australia, 2016, <http://fpdn.org.au/uncle-lester-bostock-awarded-honorary-doctorate-by-aftrs/>, accessed 23 November 2017.

28 Lester Bostock, interview by Rachael Maza, 'Best Foot Forward'.

29 M. Smith, '25 Years On, Classic Film Still Shocks', *Koori Mail*, 22 October 2008, <http://aiatsis.gov.au/collections/collections-online/digitised-collections/koori-mail/koori-mail-issues>.

30 M. Smith, '25 Years On, Classic Film Still Shocks'.

31 Australian Film, Television and Radio School, 'AFTRS Bestows Honorary Degrees on Lester Bostock and David White', <www.if.com.au/aftrs-bestows-honorary-degrees-on-lester-bostock-and-david-white>, accessed 13 January 2017.

32 Australian Film, Television and Radio School, 'AFTRS Bestows Honorary Degrees on Lester Bostock and David White'.

33 A. Heiss & P. Minter (eds), *Macquarie PEN Anthology of Aboriginal Literature*, Crows Nest, NSW: Allen & Unwin, 2008, pp. 5–6.

34 Langford Ginibi, *Don't Take Your Love to Town*, Acknowledgements.

35 Ruby Langford Ginibi, replay of 5 July 1999 interview by Margaret Throsby, ABC Radio National, 10 December 2012.

36 Wheeler, *A Companion to Australian Aboriginal Literature*, p. 1.

37 G. Bostock, 'The Reflections of My Life: George Harold (Podgie) Bostock, Aboriginal-Soldier-Playwright-Actor-Poet-Elder', unpublished memoir, p. 61.

38 Bostock, 'The Reflections of My Life', p. 63.

39 Bostock, 'The Reflections of My Life', p. 70.

40 R. Cerabona, 'Black Diggers at the Playhouse Reveals Untold Stories of World War I', *The Canberra Times*, <www.canberratimes.com.au/story/6070043/black-diggers-at-the-playhouse-reveals-untold-stories-of-world-war-i/>.

CHAPTER 10: THE TRUTH IS A HEALER

1 P. Read, 'Reflecting on the Stolen Generations', *Indigenous Law Bulletin*, July/August, vol. 8, issue 13, 2014, p. 3.

2 Maynard & Haskins, '"For the Record"', p. 134.

3 Maynard & Haskins, '"For the Record"', p. 124.

4   Maynard & Haskins, "'For the Record'", p. 124.
5   Maynard & Haskins, "'For the Record'", p. 132.
6   NSW Government, *State Records Authority of New South Wales Annual Report 2006–07*, Sydney, 2007, p. 38, <www.opengov.nsw.gov.au/publications/11729>, accessed 6 September 2021.

EPILOGUE
1   Farwell, *Squatters' Castle*, p. 322.
2   Farwell, *Squatters' Castle*, pp. 132–5.
3   P. Wohlleben, *The Hidden Life of Trees: What they feel, how they communicate*, Carlton, Vic: Black Inc., 2016, p. 249.
4   S. Harding, *Animate Earth: Science, intuition and Gaia*, 2nd edn, Devon, UK: Green Books Ltd., 2006, back cover.
5   Harding, *Animate Earth*, p. 190.
6   Paul Stamets, in Harding, *Animate Earth*, p. 195.
7   N. O'Sullivan & N. Graydon, *The Ancestral Continuum: Unlock the secrets of who you really are*, London: Simon & Schuster, 2013, pp. 128–9.
8   Reynolds, *Truth-Telling*, p. 8.
9   Thomas DeWolf, 'Dear Ben Affleck, My Ancestors Were Slaveowners, Too', *Zocalo*, 27 April 2015, <www.zocalopublicsquare.org/2015/04/27/dear-ben-affleck-my-ancestors-were-slaveowners-too/ideas/nexus/>.